Public Policy Toward Corporate Takeovers

Public Policy Toward Corporate Takeovers

Edited by
Murray L. Weidenbaum
and
Kenneth W. Chilton

Transaction Books
New Brunswick (USA) and Oxford (UK)

Library of Congress Catalog Number: 87-10750
ISBN 0-88738-166-9
Printed in the United States of America

Library of Congress Cataloging in Publication Data

Public policy toward corporate takeovers.

  Papers resulting from a research project conducted
in the winter and spring of 1986 by the Center for
the Study of American Business at Washington
University in St. Louis, Mo.
  Includes bibliographies and index.
  1. Consolidation and merger of corporations—
Government policy—United States. I. Weidenbaum,
Murray L. II. Chilton, Kenneth. III. Washington
University (Saint Louis, Mo.). Center for the
Study of American Business.
HD2795.P825   1987   338.8'3'0973   87-10750
ISBN 0-88738-166-9

Contents

Acknowledgments

The preparation of this book was supported in large measure by the Center for the Study of American Business at Washington University in St. Louis. In particular, the chapters by Mr. Cook and Professors Lehn, Sullivan, and Thompson were adapted from more detailed technical reports resulting from summer research support furnished by the Center. Mr. Pickens' and Dr. Ravenscraft's chapters are adapted from papers presented at a 7 November 1986 Conference on Public Policy toward Corporate Takeovers cosponsored by the Center and Washington University's Schools of Business and Law.

The co-editors would like to express special appreciation to the staff of the Center for the Study of American Business for their professional and enthusiastic handling of both the preparation of the manuscript and the administration of the November 7 conference. Expert manuscript typing was performed by Mrs. Donna Cole and Ms. Melinda Warren. Conference coordination was spearheaded by Mrs. Gloria Lucy. Possibly the greatest debt of gratitude for making this book possible goes to Ms. Carol Graff, who proofread many drafts of each paper and served as the overall coordinator between the publisher and the book's authors.

Introduction

One of the most widely discussed features of American business today is the battle for control of major corporations. While the natural battleground is the boardroom and stock exchange trading floor, much of the war is being fought on the business pages of daily newspapers, in national magazines, and on the evening news.

Corporate takeovers are in the news not only because they make intriguing business copy, but because the ultimate outcome in the contest for corporate control is likely to be determined by the rules of the game—public policy toward corporate takeovers. It should, therefore, not be surprising that the rhetoric describing this issue is laced with bias. Corporate executives cast disparaging remarks about corporate "raiders," "sharks," and "takeover artists." Meanwhile, the challengers assail "entrenched" managements and describe themselves as "shareholder advocates."

In the winter and spring of 1986, the Center for the Study of American Business began to formulate a research project to move the public policy debate beyond the rhetorical level and to direct it toward the issues. Most of the chapters that follow are a direct result of this research project. Two chapters, the adaptation of a luncheon talk by T. Boone Pickens, entitled "The Stockholder Revolution," and a chapter by David Ravenscraft and E. M. Scherer, entitled "The Long-Run Performance of Mergers and Takeovers," resulted from a November 1986 conference hosted by the CSAB and the Schools of Business and Law at Washington University.

The significant questions raised and studied in the CSAB's research project were:

- What is the Current Status of Public Policy in Corporate Takeovers?
  1. Direct and intentional.
  2. Indirect and unintentional.
- What are the Key Public and Professional Concerns?
  1. Are takeovers promoting business efficiency?
  2. Are they decapitalizing American business?
  3. Are they reducing the liquidity of business to a dangerous degree?
  4. Are they forcing more short-term orientation of business decisionmaking?

- What are the Pros and Cons of Proposed Changes in Public Policy Toward Takeovers?
  1. Restricting the issuance of junk bonds.
  2. Reducing the tax advantages of takeovers.
  3. Increasing the federal role in corporate governance.
  4. Shifting the focus of antitrust enforcement.

Many of these questions are economic in nature, but some are legal issues, such as: What is the proper role for state and federal governments in determining the rules governing takeover contests? and What is the most effective approach to be taken by federal regulators such as the Antitrust Division of the Justice Department? These two legal topics are addressed by Robert B. Thompson, ''Tender Offer Regulation and the Federalization of State Corporate Law'' (Chapter 6), and E. Thomas Sullivan, ''The Antitrust Division as a Regulatory Agency: An Enforcement Policy in Transition'' (Chapter 7).

The economic questions are very familiar to academics, but that does not mean that there is unanimity regarding the implications of the economic analysis conducted to date. Richard E. Cook examines ''What the Economics Literature Has to Say About Takeovers'' in Chapter 1. The primary focus of the studies analyzed is whether or not takeovers promote economic efficiency.

By far, the greatest amount of research has been directed at how takeovers affect stockholders. One of the primary reasons for this emphasis is that data on stock prices are readily available (except when a leveraged buyout takes a public firm private) and amenable to attractive new economic tools such as event analysis—measuring stock price movements before and after significant events.

However, two major questions have been raised about event studies. First of all, they are based on the assumption that the stock market is ''efficient.'' In essence, investors are credited with perfect knowledge of the value of every major corporation—the value under current management and the value if new management gains control of the assets. Therefore, positive movement in stock prices as a result of takeover bids are presumed to be an unambiguous good, and a suitable proxy for the enhancement of economic efficiency which is supposed to occur.

The other aspect of concern about event research is that stock price movements for the target firm have received far more scrutiny and attention than changes in the stock price of the firm initiating the takeover. These shortcomings are highlighted in the concluding chapter by Murray L. Weidenbaum, entitled ''Strategies for Responding to Corporate Takeovers.''

Kenneth Lehn and Annette Poulsen examine the source of stock price increases in leveraged buyouts (LBOs) in Chapter 4. The focus of their research is whether these LBOs create or merely redistribute wealth.

The economic issues addressed in this book do not cover all of the interesting questions in this area. What we have attempted to do is to present a balanced view of key aspects of the takeover issue. For instance, Chapter 5 by Dr. Weidenbaum and Richard Cook, entitled "Impacts of Takeovers on Financial Markets," neither defends nor condemns junk bond financing. Instead, it puts takeover financing in its proper perspective. Junk bonds and other forms of corporate debt issued to finance changes in control are shown to be a small portion of overall credit activities in the U.S. economy.

The results of the research conducted at the Center for the Study of American Business, collected in this volume, are intended to provide insights into an important cluster of public policy issues. Clearly, we have chosen those that are amenable to academic analysis and which could help provide a basis for sound policymaking.

Without a factual basis, new laws and regulations may well be established based upon biased rhetoric and the latest related or seemingly-related scandal. For instance, the fallout of the Ivan Boesky case may extend well beyond the issue of insider trading to the whole gamut of takeover concerns. Even worries about the trade deficit spill over into the corporate control debate, whether it is a Treasury Department official railing about "corpocracy" (a close relative of "entrenched" management) or displaced worker issues related to raiders' restructuring efforts.

The following chapter summaries are provided in this Introduction to whet the reader's appetite. A variety of viewpoints is presented. In each chapter, the authors deal with specific aspects of takeovers and reach their own conclusions.

Chapter 1: What the Economics Literature Has to Say about Takeovers

In this survey of the economics literature, CSAB research assistant Richard E. Cook's objective is not to reach heroic conclusions of his own, but to present an objective summary of recent takeover research published by the various schools of thought on the subject. He examines empirical evidence using various measures of performance, describes the variety of takeover techniques, summarizes research on the effects of defensive tactics, and reviews current public policy toward takeovers.

Cook acknowledges that the economic literature seems heavily weighted in favor of takeover activity, but he cautions that this need not be solely due to the weight of the arguments. He states, "It is also possible that researchers have reached similar conclusions because they use similar methodologies."

While the returns to the bidding firm from a takeover bid are not invariably positive, Cook finds that most economists agree that takeovers, in general, generate substantial increases in wealth for the owners of target firms. Premiums paid average over 30 percent above market value. In contrast, failed tender offers do not generate large gains for the target's shareholders.

Cook cites the work of Ravenscraft and Scherer as counter-evidence to this positive view of takeovers. In particular, their finding that 40 percent of the acquisition activity of the 1970s ended in "divorce" raises questions about long-run benefits.

With regard to the claim that takeover activities result in a short-run focus, two recent studies present results that weaken the argument. One study by Ken Lehn, et al. found that the preponderance of takeover targets are the lower-tech firms that typically are not investing in long-term research and development. Furthermore, institutional investors do not seem to be a key factor in takeovers—target firms showed a much smaller percentage of institutional ownership than the average for all firms.

The economics literature offers an interesting view of the effects of existing regulation on takeovers. "Virtually all studies find that both the Williams Act and state laws have increased the premiums paid to target shareholders." Ambiguities arise, however, because most economists also find that "by raising the costs involved in takeovers, regulation in essence, 'taxes' the information [that a bid is being made], reducing its profitability."

Cook concludes, "On balance, we seem to know less about hostile takeovers than is claimed by the seemingly certain proponents on each side of the debate. . . . What seems apparent is that the literature does not yet support any significant changes in regulation of the takeover process."

Chapter 2: The Stockholder Revolution

This strongly favorable evaluation of the benefits of a free market for corporate control is adapted from a luncheon address presented at the Conference on Public Policy toward Corporate Takeovers held at Washington University on 7 November 1986. Mr. T. Boone Pickens, Chairman and CEO of Mesa Petroleum Company, makes no apology for his one-sided view on this issue.

Pickens is particularly critical of the typical corporate manager's apparent lack of respect for shareholders. He states that one of his primary objectives in forming the United Shareholders Association is "to reestablish the principle that it is stockholders who own the companies—managers are employees."

Far from seeing companies threatened by being overly leveraged, Pickens claims, "Debt does have a disciplining effect on management. Companies start to look at things a little differently when they are not overloaded with cash."

The corporate proxy process also receives some harsh criticism from Pickens, which he cites as "the biggest obstacle to getting shareholders' rights on the table." In his view, a voting process where the incumbent sends out the ballots with the voter's name at the top, receives them back from the stockholder, counts them, and then informs the voter of the results runs counter to the American concept of democratic voting.

Pickens sees takeovers and corporate restructuring as beneficial and forecasts that, "Shareholders will restore management accountability, which, in turn will bring back a competitiveness that we have lost. Takeover activity will continue as long as corporate assets are undervalued in the marketplace."

Chapter 3: The Long-Run Performance of
Mergers and Takeovers

David J. Ravenscraft, an economist in the Bureau of Economics of the Federal Trade Commission, and F. M. Scherer, professor of economics at Swarthmore College, offer an alternative method to the stock price event analysis approach for estimating the economic effects of merger "events." Taking a longer term view, Ravenscraft and Scherer simply compare "before and after" financial results for mergers that took place in the 1950-76 time period.

The two economists first list nine principal reasons for mergers and then examine the data to see which motives appear to be supported by the facts. Their nine reasons for merging are:

1. *Management displacement.* Removal of inefficient, entrenched management.
2. *Synergies.* Efficiencies gained when two companies merge so that the total benefit exceeds the sum of the two parts.
3. *Monopoly power.* Profit potentials are increased through greater market power.
4. *Tax motivations.* Use of tax-loss carry forwards or changes in accounting rules made possible by tax code quirks.
5. *Bargain motivations.* Acting on the belief that the stock market has undervalued a company's stock.
6. *Risk diversion.* Efforts by conglomerates to dampen the cyclical swings of portions of their holdings.
7. *Hubris.* Overestimates by an acquiring firm's management of the synergies or efficiencies possible.
8. *Empire-building.* Managers seeking to enhance their own prestige and power.
9. *Speculative motivation.* Taking advantage of a stock market that faddishly awards price premiums to firms active in mergers and takeovers.

Ravenscraft and Scherer find little support for the most widely held view of these changes in corporate control—synergies or displacement of inefficient management. For instance, they cite the fact that acquiring firms in their large sample failed to significantly improve operating performance of their acquisitions, but paid substantial premiums for the privilege of trying. They state, "This result is more closely consistent with hubris, empire-building, tax avoidance or bargain theories."

Another finding is that so-called "normal" mergers were even poorer performers than tender-offer takeovers. Conglomerate mergers showed the poorest results—lower profits and higher rates of postmerger sell-offs. In addition, mergers of small innovative firms with larger corporations resulted in lower research and development to sales ratios, just the opposite result hypothesized by the proponents of mergers and takeovers.

Ravenscraft and Scherer conclude, "Our results provide little support for the hypothesis that the average merger or takeover yields significant improvements in efficiency and operating unit performance."

Chapter 4: Leveraged Buyouts—Wealth Created or Wealth Redistributed?

The research of Kenneth Lehn and Annette Poulsen focuses on answering the question, "Do the benefits to target shareholders in leveraged buyouts represent real increases in social value from more efficient allocation of resources or are they merely redistributions from bondholders, taxpayers and other 'stakeholders' in the firm?" Lehn is an assistant professor in the School of Business and a research associate at the Center for the Study of American Business at Washington University; his coauthor, Annette Poulsen, is Deputy Chief Economist at the Securities and Exchange Commission. They examined eighty-seven leveraged buyouts during 1980-84 to determine the driving factors behind these LBOs.

The two researchers first examine the wealth-creation hypothesis by relating the premium paid to target shareholders to measures of the firm's cash flow. In the view of economists who see LBOs as creating wealth, the purchase of low-growth, high-cash-flow firms causes a redeployment of this cash flow to the original stockholders and to holders of the LBO debt. This "disgorging" of cash offers better investment opportunities than continued reinvestment of earnings in the low-growth company.

Lehn and Poulsen do find a "direct and significant relationship between cash flow measures and premiums." This portion of their study, thus, supports the wealth-creation hypothesis.

Examinations of the wealth redistribution theory focused on bondholders and taxpayers. Only a small portion of the LBOs in Lehn and Poulsen's sample had bonds and preferred stocks outstanding (thirteen bond and ten preferred stock issues). Neither bond prices nor preferred stock prices suffered significant declines as the result of a leveraged buyout. If wealth is being redistributed, it appears to not be the bondholders' and preferred stockholders' wealth being transferred.

Lehn and Poulsen next analyze whether taxpayers are helping pay the premiums to target shareholders through reduced tax liabilities of LBOs compared to tax payments of the original corporation. In particular, a transaction that establishes the market value of a firm's assets can enable the entity to "step up" the value of those assets and hence increase the depreciation charges and reduce tax liability. They find that "the evidence strongly suggests that tax benefits play a significant role in leveraged buyouts."

The two economists conclude:

> These results indicate that the stockholders of the target firm are benefited by the current relatively open market for takeovers. Prohibitions . . . would reduce those benefits, thus reducing wealth creation . . . [however] a portion of [this] wealth appears to be coming from the general taxpaying public . . . [I]t [thus] may be the tax code that is "failing," not the market for corporate control.

Chapter 5: Impacts of Takeovers on Financial Markets

CSAB director Murray L. Weidenbaum and research assistant Richard Cook coauthor this examination of the significance of increases in corporate debt resulting from mergers and takeovers. Many observers share the views of Federal Reserve Chairman Paul Volcker, who has expressed ". . . concerns about the potential risks associated with mergers and takeovers when these transactions involve unusual amounts of leveraging."

Weidenbaum and Cook do find a definite increase in corporate debt as a ratio of gross national product, but they do not find takeovers to be a significant cause of this change. Bank lending for mergers and takeovers amounted to only 2 percent of the total loans outstanding at U.S. banks in December 1984. "Junk" bonds account for only 5 percent of acquisition financing and play only a minor role in financing hostile takeovers.

On the other hand, major shifts in debt and equity on individual corporate balance sheets may be a cause for concern for stockholders/stakeholders in those firms. These highly leveraged companies may well be at risk when the next business downturn reduces cash flow or if interest rates rise substantially.

As the two authors point out, the most relevant economic measure may well be the relationship between corporate indebtedness and the productive assets financed. They conclude from their analysis of the data, "It is clear that over the last decade . . . the increase in physical assets has been larger than the rise in corporate indebtedness. It seems . . . there is real value behind the rising debt load of American business.''

Chapter 6: Tender Offer Regulation and the Federalization of State Corporate Law

Washington University law professor and CSAB research associate Robert B. Thompson finds that the issue of state versus federal regulation of takeovers is very clouded. Primarily as a result of court interpretations of legislative intent of the Williams Act, a substantial federalization of corporate governance, likely never intended by Congress, is underway.

Thompson also finds this issue to be further confused by courts showing deference to the states' authority to define permissible defensive tactics for firms, but simultaneously overriding state statutes that favor defending managements over raiders. He is critical of the federal courts for not coming to grips with the larger issue of delineating the criteria for federal preemption of state statutes.

The law professor sees the original differentiation of areas of responsibility to be the best: Federal law should reign supreme with regard to the bidder's transaction with shareholders. But state law should continue as the principal regulator of shareholders' relationships with management.

Thompson does not advocate that state laws designed to protect hometown management from raiders should go unchallenged, but does believe the burden of proof should be on those seeking to override state law. Moreover, he cautions that those who read the Williams Act ''to mandate an unfettered market for corporate control and to block state regulation of shareholder-management relations are misreading the legislative history and purposes of that Act and are federalizing corporate law.''

Chapter 7: The Antitrust Division as a Regulatory Agency— An Enforcement Policy in Transition

With all the merger and takeover activity taking place in the United States, why aren't there more cases being filed by the Justice Department's Antitrust Division? Are these consumer protectors asleep at the switch?

Not according to the research of E. Thomas Sullivan, Washington University law school professor and research associate at the Center for the Study of American Business. The Antitrust Division has merely switched its emphasis from litigation to regulation. There may be fewer antitrust challenges in the courts, but the Division is very much involved in mergers and takeovers that might have anticompetitive effects.

Sullivan writes that those who believe the original intention of Congress in establishing an agency should guide its actions may justifiably be upset with the developments at the Justice Department's Antitrust Division. The debates on the Sherman and Clayton Acts clearly indicate that Congress did not contemplate that the Justice Department would be a market regulator. In particular, many antitrust lawyers question whether this change is sound policy. Sullivan, however, believes the shift is welcome and "has important implications for enforcement policy, compliance incentives, and substantive law."

The Hart-Scott-Rodino Act of 1976 provided the Justice Department with the tools to become a true economic regulator—premerger notification and review, and disclosure requirements. Professor Sullivan says that the Reagan Administration has completed the transition, challenging "only 26 out of more than 10,000 merger applications. And 13 of those cases were resolved out of court."

Sullivan disagrees with the critics of this change who would like to return to the original concept of the Antitrust Division. He cites the fact that "from the inception of the Clayton Act in 1914 until . . . 1950, the Department of Justice brought only sixteen merger cases."

In Professor Sullivan's view, the new emphasis on bargaining and "fixing" anticompetitive aspects of mergers before signaling approval "produces more voluntary compliance with merger standards at lower cost than litigation and minimizes enforcement costs." Sullivan says, "Deterrence also is fostered by the relative clarity of the [antitrust] guidelines, compared with case law ambiguities. To the extent that legal standards are clear and enforcement prompt, the efficiency of law is maximized."

Chapter 8: Strategies for Responding to Corporate Takeovers

In this chapter, Murray L. Weidenbaum examines the arguments behind calls for greater government intervention in takeover battles. He also evaluates a variety of public policy proposals ranging from a laissez-faire response to tax changes to tough new federal laws.

He finds that most of the people writing on the subject share a one-sided perspective, particularly those who hold to the "efficient markets hypothesis" as a tenet of faith. He asks, "What happens to the shareholders of the acquiring firm?" Weidenbaum states that they are often the innocent bystanders. Takeover specialists should not always be viewed as the good guys in white hats since their own shareholders often suffer reductions in stock value as a result of takeovers.

Weidenbaum opposes proposals for the government to intervene in take-overs because of its past track record in dealing with other perceived "market failures." "Study after study shows that government often does more harm than good when it interferes in private economic matters," he writes.

Such opposition does not mean that government should not try to amend tax provisions or existing regulations that create inequities between management and takeover practitioners. But it does mean that the parties closest to the situation and relevant facts—the owners and managers of the corporation—should balance management's need to act expeditiously with the shareholder's right to call that action into account. He says state and federal legislation should be last resorts.

The key is the outside directors, who are in the best position to head off further takeover bids, Weidenbaum writes. "They need to bear in mind that the future of the corporation is in their hands—as long as they serve the desires of the shareholders."

"The challenge to many boards is to pay out more cash for shareholders and to reduce outlays for low-yield projects," the CSAB's director warns. "The record is clear: If the board will not make the difficult choices that enhance the value of the corporation, the takeover artists will. Takeover mania is not a cause but a symptom of the unmet challenge."

In recent testimony on the takeover issue before the House Judiciary Committee, Weidenbaum cautioned that sensational cases, such as the Boesky scandal, make bad law. He observed that most Congressional committees devote the great bulk of their time and effort to exposing some perceived shortcoming in the status quo. Thus, they devote proportionally little attention to the policy proposal that is before them and frequently enact ill-considered and needlessly burdensome legislation. The corporate takeover issue, full of drama and front page news, could well become the next case in point.

1

What the Economics Literature Has to Say about Takeovers

Richard E. Cook

The subject of corporate acquisitions, particularly hostile takeovers, often generates passionate arguments. The popular press resounds with colorful terms such as "shark repellent," "white knight," and "greenmail," reflecting the views of takeover critics. They claim, with no uncertain hostility, that takeovers are the work of "corporate pirates" who want to plunder innocent firms. Others insist that takeovers are essential in a free-market economy, promoting efficiency and growth.

In an attempt to bring some order to the debate, this paper summarizes the arguments and results of academic studies on various aspects of takeovers. The term "takeover" is used here somewhat freely. It encompasses a wide range of corporate acquisitions, including mergers, tender offers, leveraged buyouts, proxy fights, and any other means by which the control of corporate assets changes hands.

Readers will notice that the following literature cited seems heavily weighted in favor of takeover activity. This weighting reflects the conclusions in the academic literature. Perhaps research has uncovered a "true" intrinsic value in takeover activity. It is also possible that researchers have reached similar conclusions because they use similar methodologies. Research methodology is discussed below.

Before reviewing the literature on hostile takeover activity, a general overview of merger and takeover research is provided. A substantial body of empirical literature has evolved, the vast majority of it using stock prices to measure the effect of takeover activity on individual firms. Much is known, therefore, about the impact of takeovers on the share prices of the firms involved. Much less is known about effects on other aspects of firms' performance, such as profitability, costs, and output, or about the impact on financial markets in general.

The Market for Corporate Control

In publicly owned corporations, the stockholders do not directly control decisions that affect corporate assets. Thus, a possible conflict of interest exists for managers, who have some ability to maximize their own utility at the stockholders' expense. This situation stems from the diverse ownership of public corporations. Monitoring management behavior benefits all stockholders, while only the monitors absorb the costs. This free-rider problem discourages active control of management by the shareholders.

This does not imply that management is free to act solely in its own interest. Ownership of some firms is concentrated among a few individuals, reducing the monitoring problem. Managers also have incentives to act on the shareholders' behalf. The market for corporate control provides some of these incentives, as will be seen below. Others are provided by the managerial labor market, where managers are judged according to their performance. Whether these incentives are sufficiently strong to protect shareholders' interests is part of the debate over the market for corporate control.

Takeovers Provide Incentives to Management

Merger and takeover activity induce managers to maximize shareholder wealth, according to those who oppose restrictions, by providing a means for removing managers who do not act to maximize the value of the firm. In this corporate-control market, the right to govern the use of corporate assets is allocated to those who value this right most highly. The more competitive this market, the greater the pressure applied to managers to pursue projects that maximize market value. Agents who divert resources to less-valued uses will be outbid by others.

Proponents of this view argue that an environment of low-cost corporate-control battles is needed to facilitate the efficient use of resources. Merger and takeover activity generates gains to all participants in financial markets, they say, regardless of whether they are ever directly involved in control struggles. Any interference with this activity impedes efficient resource allocation.

Aside from influencing managerial behavior, mergers and takeovers can directly increase efficiency. For example, combining firms might give rise to economies of scale or scope. As firms pool their resources, efficiencies also may result from new combinations of productive factors—gains that economists call "synergies." Furthermore, to the extent that the markets have valued assets at less than "full worth," an active takeover market can help redistribute assets toward higher-valued uses.

Takeovers Create New Problems

Opponents of takeovers argue that takeovers can weaken the economy. Quite apart from the debate over hostile activity, which many consider the "free market run amok," some argue that an excessively free takeover climate can have harmful effects.

One of the most common complaints is that takeover activity is distracting managers from the day-to-day operations of their corporations. According to this view, management must constantly watch for signs that the company is becoming a tempting target. Fears of a disappointing quarterly report lead managers to focus on any technique that will keep those reports shining, regardless of the effect on the long-term health of the firm.

The driving force behind this fear is purported to be the role institutional investors play in the market. Such large investors can devote great resources to following stock information and will, it is argued, dump their holdings at the first hint of a less-than-perfect earnings report. As these institutions play an increasing role in corporate investment, pressure for short-term performance grows.

Takeover opponents argue that such a short-run focus has reduced capital spending since investment projects incur large immediate costs but may show no return for several years. These higher costs and lower current incomes hurt quarterly reports. Similarly, research and development spending has been curtailed. Such spending has more uncertain returns, and then only after a longer time period. Of course, any company that neglects its capital outlays and its R&D cannot survive in the long run.

Another threat to firms' long-run health is thought to be the increased leverage resulting from extensive borrowing to finance takeovers. This leads to less corporate liquidity. From this view, corporations are building up levels of debt that will be impossible to service during an economic downturn, leading to higher failure rates.

In addition to the direct effects on long-term health, proponents of this "short-run focus" view note that international competition has intensified. Companies must continually improve their capital stock to remain competitive. If foreign corporations are investing more in capital, it is only a matter of time until domestic producers fall behind.

In this same vein, takeover critics point out that in many fields, American industry has stayed ahead of others by continually developing new products and technologies. Other countries may have lower labor costs or other advantages, but as long as domestic companies are the innovators, competition will not harm American firms. However, for this lead in innovation to be maintained, research and development must be pursued.

Critics say that other problems may emerge in an active takeover environment. For example, current tax law favors debt over equity by allowing the deduction of interest payments but not of dividends. Firms also are allowed to "step up" asset values upon acquisition, thereby increasing the value of depreciation. Thus, critics have claimed that firms engage in mergers and takeovers to reap gains from tax advantages, rather than for any real economic gains. It has also been argued that the gains from mergers are due mainly to greater market power, resulting from larger, combined firms.

Apart from questionable motives driving takeover activity, even well-intended takeovers can have drastic consequences. Employee pension funds may suffer. Older, loyal employees may be the first to be laid off as merged companies reduce redundant workforces. Entire communities can be harmed because a takeover may eliminate many local jobs.

Finally, the transaction costs of such actions can be substantial. A firm cannot undertake such activity without legal or investment-banking advice. After this advice has been considered and the takeover process started, the company will spend money on public relations counsel and printers in trying to lobby its shareholders for approval and attempting to convince the community that the decision is beneficial.

For example, consider the takeover of the Beatrice Companies by Kohlberg Kravis Roberts, the largest to date. It is also considered the most expensive. Estimates of the overall fees, including financing, advising, printing, and other costs run as high as $248 million.[1] While the Beatrice amount dwarfs most takeover costs and also may be small relative to the actual takeover, it is argued that such costs might not be trivial.

Empirical Evidence on Merger and Takeover Activity

Much of the pre-1983 literature has been summarized by Michael Jensen and Richard Ruback in a 1983 article for the *Journal of Financial Economics*. Most important from the standpoint of this review, Jensen and Ruback report on papers dealing with the following questions:[2]

- How should the gains to shareholders of both target and bidding firms be measured, and what are these gains?
- Does target opposition affect shareholder wealth?
- Do takeovers increase market power?
- Do proxy contests affect shareholder wealth?

The first question is central to most of the studies summarized here. The economic and financial literature, with some exceptions, considers stock price to be the best indicator of the value of a firm. This conclusion is based on the idea that shareholders ultimately hold the rights to organizational control and bear all residual risk.[3] In an efficient market, all information on the value of a firm will be embodied in the share price. Thus, stock price is taken as a measure of the impact on owners. With some exceptions (such as changes in value due to tax-induced changes in cash flow), firm value is also taken to be a good indication of social worth. In general, efficiently working markets are the goal. A few studies investigate productive performance rather than share-price gains. Unfortunately, most studies have not distinguished between hostile and friendly activity.

The Jensen and Ruback Summary

Most economists agree that successful takeovers generate substantial increases in wealth for the owners of target firms. Target shareholders are generally offered a large premium over market value. These premiums vary considerably from one takeover to another; differences also exist between mergers and tender offers. Jensen and Ruback find that, on average, the change in stock price due to tender offers is 30 percent of market value; that arising from mergers is about 20 percent. Although individual studies find great differences in the amount of the premiums, Jensen and Ruback note that all report target shareholders gaining from successful takeovers.

The results are not nearly as clear-cut for successful bidding firms. Where gains do appear, they tend to be small; according to Jensen and Ruback, the literature shows an average of only a 4 percent gain in share price in tender offers, and no gain at all to bidders in mergers.

These average results must be qualified, however. Jensen and Ruback note that three studies found bidding firms losing.[4] Jensen and Ruback theorize that these negative results might be caused by either data problems or model misspecification, since such results conflict with the efficient-markets assumption. Apparently, Jensen and Ruback do not question the theory, only data that do not support the theory. Whether such losses can be interpreted as evidence against market efficiency (i.e., that stock price is an unbiased estimate of discounted future dividend streams—the "value" of the firm) or should be taken to indicate econometric problems cannot be decided without further work. In any event, Jensen and Ruback acknowledge that the question of returns to bidding firms is still unsettled.

When merger or tender-offer attempts fail, stockholders of either bidders or targets do not reap large gains. Indeed, the literature reports slight losses to both, although most of the losses are not statistically significant. In unsuccessful tender offers, stock prices tend to remain at the new, higher level for as much as one or two years after the attempt before returning to the previous price. This tendency may be due to the information that the firm is a valuable target, Jensen and Ruback say, and the market is merely waiting for another suitor to appear. If none does, the market eventually lowers its opinion of the firm's worth.

In one curious finding, Jensen and Ruback note that proxy contests generate a moderate gain (8 percent), regardless of outcome. This seems to be the sole exception to the pattern that corporate control must actually change hands to generate increased wealth. Jensen and Ruback say this could be the result of better management in response to the threat. However, they offer no explanation why a proxy fight should prod management better than any other control battle.

Jensen and Ruback review two studies that test whether gains from mergers are due to increased market power.[5] Both report results that do not support the hypothesis. Unfortunately, neither paper identifies the actual source of gains.

Subsequent Studies

The literature since the Jensen and Ruback study reports mixed findings. Most studies continue to support the notion that target firms gain. However, Magenheim and Mueller show that results are sensitive to both the methodology used and the efficient-markets assumption. They show, for example, that gains to bidding firms depend on the time period used to evaluate the wealth effects. Negative results arise when the effects are evaluated over a longer time period after a change in control, during which the market can absorb information not available at first.[6]

Ravenscraft and Scherer also use a longer period to measure share response. They study postmerger divestitures, noting that nearly 40 percent of the acquisition activity of the 1970s ended in "divorce." Shareholders of early entrants into the merger wave of the 1960s fared quite well, while later entrants lost substantially.[7]

For these negative results to hold, financial markets cannot be "efficient." The basic premise of market efficiency is that if a stock were systematically under- (or over-) priced, the availability of arbitrage profits would encourage a "correction" of the stock's price. Virtually all other studies are based on this assumption of market efficiency. Of course, the popularity of this assumption does not guarantee its validity. For example, Shiller presents evidence that flows of new information on expected earnings cannot account for the volatility of stock-price movements, weakening the assumption of efficient markets.[8]

Studies using the efficient-markets hypothesis typically measure share-price response over a period of one to three days following the event. If markets are "efficient," this time period is sufficient for measuring the event's potential impact on stockholders. Of course, if the market is not so efficient, such studies would measure nothing more than random fluctuations in market value of the firm. Scherer also objects to using such a short time period. His findings are reviewed below.

Earlier studies that found no gains to bidding firms are criticized by Schipper and Thompson who differentiate between individual acquisitions and acquisition programs.[9] They argue that when a firm announces its intention to engage in a program of merger activity, the stock market evaluates the expected gains from the overall program. Each merger in the program then generates stock-price changes caused by "surprise" elements, which are likely to be random. Therefore, measuring gains at the time of individual events will only measure this random surprise return, not the return to the overall program.

For example, upon announcement of a merger that is not as valuable as the market expected, the surprise element will be a negative reaction in share value. This occurs even though the merger is profitable to the bidding firm. Schipper and Thompson note that previous studies focused on single events rather than treating takeovers as part of an ongoing project. Thus, they argue that findings of no gain or even losses to bidders are not measures of the true value of acquisition programs.

Schipper and Thompson report significant positive returns to announcements of plans for series of mergers. These gains vary from approximately 12 percent to 20 percent, depending on the time period involved.

Bradley, Desai, and Kim also report results at odds with earlier findings.[10] They find that some control contests leave bidding firms with significant losses. Their tests compared unsuccessful offers for firms that were eventually taken over by a third party with those in which the target did not subsequently change hands. The first group of unsuccessful bidders showed significant wealth losses, occurring around the announcement date of the control change. On the other hand, firms bidding for companies that remained independent suffered no loss.

Bradley et al. interpret these results to mean that the wealth effects are due to synergies of combined resources. These synergies allow the merged firm to operate more efficiently than the unsuccessful bidder, eventually putting the bidder at a disadvantage in the product market. The wealth losses are claimed to reflect this disadvantage. Of course, for this result to hold, the merged firm and the original bidder must be competitors in the same product markets.

Takeovers and a Short-Run Focus

Researchers have only recently begun analyzing whether takeover activity is causing a short-run focus among corporate managers. Two studies have surfaced so far.[11] These papers focus on the relationships between institutional investors, takeover activity, and long-term effects. Both papers present several results that weaken the argument that takeovers lead to managing for short-run financial results.

Institutional investors, because of their size and resources, have been blamed for causing this short-run focus. However, these two studies find that institutional ownership increased industrywide concurrent with greater R&D spending in the industries examined. This pattern holds too for individual firms within these industries. Also, share prices showed a slight rise (1 percent–2 percent) upon the announcement of new research and development projects. None of these results supports the short-run argument.

Furthermore, target firms showed a much smaller percentage of institutional ownership (19.3 percent) than the average (33.7 percent) for all firms. If institutions were a major force in changing corporate control, one would expect to see increased institutional ownership of a firm leading to a higher probability of that company becoming a target. Finally, in yet another attack on the short-run argument, Pound et al. find that target firms spend much less on R&D than others in their industry. A substantial majority of the targets in their sample (160 out of 217) report that R&D expenditures are "not material"; the rest average R&D-to-revenue ratios that are only half that of their respective industries.

Macroeconomic data also cast doubt on the short-run claim. Weidenbaum, citing data from the National Science Foundation (NSF), finds company-funded R&D investment has been rising, about 12 percent in 1985 and another 9 percent expected in 1986. The average annual increase between 1984 and 1986 adjusted for inflation is about 5.9 percent. He notes that this trend is similar to that of the 1974–81 period. Furthermore, the NSF blames the slight slowdown in 1986 on uncertainty about the macroeconomic outlook, rather than any response to takeover threats. It is possible that R&D spending might have grown more rapidly in a climate of fewer takeovers, but the growth rate is still healthy.

In spite of the above evidence, many corporate executives insist they are under tremendous pressure to maintain an attractive balance sheet, even at the risk of the long-run health of their firms. For example, a recent *New York Times* article quotes the CEOs of several large corporations who claim that the quarterly report is nearly all that matters. At the same time, these CEOs note that their companies would be better off if quarterly earnings were ignored, while long-term projects received management's undivided attention.[12] The irony of these comments is that many CEOs place similar "quarterly pressure" on the institutions that manage their firms' pension funds.

If the market evaluates companies accurately, the expected performance of a company over a longer time period will weigh much more heavily in the stock price than will the quarterly report. In addition, actions that boost quarterly earnings while harming long-run health would have the perverse effect of worsening share-price performance. As noted above, this claim of a short-run focus requires further scrutiny.

Other Measures of Performance

The prior studies reviewed all use share-price movements as a gauge of firm performance. A different picture emerges from another approach, using measures of industrial rather than share-price performance. Scherer raises two main objections to the share-price approach. First, the time frame of these studies is short. Scherer cites evidence that over a period of two years or more after the event, share value for acquiring firms declined relative to the market. This result is consistent with others using a long time frame. Second, increases in stock price do not necessarily reflect gains in economic efficiency. For example, tax savings may benefit individual firms at the expense of other taxpayers.[13]

Scherer found that target companies are not, on average, less profitable than their counterparts. He cites two other profitability studies that report similar results.[14] These findings contradict the notion that takeovers replace inefficient management. Furthermore, the profitability of acquiring firms declined substantially. Scherer reports that ratios of operating income to assets for these firms were 22 percent lower after the acquisition than for comparable firms. Further work is needed to reconcile this apparent discrepancy between these other performance measures and share-price results.

While much work has been done on the broad topic of mergers and takeovers, recent developments have narrowed the focus of some research to hostile takeover activity, which is covered in the next section.

Hostile Takeover Activity

As the literature reflects, recent trends in takeovers have caused academics to distinguish between friendly and hostile activity. For our purposes, a "hostile" takeover is any control contest that has not been approved by the target company's management or board of directors. While the end results may be the same for either method, major differences often occur in the actual process. This leads many economists to question whether hostile activity increases or decreases efficiency separately from the stock-price gains or losses generated by merger and takeover activity in general. This narrower topic is the focus of the remainder of this paper.

As noted, the principal distinguishing feature of hostile takeovers is that a target company's management and board do not approve of the change. While managers and boards are expected to ensure that the shareholders' interests are upheld, hostile activity allows the market mechanism to bypass these agents. Stockholders of the target company individually make the decision on transfer of control. This difference raises two important questions:

• Can the individual owners make the decision better or worse than their agents?
• Do those in control act in the best interest of the owners, or do they treat the company's resources as a means of keeping themselves in power?

Economists want to know whether the corporate-control market performs efficiently; if not, can it be improved? Some claim that the high pressure of a fast-moving control battle reduces the capacity of owners to make wise decisions. Others argue that the inherent conflict of interest between owners and managers makes the shareholders the best decision makers. Still others insist that the market exerts sufficient forces to ensure that optimal results will be achieved. Before these questions are addressed, hostile activity is described briefly.

Takeover Techniques

The most common techniques for hostile takeovers are tender offers and proxy battles, with tender offers comprising the bulk of the activity. Proxy battles, by nature, are hostile. Tender offers can be either hostile or friendly. Theoretical arguments distinguish between friendly and hostile offers; however, most of the empirical work does not.

Proxy battles are usually not an effective means of changing corporate control. In theory, the possibility of proxy fights imposes restraint on incumbent managers and boards. If these corporate officers perform in an unsatisfactory manner, shareholders can elect other members to the board, ensuring better owner representation. In fact, proxy battles are a small part of takeover activity, for reasons of both economics and corporate law.

Faced with a proxy challenge, incumbent management generally has the resources of the firm at its disposal in resisting. Shareholders forcing the issue must devote their own resources. In addition, gains to a successful quest would accrue to all owners, while the costs (which can be great) would be borne solely by those forcing the issue. This substantial free-rider problem makes proxy fights difficult for unhappy shareholders, making tender offers the more attractive alternative.[15]

Tender offers are not all created equal, and the differences can be important. The simplest is the any-or-all offer. The bidder agrees to purchase every share tendered at a given price. As with virtually all tender offers, this price far exceeds the current trading price of the stock. The bid may be in cash, in securities of the bidding firm, or some combination of cash and securities. The market exhibits tremendous creativity in its offers, with many containing unique twists.

Not only does the form of the bid vary considerably, the action may be further confused if not all shares are purchased at this price. Under partial tender offers, bidders agree to buy a certain percentage of outstanding shares, usually just enough to assure a controlling interest. Even more complex are two-tier offers, in which a bidder specifies two prices. The higher first-tier price, usually cash, applies until the buyer has a set percentage of the stock, usually a controlling interest. After this, the price offered for the remaining shares falls considerably, and often contains more securities than cash.

Of course, not all tender offers take on these complex forms. Indeed, as noted earlier, many are not even hostile, resulting from negotiations between target management and the bidder. According to a 1985 SEC study, half of the tender offers during 1981-84 began as negotiated offers.[16] Those offers that are not friendly are examined below.

Hostile Takeovers

As noted earlier, management may be able to act in its own interest. In this case, management cannot be expected to operate companies most efficiently. According to this view, the possibility of sidestepping incumbent management is essential for an efficient market for corporate-control. Most of the economics literature strongly favors unfettered hostile activity. The main argument is that hostile takeovers may be the only effective means of removing corporate control from the hands of entrenched, inefficient management.

On the other hand, hostile activity can generate more harm than good. Most of the arguments already noted against general takeover activity are claimed to apply even more strongly against hostile ventures. For example, the claim that the takeover threat fosters a short-run focus among incumbent management becomes even more forceful when one envisions hostile corporate "pirates" on the prowl for undervalued prey.

Rather than rehash this debate, let us now investigate arguments dealing with different types of hostile activity. Specifically, it is often argued that the form an offer takes can imply different social and economic impacts.

Some claim that certain tender offers are coercive, leading shareholders to make bad decisions. For example, partial and two-tier (front-end loaded) offers are thought to pressure investors into selling early in order to ensure themselves against being left out. Owners are thus pushed into accepting a lower bid than they could obtain in an any-or-all offer. In particular, it is the small investor, lacking sufficient resources to evaluate all offers fully, who is most likely to be harmed, according to this view.

In a 1985 study dealing with various forms of tender offers, evidence is presented against the argument that two-tier offers coerce shareholders. They reveal that the gains to target shareholders are of similar magnitudes for any-or-all or two-tier offers. However, partial offers do yield significantly smaller premiums. The study further notes that the proportion of outstanding shares tendered is higher in any-or-all offers (73 percent) than in two-tier (62 percent) or partial offers (34 percent). The authors claim these figures do not support the idea that front-end-loaded offers cause a stampede among shareholders to tender.[17]

Comment et al. skirt one issue. They deal with numbers of shares, ignoring the possibility of distributional effects. Policymakers might view the question as "the man on the street" versus institutions. The study does not distinguish between these different types of investors. However, the distinction is not as clear-cut as it may seem. Many large institutions are pension funds, insurance companies and other investment funds, some of which represent many small investors.

Defensive Tactics

Given the variety of arguments in other facets of the takeover debate, it is no surprise that defensive maneuvers likewise generate widespread disagreement.

On the surface, the question of defenses seems to be simply a matter of whether takeovers enhance the efficiency of financial markets. If so, defenses hinder the market. But if takeovers cause disorderly markets, defensive action can bring stability.

However, surface appearance merely disguises the depth of the debate. A considerable literature has evolved on this topic, revealing subtle and complex points. Space does not allow a thorough presentation of all the nuances of the debate, but this section attempts to cover the important points.

Let us begin by looking at theoretical arguments, concerning first the effects on individual firms and then the impact on financial markets in general. Empirical evidence follows the theoretical discussion.

Owners' Benefits

One of the important distinguishing features of managerial opposition to takeover attempts is whether such actions merely delay the change in control, or entirely thwart the takeover bid. Proponents of defensive tactics generally support those actions that act as delays, although there are exceptions.

By delaying the takeover bid, management can boost the gain to shareholders, advocates say. A delay allows time for a competing bidder to enter the auction with a higher bid, perhaps forcing the original bid up. Target owners can then reap a higher premium. Some claim that this delay prevents "raiders" from acquiring corporate assets at extremely low prices. At any rate, the delay allows owners more time to analyze the offer, enabling target shareholders to act in a more orderly fashion.

Less obvious points have also been made. Jensen and others argue that managers must invest in firm-specific human capital (knowledge of the individual company) in order to operate the firm most effectively.[18] Corporate officers may be less inclined to make such a personal investment if they are uncertain about retaining their jobs. Certain defensive actions, such as charter amendments that make takeovers more difficult, can help to alleviate this doubt. Also, golden parachutes (lump-sum payments to managers whose jobs end after a takeover) can guarantee that in the event of a change in control, managers will be rewarded for their investment in human capital, regardless of whether they are retained.[19] This is essentially a form of long-term contract between owners and management.

Knoeber notes also that managerial performance may be difficult to monitor over a short period, because results from long-term projects must be evaluated. Companies that face this monitoring difficulty might defer payment until performance can be better measured. Unprotected managers will not accept such a deferral without some assurance that they will not simply be fired before the payment can be made. Knoeber argues that golden parachutes can be effective in providing this guarantee. However, he also notes that large lump-sum payments can reduce the influence of the managerial labor market on management behavior; too much gold in the parachute can encourage management to sell to the first bidder.[20]

A further argument favoring managerial opposition is made by Jarrell and Bradley, and DeAngelo and Rice. They argue that individual shareholders acting to maximize their own wealth can receive lower premiums than they could achieve by working together. The argument is essentially another version of the well-known prisoners' dilemma of game theory. In this case, management can bargain for the stockholders so that more of the gain will accrue to the target.[21]

Management's Gain is Owners' Loss

Of course, not all academics agree that defenses are of value to target stockholders. Many argue that opposition to takeovers harms target shareholders. The most obvious claim is the "entrenched management" hypothesis—that is, managers are merely trying to protect their jobs.[22] By reducing the likelihood that shareholders will be able to sell at a substantial premium, defensive tactics lower the value of target stock.

As mentioned earlier, many supporters of defensive maneuvers separate such tactics into delaying methods versus preventive defenses. Generally, they find preventive tactics tend to affect adversely shareholders' wealth.[23]

A third approach, taken by several researchers, notes that shareholders often vote for management actions that are purely defensive. This tendency could be due to a lack of information available to investors, less-than-full disclosure by management, or the transaction costs of gaining further information that may outweigh the benefits to shareholders of doing so. On the other hand, perhaps owners perceive some benefit in such actions. Many economists argue that if parties to a transaction all act freely, each must believe he gains from (or at least, is not made worse off by) the transaction. Several economists have applied this argument to takeover defenses.[24]

DeAngelo and Rice categorize investors as informed or uninformed. The uninformed investor may face high transaction costs and thus might vote with management, while informed owners vote against.[25]

Brown offers an explanation based on the tax code. Investors who face high capital-gains tax payments could be hurt by a takeover. If the premium insufficiently compensates them for their higher tax bill, their after-tax wealth will fall despite the higher share price. These investors could choose antitakeover amendments that reduce the possibility of a takeover yielding a small premium.[26]

Jarrell, Ryngaert, and Poulsen consider another possibility. If investors expect to deal with management (e.g., suppliers), these owners may find that the loss from a defense may be outweighed by the gain from supporting management.[27]

Several authors divide takeover-opposition tactics into two groups: those approved by shareholders and unapproved acts imposed by management. These economists generally see no problem with any management action that the owners back. However, managers who act without the consent of shareholders might act in their own self-interest.[28]

Effects on Financial Markets

It is apparent that the influence of defensive actions on individual firms has not been settled. Likewise, the impact on financial markets is still open to debate. Some claim that "raiders' " activities disrupt the markets, while actions that slow the pace of takeovers calm the markets somewhat.[29]

In addition, delays can enhance the flow of information through the markets. This view posits that information is costly to acquire, and that bidders must expect to regain those costs through takeover attempts. Targeted repurchases (greenmail) are a possible method for spreading such costs throughout the market; all investors gain from efficient markets, so all should help cover the costs of maintaining that efficiency.[30] Furthermore, if bidders perceive the possibility of receiving such payments, bidding might be further encouraged. This argument, of course, assumes that takeover activity per se is good for the markets.

Others argue exactly the opposite. Many academicians say defensive actions reduce activity, as potential bidders see opposition raising the costs of takeovers. Indeed, Easterbrook and Fischel argue against any sort of delaying tactic. The idea is that takeover attempts are a way of spreading information on potentially good target firms. Easterbrook and Fischel propose that when a takeover is attempted, the information has been released. Any further bidding may result in redistributing the gains from a takeover but does not provide fresh information to the market. Therefore, resources used in competing bids are wasted because society no longer gains. Easterbrook and Fischel claim that allowing competing bids encourages free riders; that is, some investors can simply wait until others have identified profitable targets and then attempt to wrest the gains away from those who spent resources uncovering the information.[31]

This argument assumes that all competing bidders have the same potential for running a firm. If differences do exist between bidders, competition may allow the best-suited managers to outbid the others, yielding a more efficient corporation. Perhaps company performance should be considered in addition to information flow.

However, it is not certain that the highest bidder must be the most efficient user. For example, if gains are caused by different tax treatments, the highest bidder may be the firm that achieves the greatest tax savings; economic efficiency might not be maximized.

Public Policy Toward Takeovers

Public policy affects takeover activity through several channels. Most obvious is the direct regulation through the Williams Act at the federal level and numerous state laws. Antitrust enforcement is also important.

Takeover activity is also affected by the tax code. Direct effects stem from rules governing the sale of stock or other assets. The indirect impact is also potentially important. Such factors as corporate and personal income taxes, the treatment of capital gains, and estate taxes can all influence the market for corporate control.

Most of the relevant literature deals with the direct effects of regulation, while some investigates the influence of taxes. Although antitrust action affects mergers and takeovers, it is peripheral to this report and will be ignored here. Studies of the effects of the Williams Act and various state laws are summarized below, followed by those dealing with the effects of the tax code.

The main provisions of the Williams Act and its amendments are disclosure requirements, a minimum tender period, and antifraud provisions. A bidding firm or individual is required to report its plans and sources of funds for its acquisitions and must leave open any tender offer for a minimum of twenty days. The act further includes a broad range of requirements intended to eliminate fraud.[32]

The states have joined the fray more recently. Before 1968, no state had any statute on tender offers. A 1980 count revealed thirty-six states regulating tenders. According to Jarrell and Bradley, the state acts are generally similar to the Williams Act, although most require more extensive disclosures and allow for longer delays. Furthermore, many state laws also regulate two-tier and partial tender offers, which are ignored at the federal level.[33]

Regulation Raises the Cost of Takeovers

Virtually all studies find that both the Williams Act and state laws have increased the premiums paid to target shareholders, making those stock owners better off. Researchers are divided, however, on whether such regulation benefits the takeover market. The market must be considered in its entirety before concluding how efficient it is. Although target shareholders gain, many researchers claim that the market has suffered, with the loss outweighing the gain to targets. Much of the difference in views seems to be based on whether the principal concern of the researcher is market efficiency or "fairness" and on differing views of the efficiency of the market in valuing equity.

Fischel argues against regulation, although he tends to focus on mismanagement as the primary reason that companies become targets. Fischel notes that in most U.S. law, information is treated as property, with its attendant property rights. Forced disclosure in tender offers violates those rights. Also, incumbent management is not required to reveal its plans. Thus, the claim that disclosure gives all parties an "equal footing" is weakened. Furthermore, even if the disclosure requirement did give all players an equal footing, the notion that all parties to a tender offer should have the same information differs from the situation in most other transactions.[34]

Most empirical economic literature finds that these regulations have hurt the takeover market. Jarrell and Bradley find that the Williams Act and related state laws significantly raised the average premiums paid in takeovers. Their study notes an increase in each of the three main components of takeover costs: the average premium, the average fraction of shares purchased, and the average revaluation of unpurchased shares after the transaction.[35]

This affects results, they argue, because information is costly to acquire. Potential bidders seek data on which firms would be good targets and hope to earn a return to this information search by acquiring the assets of targets and putting them to more valuable uses. By raising the costs involved in takeovers, regulation in essence ''taxes'' the information, reducing its profitability. Jarrell and Bradley report that the Williams Act raised average premiums by about twenty percentage points, and that typical state laws increased premiums by another twenty percentage points.

Other economic researchers support these findings. Schipper and Thompson find that the Williams Act and other similar regulatory changes had a significant negative effect on share values of acquiring firms.[36] Also, Jensen and Ruback note earlier reports that reached similar conclusions.[37] Smiley, and Asquith, Bruner and Mullins claim the increased returns to targets come at the expense of bidders.[38] However, Jensen and Ruback insist that the tests cannot draw this conclusion because of possible elimination of takeover attempts. That is, less profitable attempts may not be pursued because of the higher costs and thus do not show up in the samples.

Jensen and Ruback argue that this reduction in takeover activity inhibits market efficiency. They claim that any profitable takeover produces a net gain to society by redistributing assets toward more valuable uses. If regulation stifles attempts that are less profitable than others but profitable nonetheless, some of the needed reallocation of resources will not take place.

The Fischel and the Jensen and Ruback studies note further evidence against the need for regulation. A common argument is that takeovers are the actions of corporate ''pirates'' who will plunder target companies. If this were the case, one would expect to see share value fall after a company has been acquired; however, most researchers find that target stock price increases after the takeover, at least in the short run.[39]

Regulation Brings Order to the Market

Proponents of takeover regulation see the possible validity of the above arguments, but insist that questions of fairness must override those of economic efficiency. Greene and Junewicz claim that informed shareholder decision making is impossible in the frenzied atmosphere of takeover attempts. They are concerned about the possibility of coerced stockholders, as some may rush to sell to avoid being minority owners. Others may sell simply to take advantage of the higher price. In any event, Greene and Junewicz say that regulation slows the pace of a takeover attempt and thus allows for a more orderly market.[40]

In addition, Lowenstein asserts that any decision affecting the structure of the firm should not be made in less time than the firm would spend on its capital budget planning. Lowenstein favors increasing the minimum period during which an offer must remain open.[41]

Greene and Junewicz recommend that the Williams Act be expanded in another direction. They note that by addressing only tender offers, the act distorts the choice between types of takeover activity. Greene and Junewicz insist that the choice of method should be decided on economic grounds, not on whichever method is least regulated. Regulation requiring a minimum offer period is thus desirable not only for tender offers, to which the Williams Act applies, but for open-market stock purchases as well.

Taxation and Takeovers

Both sides of the Williams Act debate agree that such direct regulation affects the takeover market. Policy further influences takeovers through the tax code. According to the congressional Joint Committee on Taxation, the three most significant ways in which federal tax laws affect takeover activity are: 1) differential tax treatment of acquisitions of entire corporations versus individual assets, 2) differential taxation of interest, dividends, and long-term capital gains, and 3) the need for sufficient taxable income to use available tax preferences.[42]

Schipper and Thompson include the 1969 Tax Reform Act in their tests of the effect of regulatory changes on share prices, reporting a significant adverse effect on the value of acquiring firms.[43]

Smirlock addresses the tax incentives that might encourage corporations to pursue merger activity. He claims that earlier tests tended to focus on the target firms, whereas the combined effects on both firms must be considered. In addition, personal taxation on both income and capital gains should enter the analysis. A corporation will choose payment plans that maximize its owners' after-tax incomes. Therefore, the total effect of all applicable taxes should be considered in determining whether tax policy influences merger activity.

Smirlock further notes that for tax preferences to drive corporations to merge, the actual consummation of the merger must be required for the tax gains to accrue and no lower-cost alternatives must exist. He recommends that takeover activity and the choice of method should not depend on tax policy; it should result from economic considerations.[44]

Further theoretical arguments are presented by Gilson, Scholes, and Wolfson. They separate the claims of tax effects on takeovers into three levels. First, an acquisition simply increases after-tax cash flows, while leaving pre-tax flows unchanged. Second, and somewhat stronger, is the idea that merging is the best route to the tax gains in question. The strongest claim is that taxes explain the size of premiums in takeovers. Gilson and his coauthors propose tests of these various hypotheses.[45]

Conclusion

The financial economics literature addresses many questions regarding the market for corporate control. Few, if any, of these questions apparently have been answered to the satisfaction of all parties in the debate.

Much evidence has been gathered on the effects of both friendly and hostile activity on share prices. The usefulness of this data heavily depends on the efficiency of the market in absorbing new information. Unfortunately, this evidence from stock prices tends to diminish rapidly over time, as the difficulty of isolating individual influences on stock price grows quickly.

Little knowledge has been gained, however, on the effects of hostile takeover activity on firms' economic performance. Changes in such areas as production, sales, profits, and growth are all important aspects that need to be addressed. Of the few studies that have investigated these questions, several results conflict with some evidence from stock prices. This discrepancy needs closer examination.

On balance, we seem to know less about hostile takeovers than is claimed by the seemingly certain proponents on each side of the debate. Many key points are still unsettled. What seems apparent is that the literature does not yet support any significant changes in regulation of the takeover process. Further control of takeovers could only be justified by evidence that certain parties are harmed beyond the risk they have willingly accepted. At the same time, with no supporting evidence other than share-price data, it would also be premature to remove existing controls.

Notes

The author thanks Lee Benham, Art Denzau, and Ken Lehn for comments, Murray L. Weidenbaum for suggestions and encouragement, and the staff of the Center for the Study of American Business.

1. John Williams, ''Kohlberg Kravis to Get $45 Million Fee if its Purchase of Beatrice is Completed,'' *Wall Street Journal,* 19 March 1986, p. 4.

2. Michael Jensen and Richard Ruback, "The Market for Corporate Control," *Journal of Financial Economics*, Vol. 11, 1983, pp. 5–50.
3. Michael Jensen, "Takeovers: Folklore and Science," *Harvard Business Review*, November-December 1984, pp. 109–21.
4. T. Langetieg, "An Application of a Three-Factor Performance Index to Measure Stockholder Gains from Merger," *Journal of Financial Economics*, Vol. 6, 1978, pp. 365–84; Paul Asquith, "Merger Bids, Uncertainty, and Stockholder Returns," *Journal of Financial Economics*, Vol. 11, 1983, pp. 51–83; Paul Malatesta, "The Wealth of Merger Activity and the Objective Functions of Merging Firms," *Journal of Financial Economics*, Vol. 11, 1983, pp. 155–81.
5. B. Espen Eckbo, "Horizontal Mergers, Collusion, and Stockholder Wealth," *Journal of Financial Economics*, Vol. 11, 1983, pp. 241–73; Robert Stillman, "Examining Antitrust Policy Toward Horizontal Mergers," *Journal of Financial Economics*, Vol. 11, 1983.
6. Ellen Magenheim and Dennis Mueller, "On Measuring the Effect of Acquisitions on Acquiring Firm Shareholders," manuscript, University of Maryland, p. 24.
7. David Ravenscraft and F. M. Scherer, "Mergers and Managerial Performance," Working Paper No. 137 (Washington, D.C.: Bureau of Economics, Federal Trade Commission, 1986), pp. 1–38.
8. Robert Shiller, "Do Stock Prices Move Too Much to be Justified by Subsequent Changes in Dividends," *American Economic Review*, Vol. 71, 1981, pp. 421–36.
9. Katherine Schipper and Rex Thompson, "Evidence on the Capitalized Value of Merger Activity for Acquiring Firms," *Journal of Financial Economics*, Vol. 11, 1983, pp. 85–119.
10. Michael Bradley, Anand Desai, and E. Han Kim, "The Rationale Behind Interfirm Tender Offers: Information or Synergy," *Journal of Financial Economics*, Vol. 11, 1983, pp. 186–87.
11. Gregg Jarrell, Ken Lehn, and Wayne Marr, *Institutional Ownership, Tender Offers, and Long-term Investments* (Washington, D.C.: The Office of the Chief Economist, Securities and Exchange Commission, 1985), pp. 1–15; John Pound, Ken Lehn, and Gregg Jarrell, *Is the Takeover Market Rational? Some New Evidence* (Washington, D.C.: The Office of the Chief Economist, Securities and Exchange Commission, 1985), p. 6.
12. Steven Greenhouse, "The Folly of Inflating Quarterly Profits," *New York Times*, 2 March 1986, p. F1.
13. F. M. Scherer, "Takeovers: Present and Future Dangers," *The Brookings Review*, Winter/Spring 1986, p. 17.
14. Edward Herman and Louis Lowenstein, "The Efficiency Effects of Hostile Takeovers: An Empirical Study," Working Paper no. 20, Columbia University Law School, November 1985, p. 67; John Pound, *Are Takeover Targets Undervalued? An Empirical Examination of the Financial Characteristics of Target Companies*, Investor Responsibility Center, January 1986, pp. 1–2.
15. Ronald Gilson, "A Structural Approach to Corporations: The Case Against Defensive Tactics in Tender Offers," *Stanford Law Review*, Vol. 33, May 1982, pp. 819–91.
16. Robert Comment et al. *The Economics of Any-or-All, Partial, and Two-Tier Tender Offers* (Washington, D.C.: The Office of the Chief Economist, Securities and Exchange Commission, 1985), p. 2.
17. Robert Comment et al., pp. 17–22.

18. Michael Jensen, "When Unocal Won Over Pickens, Shareholders and Society Lost," *Financier*, November 1985.

19. Daniel Fischel, "Efficient Capital Market Theory, the Market for Corporate Control, and the Regulation of Cash Tender Offers," *Texas Law Review*, Vol. 57, 1978, p. 1–46; Mark Hirschey, "Mergers, Buyouts and Fakeouts," *American Economic Review*, Vol. 76, May 1986, pp. 317–22.

20. Charles Knoeber, "Golden Parachutes, Shark Repellents and Hostile Tender Offers, *American Economic Review*, Vol. 76, 1986, pp. 155–67.

21. Gregg Jarrell and Michael Bradley, "The Economic Effects of Federal and State Regulation of Cash Tender Offers," *Journal of Law and Economics*, Vol. 23, 1980, pp. 371–404; Harry DeAngelo and Edward Rice, "Antitakeover Charter Amendments and Stockholder Wealth," *Journal of Financial Economics*, Vol. 11, 1983, pp. 336–38.

22. For example, Larry Dann and Harry DeAngelo, "Corporate Financial Policy and Corporate Control: A Study of Defensive Adjustments in Asset and Ownership Structure," unpublished, although this argument goes back at least to Adam Smith.

23. Jensen and Ruback, pp. 5–50.

24. Fischel, pp. 31–2; Hirschey, pp. 319–21.

25. DeAngelo and Rice, p. 334.

26. David Brown, "Shareholder Preference and Voting Rules: A Theoretical and Empirical Examination of Voting in Corporate Control Contests," dissertation, Washington University, 1986, pp. 13–28.

27. Gregg Jarrell, Michael Ryngaert, and Annette Poulsen, *Shark Repellents: The Role and Impact of Antitakeover Charter Amendments* (Washington, D.C.: The Office of the Chief Economist, Securities and Exchange Commission, 1984), pp. 7–9.

28. "Summary of Remarks by Presenters of SEC Economic Forum on Tender Offers" (Washington, D.C.: Securities and Exchange Commission, 20 February 1985), pp. 1–3; Jensen and Ruback, p. 33.

29. Edward Greene and James Junewicz, "A Reappraisal of Current Regulation of Mergers and Acquisitions," *University of Pennsylvania Law Review*, Vol. 132, No. 4, April 1984, pp. 647–739.

30. "Greenmail: Targeted Stock Repurchases and the Management-Entrenchment Hypothesis," *Harvard Law Review*, Vol. 98, 1985, pp. 1045–65.

31. Frank Easterbrook and Daniel Fischel, "The Proper Role of a Target's Management in Responding to a Tender Offer," *Harvard Law Review*, Vol. 94, 1981, pp. 1161–1204.

32. Jarrell and Bradley, pp. 371–72.

33. Green and Junewicz, p. 686.

34. Fischel, pp. 10–15.

35. Jarrell and Bradley, p. 393.

36. Schipper and Thompson, pp. 109–19.

37. Jensen and Ruback, pp. 28–9.

38. Robert Smiley, "The Effect of the Williams Amendment and Other Factors on Transaction Costs in Tender Offers," *Industrial Organization Review*, Vol. 3, 1975; Paul Asquith, Robert Bruner, and David Mullins, "The Gains to Bidding Firms From Merger," *Journal of Financial Economics*, Vol. 11, 1983, pp. 121–39.

39. Fischel, pp. 17–8; Jensen and Ruback, p. 10.

40. Greene and Junewicz, p. 658.
41. Louis Lowenstein, letter to Representative Timothy Wirth, 14 February 1984; Louis Lowenstein, "Pruning Deadwood in Hostile Takeovers: A Proposal for Legislation," *Columbia Law Review*, Vol. 83, March 1983, pp. 249–334.
42. Joint Committee on Taxation, *Federal Income Tax Aspects of Mergers and Acquisitions* (Washington, D.C.: U.S. Government Printing Office, 1985), p. 4.
43. Schipper and Thompson, pp. 109–18.
44. Michael Smirlock, "A Survey of the Tax Incentives for Mergers," manuscript, University of Pennsylvania, p. 19.
45. Ronald Gilson, Myron Scholes and Mark Wolfsen, "Taxation and the Dynamics of Corporate Control: The Uncertain Case for Tax Motivated Acquisitions," manuscript, Stanford University, pp. 1–2.

Bibliography

Asquith, Paul, 1983. "Merger Bids, Uncertainty, and Stockholder Returns," *Journal of Financial Economics*, 11.

Asquith, Paul, Robert Bruner, and David Mullins, 1983. "The Gains to Bidding Firms From Merger," *Journal of Financial Economics*, 11.

Bradley, Michael, Anand Desai, and E. Han Kim, 1983. "The Rationale Behind Interfirm Tender Offers: Information or Synergy," *Journal of Financial Economics*, 11.

Brown, David, 1986. "Shareholder Preferences and Voting Rules: A Theoretical and Empirical Examination of Voting in Corporate Control Contests," Dissertation, Washington University, St. Louis.

Cleveland, Gaines, 1982. "Developments in Corporate Takeover Techniques: Creeping Tender Offers, Lockup Arrangements, and Standstill Agreements," *Washington and Lee Law Review*, 39.

Comment, Robert, et al. 1985. "The Economics of Any-or-All, Partial, and Two-tier Tender Offers," The Office of the Chief Economist, Securities and Exchange Commission, Washington, D.C.

Dann, Larry, and Harry DeAngelo, 1985. "Corporate Financial Policy and Corporate Control: A Study of Defensive Adjustments in Asset and Ownership Structure," manuscript.

DeAngelo, Harry, and Edward Rice, 1983. "Antitakeover Charter Amendments and Stockholder Wealth," *Journal of Financial Economics*, 11.

Dodd, Peter, and Richard Ruback, 1977. "Tender Offers and Stockholder Returns," *Journal of Financial Economics*, 5.

Easterbrook, Frank, and Daniel Fischel, 1981. "The Proper Role of a Target's Management in Responding to a Tender Offer," *Harvard Law Review*, 94.

Eckbo, B. Espen, 1983. "Horizontal Mergers, Collusion, and Stockholder Wealth," *Journal of Financial Economics*, 11.

Fischel, Daniel, 1978. "Efficient Capital Market Theory, the Market for Corporate Control, and the Regulation of Cash Tender Offers," *Texas Law Review*, 57.

Gilson, Ronald, 1982. "A Structural Approach to Corporations: The Case Against Defensive Tactics in Tender Offers," *Stanford Law Review*, 33.

Gilson, Ronald, Myron Scholes, and Mark Wolfson, "Taxation and the Dynamics of Corporate Control: The Uncertain Case For Tax Motivated Acquisitions," manuscript, Stanford University, undated.

Greene, Edward, and James Junewicz, 1984. "A Reappraisal of Current Regulation of Mergers and Acquisitions," *University of Pennsylvania Law Review*, 132.

Greenhouse, Steven, 1986. "The Folly of Inflating Quarterly Profits," *New York Times*, 2 March 1986, p. F1.

"Greenmail: Targeted Stock Repurchases and the Management-Entrenchment Hypothesis," *Harvard Law Review*, 98 (1985).

Herman, Edward, and Louis Lowenstein, "The Efficiency Effects of Hostile Takeovers: An Empirical Study," presented at a Columbia University Law School Conference on Takeovers and Contests for Corporate Control, November 1985.

Hirschey, Mark, 1985. "Mergers, Buyouts, and Fakeouts," University of Colorado at Denver, Working Paper 1985-10.

Jarrell, Gregg, and Michael Bradley, 1980. "The Economic Effects of Federal and State Regulation of Cash Tender Offers," *Journal of Law and Economics*, 23.

Jarrell, Gregg, Ken Lehn, and Wayne Marr, 1985. "Institutional Ownership, Tender Offers, and Long-term Investments," The Office of the Chief Economist, Securities and Exchange Commission, Washington, D.C.

Jarrell, Gregg, and Michael Ryngaert, 1984. "The Impact of Targeted Share Repurchases (Greenmail) on Stock Prices," The Office of the Chief Economist, Securities and Exchange Commission, Washington, D.C.

Jarrell, Gregg, Michael Ryngaert, and Annette Poulsen, 1984. "Shark Repellents: The Role and Impact of Antitakeover Charter Amendments," The Office of the Chief Economist, Securities and Exchange Commission, Washington, D.C.

Jensen, Michael, 1984. "Takeovers: Folklore and Science," *Harvard Business Review*.

———, 1985. "When Unocal Won Over Pickens, Shareholders and Society Lost," *Financier*, November 1985.

———, 1986. "Agency Costs of Free Cash Flow, Corporate Finance, and Takeovers," *American Economic Review*, 76.

Jensen, Michael, and Richard Ruback, 1983. "The Market for Corporate Control," *Journal of Financial Economics*, 11.

Joint Committee on Taxation, "Federal Income Tax Aspects of Mergers and Acquisitions," U.S. Government Printing Office, Washington, D.C., 1985.

Knoeber, Charles, 1986. "Golden Parachutes, Shark Repellents, and Hostile Tender Offers," *American Economic Review*, 76.

Langetieg, T., 1978. "An Application of a Three-Factor Performance Index to Measure Stockholder Gains from Merger," *Journal of Financial Economics*, 6.

Lowenstein, Louis, 1983. "Pruning Deadwood in Hostile Takeovers: A Proposal for Legislation," *Columbia Law Review*, 83.

———, 1984. Letter to Representative Timothy Wirth, February 14.

Magenheim, Ellen, and Dennis Mueller, "On Measuring The Effect of Acquisitions on Acquiring Firm Shareholders," manuscript, University of Maryland, undated.

Malatesta, Paul, 1983. "The Wealth Effect of Merger Activity and the Objective Functions of Merging Firms," *Journal of Financial Economics*, 11.

Pound, John, 1986. "Are Takeover Targets Undervalued? An Empirical Examination of the Financial Characteristics of Target Companies," Investor Responsibility Research Center, January, 1986.

Pound, John, Ken Lehn, and Gregg Jarrell, 1986. "Is the Takeover Market Rational? Some New Evidence," The Office of the Chief Economist, Securities and Exchange Commission, Washington, D.C.

Ravenscraft, David, and F. M. Scherer, 1986. "Mergers and Managerial Performance," Federal Trade Commission, Working Paper No. 137.
Scherer, F. M., 1986. "Takeovers: Present and Future Dangers," *The Brookings Re-
view*, Winter/Spring, 1986.
Schipper, Katherine, and Rex Thompson, 1983. "Evidence on the Capitalized Value
of Merger Activity for Acquiring Firms," *Journal of Financial Economics*, 11.
Shiller, Robert, 1981. "Do Stock Prices Move Too Much to be Justified by Subse-
quent Changes in Dividends?" *American Economic Review*, 71.
Smiley, Robert, 1975. "The Effect of the Williams Amendment and Other Factors on
Transactions Costs in Tender Offers," *Industrial Organization Review*, 3.
Smirlock, Michael, 1985. "A Survey of the Tax Incentives for Mergers," manuscript,
University of Pennsylvania.
Stillman, Robert, 1983. "Examining Antitrust Policy Toward Horizontal Mergers,"
Journal of Financial Economics, 11.
"Summary of Remarks by Presenters of SEC Economic Forum on Tender Offers,"
Securities and Exchange Commission, Washington, D.C., 20 February 1985.
Williams, John, "Kohlberg Kravis to Get $45 million Fee if its Purchase of Beatrice is
Completed," *Wall Street Journal*, 19 March 1986.

2

The Stockholder Revolution

T. Boone Pickens

The current shareholder movement in America, which has been described as "the civil rights movement of the 1980s," borders on a revolution. Being very involved in this movement, I get a lot of mail. In fact, I received over 3,000 unsolicited letters from stockholders from 46 states and seven foreign countries in a matter of 30 days after announcing the founding of United Shareholders Association.

My stand on corporate takeovers is no secret. I believe that takeover activity is vital to the business system and provides the checks and balances that keep corporate America on an even keel. If takeovers are eliminated, or overly restricted, there will be no effective check on poor management. Without a check on subpar performance, the economy is going to suffer.

When you look at the performance of America's largest corporations—the Fortune 500—during the past five years, you can see that profits fell by 17 percent and payrolls shrank by 12 percent. That means that 2 million people were put out of work by those companies over the period 1980 to 1985.

The Fortune 500's poor performance reflects, I believe, a lack of management accountability. This accountability problem started with the advent of professional managers after World War II. That is when the interests of managers and stockholders seemed to drift apart. It has gotten progressively worse. It is probably much worse today than it was even three years ago. Executives became preoccupied with their perks—salaries, bonuses, and whatever else was available to them—but not with performance of their company's stock, and not with serving the interests of the stockholders.

When I talked to the chief executive of a major company recently, he said, "I hope you will keep doing the things that you're doing. It really is making a difference." I asked, "Are you an isolated case, or are there others in similar positions who feel that way?" He replied, "I can assure you that you are making a difference. It hurts but we are a lot better today than we were three years ago because of the changes and restructuring that we have done."

In my experience with managements, I have seen quite a few managers who should have been turned out to pasture. That is not to say that everybody in corporate America is a poor manager, but there is a substantial number who are making us noncompetitive in world trade. Some managers are so brazen in their attitude toward stockholders that they simply turn their backs.

If I do not establish anything else as a result of forming the United Shareholders Association, I hope to reestablish the principle that it is stockholders who own the companies—managers are employees. I am an employee of Mesa Petroleum and, when I took that company public in 1964, I knew very well what I was doing. I got several thousand stockholders at that time, and today there are several hundred thousand stockholders. I know exactly where I stand with them. If someone else can do a better job, I should be removed.

If anyone ever makes a successful offer for Mesa Petroleum, the transition will take place in a very orderly, professional fashion. If someone wants to make an offer today, I will not make one telephone call or spend one dime to keep that offer from going to the stockholders. I would have one mission at that point: to get that person to raise the offer or to get someone else to make a better offer. If the stockholders want to change the management, then it will happen. And I can tell you that I will not even take the pen set off the desk when I leave, it belongs to the stockholders, too.

There are no golden parachutes at Mesa Petroleum. We do have a staggered board, but the stagger drops immediately when an offer is made for the company unless it is in a countertender offer context. If Mesa makes an offer for a company and the company counter offers, we do have to stay in the fight until the finish. That is the only reason that we have a staggered board. We have all seen instances where managers and CEOs have believed they owned the company. However, stockholders take the financial risk; they are the true owners.

Some big thinkers will tell you that there are four different constituencies in a company—the employees, the long-term suppliers, the consumer, and the fourth is the stockholder. But when a company takes a big write-down, do any of these other three constituents take any part of that write-down, or is it just the stockholders? Only the stockholders suffer that loss, we know that.

If management does a good job, then the stockholders are well served, the employees have a secure place to work, and cities and towns where the companies are located do well. But delivery for the stockholders is number one. The only things at risk for most managements are their jobs. That is not an insignificant thing, I understand that. But they do not have their own money at risk in a publicly owned company.

After a Japanese airline disaster killed over 500 people a year or so ago, the CEO of that airline resigned. He assumed responsibility even though he was not the one who worked on the tail section of the plane, which was the cause of the accident. He felt responsible for the total operation of the airline and he resigned. Responses like that do not happen in this country any more. I do not believe there is a CEO in America who would resign if a tail fell off one of the company's airplanes. I have seen companies take $2 billion write-downs with hardly a press release. They just readjust the balance sheet a little bit, write off $2 billion, but nobody leaves.

Takeover activity is restoring management accountability and corporate competitiveness. There is no question that the shareholder movement has been good for the economy. A Goldman-Sachs study for the period 1984-85 attributes one-third of the stock market gain to the restructuring of corporate America. Professor Michael Jensen, at the University of Rochester, says that mergers and acquisitions generated $75 billion in gains to shareholders in 1984 and 1985. Well, that's not peanuts. MIT Professor Alan Jacobs says that additional restructuring in the oil industry alone could generate $200 billion in benefits to the economy.

Some critics dismiss these gains as so-called paper profits, achieved by simply transferring money from one pocket to another, but they are wrong. Takeover activity has caused companies to reduce uneconomic investments, upgrade or divest underutilized assets, and increase operating efficiency. In most cases, these companies returned a portion of their equity to the share-holders, and that is the most sensible strategy for mature, overcapitalized corporations.

Sometimes an outside push is needed to get this done. A takeover bid or even the possibility of a takeover provides that incentive. Takeovers are simply another form of competition—competition for control of the corporation.

Of course, many executives are scared stiff by competition. A leading spokesman for the Business Roundtable (and CEO of a major company) was quoted in the *Los Angeles Times* in May of 1986 as saying, ''We had better start looking at ways to protect the American economic system from the shareholders.''

Just this week, in a *Washington Post* interview, the same CEO described the typical chief executive: ''We are all products of a bureaucracy,'' he said. ''At some stage, we all get expensive suits and look alike, but none of us are really sharp in public debate.'' That was a most unusual admission. Last year, a Weyerhauser executive offered the ultimate argument against takeovers when he said, ''There is no telling what stockholders will do when faced with the prospect of a profit.''

Entrenched managers have come up with all sorts of defenses. They argue that restructuring creates too much debt. They cried about Phillips Petroleum being buried under a mountain of debt. Remember that the decision to borrow $5 billion was made by the management of Phillips in an effort to repel our tender offer. Mesa Petroleum was involved in that deal but the plan they used was not ours. What happened to the $5 billion? Did it disappear from the economy?

I had an interesting discussion on this subject with a senator in Washington, not in relation to the Phillips deal, but to Gulf Oil Corporation. He is an astute fellow from an oil producing state so he knows a lot about the oil business. He said, ''I think that Chevron is paying too much for Gulf.'' I found that an interesting statement. Was this just an idle observation of his or was he thinking about legislation to prohibit somebody from paying too much for something? I replied, ''Tell me more about why you think they are paying too much.'' He said, ''If the price of oil goes down and interest rates go up, they would have paid too much.'' I said, ''I don't see where that is really a discussion that we should be having in this particular situation.''

If I had gone to George Keller, who is CEO of Chevron, and said, ''You may be paying too much for Gulf,'' he would have thrown me out the door. I told the senator that there was no way that George Keller would even pay any attention to me and probably should not. I said, ''Thirteen billion dollars sounds like a lot of money, but Chevron has a very strong balance sheet and Gulf has a lot of assets. So you have to look at it in the proper context. Somebody paying $10,000 for a corner filling station may be paying relatively more than what Chevron is paying for Gulf Oil.''

''Furthermore,'' I pointed out to the senator, ''the $13 billion that Chevron is paying is going to the pockets of 400,000 stockholders at Gulf.'' You could tell it was the first time he had thought of that. ''You don't think that $13 billion just disappears, do you?'' ''No,'' he said, ''that's right; 400,000 people get it.'' I said, ''It goes into hot hands, too, that are getting ready to buy something. You'll see it go back into other investments, or you'll see it go into a home, automobiles, or whatever else.'' It was a surprise to him that this was an immediate infusion right back into the economy. And the $5 billion that Phillips borrowed went right back into the pockets of 150,000 stockholders at Phillips.

Debt does have a disciplining effect on management. Companies start to look at things a little differently when they are not overloaded with cash. George Keller was quoted in a recent *Wall Street Journal* article as saying that the oil industry over the period 1980-85 was faced with too much cash and limited investment opportunity. I made a speech in 1980 saying that was what the industry was headed for, that we did not have a place to spend the money. We are about to go through another period in this restructuring movement where managements are starting to figure out how, in mature situations, they can get money to the stockholders.

Managements complain that you are liquidating the company when you make acquisitions. I have been accused of that. The noted attorney Martin

Lipton, at a hearing in Washington, said, ''Boone Pickens is likely to turn one of these oil companies into a dust bowl.'' Mesa Petroleum started out with no production at all and $2,500 paid in capital in 1956, and today we are larger than we have ever been in our history. We are the largest independent oil company in the United States. Now, that is hardly turning things into dust bowls.

When I got a chance to give my testimony, I told Lipton, ''I may know more about dust bowls than anybody in this room. I was born in Oklahoma in 1928, right in the dust bowl.'' No one is going to pay millions or billions of dollars for something and then destroy it. It is absurd to think that is going to happen.

A part of the Phillips restructuring was to sell off $2 billion worth of assets, including hotels and some other things that did not really fit an oil company. They would have been some of the first assets we would have sold off, also. Interestingly enough, Phillips made a statement to the *Wall Street Journal*, saying the sale of these assets did not reduce the cash flow, an unusual admission. What were they doing with $2 billion worth of assets that were not contributing to the cash flow?

Furthermore, somebody bought the $2 billion worth of assets. What did they do with them? The $2 billion was sold off in five or six packages of maybe $300 to $600 million each. But each one of those packages is really the nucleus of another company that employs people, creates profits, and makes the economy work. I could see only good coming from what happened in the sale of those $2 billion worth of assets.

Phillips is not an isolated case. There are billions of assets in similar underutilized condition all over corporate America. An executive with a major West Coast railroad told me about his duck hunting trip to California. The duck shooting had been absolutely terrific. When he asked who had owned the place, he was told that it was leased. Finally, after much effort, over a period of nearly a year, he discovered that his railroad owned it. The land had been set up in a corporation 30 or 40 years ago for some special purpose and they did not want anyone to know about it. This man had been hunting there two or three times over that year, and it took him that long to find out that he was on his own company's land.

In 1981, I made a speech with regard to knowing your assets. I think that it is reasonable to say that there are managements who do not realize what they have. At Mesa, we know what we have. The reason we do is that we are frequently highly leveraged. We have gotten to know our assets very well because we put them all on the table from time to time to examine them.

People opposed to takeovers sometimes say that restructuring places too much emphasis on the short term. Of course, today's results are the product of yesterday's long-term planning; if you want to see how well a company's management does in long-term planning, examine the short-term results. In the last two years, the U.S. oil industry alone wrote off $16 billion worth of assets. If that is long-term planning, I question how much of it the stockholders can stand.

Managements tell stockholders that they can always sell if they do not like the way the company is run. That suggestion reminds me of a story involving a good friend of mine, Arnold Schmeidler. He had 600,000 shares of Unocal and he voted against Unocal management in the April 1985 proxy fight. Unocal promptly sent a team of people to talk to Schmeidler. They said, "We learned our lesson. We are going to treat stockholders better now." Schmeidler said, "Well, I am still going to vote against management." They answered in a less friendly tone, "You won't have any access to management if you vote against us, you will be cut off." "I am still going to vote against you," Schmeidler responded. Finally, in frustration they told him, "If you don't like the way we are running the company, sell your stock. That would be the thing for you to do."

Schmeidler then told them a story to illustrate what he thought of their suggestion. He said, "If I had an estate and I didn't like the way that my gardener was cutting the lawn, I wouldn't sell the estate; are you getting the picture here?" One in the group said, "I think I am." Schmeidler added, "Well, let me make it clearer. Tell your chairman to identify himself as the gardener in this particular story."

America's large corporations are scrambling to stop the shareholder movement. Over 300 of the Fortune 500 companies have adopted antishareholder proposals. More than a hundred of them have instituted poison pills and only one of these companies submitted its pill to the stockholders for a vote. That is a pretty highhanded way to treat the owners of a firm.

In August, when we announced the founding of the United Shareholders Association (USA), we thought there might be 20 people at the Washington Press Club where we held our press conference. We had 115 in attendance; we could not squeeze 25 of them in the room.

We have received a tremendous response to our stand on the one-share, one-vote issue. The Securities and Exchange Commission (SEC) is holding hearings on December 16 and 17. This is only the second time in the fifty-nine year history of the SEC that they have held hearings. The United Shareholders Association turned the heat up on this issue by calling for members to contact the SEC to request open and in-depth hearings.

The corporate proxy process is the next big issue for USA. We recently commissioned an academic study on this subject. The proxy process seems to be the biggest obstacle to getting shareholders' rights on the table.

Current proxy procedures run counter to the American concept of democratic voting. The incumbent actually sends ballots to each shareholder with the shareholder's name prominently at the top, along with the number of shares he or she owns. Then, each shareholder votes with or against management, signs his or her name to the ballot, returns it to the incumbent, and waits to hear how the election turned out.

My concept of a fair vote goes all the way back to the 5th grade, when I ran for homeroom president. The ballots were all placed in a cigar box on the teacher's desk. When I came home that night my mother asked, "Did you win?" I said, "No, I lost, but they put the ballots in a box." She then asked, "What are you telling me?" I answered, "I know that I would have won if they would have raised their hands." "Well, why do you think you would have won?" she asked. I told her, "They were all my friends." And then she pointed out, "The other person probably thought they were all his friends, too, and the other person did win." That is the first time I was involved in a secret ballot. In America we vote by secret ballot; it is not anybody else's business to know how we vote.

When Mesa was battling Unocal, a man who has a thousand shares of Unocal stock said to me, "I am not going to vote against Fred Hartley even though I disagree with him." I asked, "Why not?" He said, "Because he will take my card and look at it." I asked, "Why does that make any difference?" He answered, "He is on the board at my bank, and I have problems there. I am not sure what he will do about my loans at the bank if I vote against him."

This man's concern is a valid one. I ask my people to show me all the "no" votes on proxies that we send out at Mesa. I like to know who votes against me. We all look at those things. We have our private fiefdoms and there needs to be some check on us.

I have never tampered with the votes, of course. I just thumb through the cards, and then drop them back in the out box to go to data processing. I never look at the "yes" votes because those votes are cast by the smart people.

As I mentioned, we have commissioned a study which will come out in 1987. One suggestion is to infuse more "sunshine" into the voting process. In other words, everybody would have to show exactly how they vote, especially institutional holders of stock. Maybe the answer is to let people who are institutional holders specify whether they want a confidential vote or an open vote. After all, if I vote for Ronald Reagan, I do not have to keep it confidential.

We need to change the proxy process. This is the biggest corporate governance problem we are faced with today.

At any rate, the restructuring movement has momentum. Shareholders will restore management accountability, which, in turn, will bring back a competitiveness that we have lost. Takeover activity will continue as long as corporate assets are undervalued in the marketplace. When a corporation's management gets the price of stock up to the appraised value of the assets, they are no longer vulnerable. But if the stock sells at a discount to the appraised value, there will be takeover activity.

A few years ago, when big companies were taking over smaller ones, the Business Roundtable was lobbying in Washington in favor of takeovers. They said that takeovers were "an example of the free enterprise system working at its very best." But when someone figured out how a small company could gain control of a larger one, they changed their tune. They now claim, "This new type of takeover activity is tearing down America, and is a threat to the free enterprise system."

Meanwhile, the 200 largest corporations in America are fighting hard to be assured of the opportunity to acquire other firms. They call their takeovers "friendly." Friendly takeovers are okay but hostile takeovers are not. But what is friendly or what is hostile is only in the mind of the target company's chairman. Stockholders never think these takeovers are hostile.

After a committee hearing in Washington, one of seventeen times that I testified on takeover activity over an eighteen month period, an older gentleman got my attention. We walked out together and he said, "Mr. Pickens, Fred Hartley (the chairman of Unocal) may consider your offer to be hostile for the company, but I am a Unocal stockholder and I consider it to be downright friendly."

I was attending a party at the Augusta National Golf Course in April 1986 and a fellow who was a retired CEO of a major oil company called me aside and asked, "Do you think there is any chance for our company?" I knew what he meant, but I wanted him to explain, so I said, "What do you mean?" "Well, is there any chance that an offer will be made for our company?" he asked. I responded, "I don't know. Why do you want an offer made for your company?" He said, "Well, I have 90 percent of my net worth in the company stock." I told him, "I admire you for that, I really do. How long have you felt this way?" "About 30 days after I retired," was his reply.

Quite frequently, I am asked if this takeover process has gone far enough or possibly too far. This question reminds me of a story I have heard told about Sam Snead playing with a foursome of amateurs twenty years ago at a PGA golf Pro-Am event. One of the amateurs in the foursome was an enthusiastic, high-handicap golfer who was determined to make a friend out of Sam Snead. Snead was not interested in developing a friendship. By the time they got to the tenth hole, this fellow was still trying. Snead hit a 3-iron about 230-40 yards. It was a beautiful high shot. When it hit the green, it actually stopped, checked, and then backed up. The amateur could not believe it. He said, "In my whole life, I have never had a 3-iron stop like that." Sam Snead asked, "How far do you hit a 3-iron, anyway?" He said, "About 150 yards." Sam drolled, "Why in the world would you want to stop it?"

That is how I feel about takeover activity and the restructuring of American corporations that is taking place today. With all the benefits that come as a result of this relatively free market for corporate control, ''Why in the world would you want to stop it?''

Note

This chapter is adapted from the author's address at the Conference on Public Policy Toward Corporate Takeovers held at Washington University in St. Louis on 7 November 1986.

3

The Long-Run Performance of
Mergers and Takeovers

David J. Ravenscraft and F. M. Scherer

Decidedly divergent opinions exist on the economic consequences of takeovers. One school of thought, including takeover entrepreneurs, the President's Council of Economic Advisers, and many scholars, views mergers and tender-offer takeovers as a tremendous contributor to American economic dynamism. Another school, including many corporate executives, the Business Roundtable, consultant Peter Drucker, and a smaller band of academicians believes that hostile takeovers, in particular, are destroying American competitiveness. Where does truth reside?

Our identification as research economists is with the scholarly factions of the merger-and-takeover debate. Our approach in this chapter is to examine with a more than usually critical eye one side of the scholarly debate and then to summarize what light our recent research sheds on the issues.

The Motives for Mergers and Takeovers

To understand the consequences of mergers and takeovers, it is necessary but not sufficient to understand why they occur. There are many motives for merging. The principal variants can be characterized simply in nine main categories:

Management displacement. Since seminal articles by Robin Marris and Henry G. Manne appeared during the 1960s,[1] mergers have been seen as a vehicle for displacing managers who are either intrinsically inefficient, or who have chosen business policies inconsistent with those (usually identified with profit maximization) desired by corporate shareholders. The transfer of corporate assets to more capable hands might occur voluntarily, as incumbent

34

managers see the light and arrange a merger, but involuntary takeovers are perceived as an important instrument of displacement when entrenched management refuses to change its ways.

Synergies. The synergy theory asserts that two enterprises have greater profit-earning power when they are combined than when they operate separately. There are many conceivable ways in which this improvement can be achieved: through fuller utilization of some critical resource, human, physical, or financial; through realization of favorable network effects when organizations, facilities, or research capabilities are meshed; due to sharing corporate overhead functions; and from pooling risks, which may in turn lead to lower capital costs. Such changes characteristically entail increases in efficiency, which most economists consider beneficial to society as well as to the merging companies.

Monopoly power. A special kind of "synergy" arises when the merger of two or more enterprises yields greater power over output or input prices, so that profits can be increased through monopolistic (or monopsonistic) tactics. Unlike other synergies, these consequences of merger may, by distorting the allocation of resources, be efficiency-reducing rather than efficiency-increasing.

Tax motivations. Mergers may increase profits by permitting tax savings. A profitable company may be combined with one possessing otherwise unusable loss carry-forwards. The merger may make it possible to step up merged asset bases and shift to accelerated depreciation. Or the new entity may create internal capital markets in which cash flows are reallocated and reinvested without being subjected to dividend taxation. Such changes have ambiguous efficiency implications. They may be merely a zero-sum game against the Treasury, they may help otherwise doomed enterprises survive, or they may encourage investment decisions that would not otherwise pass a market test. These changes are likely to be less important in the future as a result of sweeping income tax reform.

Bargain motivations. Mergers may occur because certain investors believe the stock market (or the stockholders of nonpublic companies) have undervalued a company's common stock shares, making acquisition of the company a bargain too good to be passed up.

Risk diversification. Conglomerate acquisitions, in particular, are often undertaken to smooth the earnings performance of companies in cyclical businesses. Or, in cases where the acquiring company is in a declining industry, diversification may be seen as a means for ensuring the company's long-run viability. However, it is not clear that shareholders gain from these diversification efforts since they can lower risks through a stock portfolio.

Hubris. Company managers at acquiring firms may overestimate their ability to achieve synergies and to manage acquired entities better than they were managed before the acquisition. Such optimism can lead to mergers that are attractive ex ante but not ex post.

Empire building. Mergers might also occur because managers seek to enhance their own prestige and power, making acquisitions even though they reduce the wealth of their shareholders.

Speculative motivations. Mergers may take advantage of a stock market that faddishly views merger activity as desirable, awarding price premiums to companies that are particularly active at the game. Or merger-makers may be willing to take sizable risks with stockholders' money in the hope of large but only occasional gains.

Some of the motives for merger imply results that are unambiguously beneficial to the economy as a whole, some imply detrimental results, and some are ambiguous in their consequences. It is therefore crucial to determine the relative importance of each motive and the degree to which original intent was realized. Here scholars diverge. As is not uncommon in scholarly debates, there are sharp differences of opinion as to the methodologies appropriate to this task. One school of thought stresses the analysis of stock price changes at the time of merger "events" as the most suitable means of pinpointing the expected consequences of merger. Another school is more eclectic, focusing on what actually happens after a merger occurs, and attempting to see how the merger mattered through qualitative case studies and analyses of postmerger financial performance information. What one learns about the economic efficiency of mergers depends upon the methodology employed in the analysis; therefore, it is necessary to consider what each approach teaches.

The Stock Price Approach

By far the most widely-practiced method of evaluating the economic effects of mergers is analysis of how stock prices react to the announcement of various types of merger "events." Since a pioneering contribution by Gershon Mandelker appeared in 1974,[2] there have been dozens of merger event studies,[3] and if anything, the pace appears to be accelerating. The approach is popular, in part, because the key data exist in computer-readable form, and the techniques are fairly easily mastered.

The central premise is that the announcement of various "events" in merger history—a tender offer, a negotiated "deal," rejection of an offer, the appearance of a contending bidder, an antitrust challenge, the settlement of disputed legal issues, and actual consummation—adds "news" to which common stock investors react. From changes in acquiring, acquired, and competitive company stock prices at the time of these events, inferences are drawn about investor expectations of the merger's consequences. Because the stock market is populated with investors who exert considerable effort to discern what the consequences of new events will be, and because arbitrage gains can be made by trading on the basis of superior information and/or prognostications, stock price movements are said to be unbiased estimators of anticipated consequences.

Beginning from the premise that the stock market is "efficient" in this way, the bargain and speculative motives for mergers are ruled out axiomatically by merger "event" analysts. If traders are constantly using all the information at their disposal, there can be no bargains, for any shares that are undervalued will have been sought out by eager traders until their price has been bid up above the bargain level. Similarly, merger "bubbles" are deemed improbable or impossible. The reasoning is as follows: astute traders, realizing that merging companies' shares are valued highly for reasons not rooted in "fundamentals," will sell the overvalued shares short until their value is brought back into line with an unbiased projection of anticipated cash flows.

Various objections have been raised to this view. Two of these objections deserve immediate mention. For one, markets might well be efficient in eliminating all palpable bargains. But if there is a substantial class of entrepreneurs who (wrongly) hold contrary views, they may make mergers in the misguided belief that they are buying undervalued assets. Eventually, the error of their ways will be shown, but that may take considerable time, and in the meantime, a considerable quantity of merger activity can have occurred.

Also, merger event analysts have been vague about the degree of precision embodied in the notion that efficient markets leave no bargains, i.e., stocks priced below fundamental values. The tradition of vagueness has recently been broken by Fischer Black in his presidential address to the American Finance Association:[4]

> All estimates of value are noisy, so we can never know how far away price is from value. However, we might define an efficient market as one in which price is within a factor of two of value, i.e., the price is more than half of value and less than twice value. . . . By this definition, I think almost all markets are efficient almost all of the time. "Almost all" means at least 90%.

If stock prices can diverge from their true value by as much as Black believes, the proposition that mergers may be motivated by a search for bargains remains strongly viable. Large gains can be made by those who, by superior perspicacity, can identify companies that are undervalued by the market by a factor of two. The gains are all the more impressive for the acquiring company that has "insider information" leading it to believe that its own shares are overvalued, providing a uniquely economical currency for acquiring undervalued bargains (or raising the cash to acquire them).

Ignoring these difficulties, the stock market event analysts see mergers as preponderantly efficiency-increasing, because increases in common stock values tend to be coincident with merger news hitting the market. These stock price increases have a fairly characteristic pattern. The shares of the acquired firm typically rise sharply, reflecting the fact that a premium over prevailing market prices is usually offered to induce target companies either to tender their shares or (for negotiated mergers) to vote in favor of merger.

For the acquiring firm, the evidence is less compelling. The prevalent finding is that the acquiring company's shares neither increase nor decrease in value during the few days surrounding announcement of an acquisition. With no change in the acquirer's share values and a strong increase in the acquired company's share values, the merger is deemed value-enhancing. The failure of the acquirer's share price to rise is often explained as a result of a competitive market for mergers. In order to realize the benefits of merger, the acquirer must bid against other firms offering similar benefits, and it bids so vigorously (perhaps even incurring "the winner's curse") that the shareholders of the acquired company capture all of the benefits.

An alternate explanation for the lack of movement in the acquiring company's stock price is that acquirers are usually much larger than the firms they acquire. If this is the case, benefits accruing to acquirer shareholders are sufficiently small in relation to the acquiring company's total stock value that they simply cannot be discerned. A few studies focusing on mergers in which the target was large in relation to the acquirer claim to detect positive acquirer gains. But the number of firms analyzed in such cases is necessarily small and perhaps not representative.[5]

These stock price patterns are common to both tender offer takeovers and negotiated mergers. However, one special characteristic of tender offer takeovers is that they are rebuffed with some frequency. Moreover, there is evidence that when no new takeover attempt materializes within the next year or two, the stock price of the target firm drifts downward to the pre-tender offer level. This evidence is cited by event analysts as proof that the targets were properly valued by the market given the original management team. However, this argument ignores a potential selection bias. The stock price decline for tender offer survivors might imply that they, unlike the companies actually taken over, have been subjected to a series of market tests while "in play" and found *not* to have been undervalued.

The typical merger event study has proceeded on the assumption that securities investors make unbiased estimates of a merger's consequences quickly, i.e., in the first few days following a merger announcement. When this assumption is relaxed and a longer postmerger time frame is used, important anomalies appear. In particular, there seems to be a weak tendency for the stock prices of acquiring companies to decline over the one to three years following consummation of a merger. The magnitude of this decline depends upon the methodology used to measure postmerger returns. Assuming a continuation of trends during the three years preceding merger, Mueller and Magenheim found acquirer return deficiencies of 42 percent, whereas the drop was 16 percent if the acquirers were evaluated only against the record of similarly risky companies, without regard to prior history.[6]

The negative returns observed in the postmerger period have been of low statistical reliability, because the longer one observes a stock price series, the more factors other than those under study begin to cloud the evaluation. Nevertheless, as Jensen and Ruback concede in their survey of the literature:[7]

> These post-outcome negative abnormal returns are unsettling because they are inconsistent with market efficiency and suggest that changes in stock price during takeovers overestimate the future efficiency gains from mergers. . . . Explanation of these post-event negative abnormal returns is currently an unsettled issue.

To the extent that acquirer returns are in fact negative, the simple generalizations drawn from merger event studies no longer apply. When the acquiring firm is much larger than the acquired company, even small negative acquirer returns can swamp the positive returns of the acquired company.

Finally, there is little or no evidence that the stock market is an accurate predictor of a merger's long-run success or failure. The efficient market hypothesis suggests that stock prices are an unbiased predictor of future performance. But, lack of bias is only one characteristic of a good predictor. Flipping a coin can be an unbiased predictor of an uncertain binomial event, but it also will be wrong half the time.

Can the stock market accurately predict the long-run success or failure of a merger? Our preliminary evidence from an analysis of 251 mergers suggests that the premerger stock price gains for shareholders of firms that were acquired and subsequently divested were slightly smaller than those of retained firms. A possible interpretation is that the acquirers knew they were getting into something they could not manage well and therefore bid smaller acquisition premiums. This information does not appear to be reflected in the acquirer's stock price at the time of the merger announcement. Subsequent divestiture of the acquired company had no effect on the acquiring company's premerger abnormal return.

The Ravenscraft-Scherer Research

Merger ''event'' analysts have been surprisingly reluctant to probe into the within-corporation behavior that follows mergers and takeovers. We have been less reluctant, or some might say, more foolhardy. In an effort to find out

what actually happened after a merger occurred, we have compiled and analyzed a large statistical data base encompassing approximately 6,000 acquisitions traced to several thousand manufacturing "lines of business" operated
by 471 characteristically large U.S. corporations. The sample corporations
accounted for three-fourths of all recorded manufacturing and mining industry
mergers, by asset value, over the years 1950-76. With this sample, it was
possible to analyze the incidence of acquired line sell-offs, and for the surviv-
ing product lines, how 1975-77 profitability varied with diverse kinds of merger experience. In addition, field case studies were conducted for 15 mergers
(or clusters of mergers) that were subsequently undone through sell-offs. In
what follows, we distill the principal findings of our research.[8]

The principal thrust of our effort was to narrow the range of ambiguity as to
whether mergers and takeovers were on average efficiency-increasing. Several hypotheses underlie the work. If mergers are efficiency-increasing, one
would expect postmerger profitability, adjusted for relevant accounting
changes, to be higher than it was either premerger or in relation to "control
groups" of activities in the same industry with similar market shares, but
without (or with less intensive) merger histories. A focus on operating income, rather than net income after taxes, allowed us to determine whether
mergers induced changes in the pattern of companies' productive operations,
as distinguished from effects embodied in tax liabilities or financial structures.
If mergers are an important means of displacing inefficient managers, one expects the premerger profitability of acquired entities to be inferior to that of
peer companies in similar industry branches.

The Sell-Off of Merged Units

To assess the consequences of merger, one must deal with the important
question of sell-off. Our research reveals that the two phenomena are closely
related. The conglomerate merger wave of the 1960s peaked in 1968.[9] The
number of sell-offs, as recorded by W.T. Grimm and Co., rose in tandem and
peaked three years later, in 1971. After a hiatus, merger activity resumed its
upward swing in 1976 and 1977, and sell-off activity bottomed out and then
began rising sharply after 1980. Our multivariate analysis of divisional sell-
offs reveals that a divestiture was twice as likely for lines with a merger history than for those without, all else being equal. Although the great cyclical
variability of merger activity makes precise estimation impossible, our
1950-76 merger and 1975-81 sell-off data series suggest that approximately
one merger in three ended in divestiture.

Sell-off during the 1970s was clearly an indication of managerial failure.
Three to five years before divisional sell-offs commenced, profitability of the
affected unit went into a sharp decline. In the year before the full sell-off of a

line of business, the average ratio of operating income to assets was *minus* 1.09 percent. Whether the conditions that led to a sell-off had premerger antecedents is less clear. For a sample of 215 acquisitions that were subsequently sold off, premerger profitability differed trivially from that of acquired but retained companies, holding constant firm size and the method of accounting used in recording the value of acquired assets.

Our case studies of mergers that were subsequently undone through divestiture included two hostile takeover cases. In those two cases, it was clear that the circumstances accompanying the unwelcome tender offers made identification of latent or festering problems difficult for the "raiders." With a friendly merger, target company management opens its doors and its books to the would-be acquirer, so that a careful inspection can reveal some of the more serious risks. With Lykes's takeover of Jones & Laughlin and Inco's takeover of ESB, this was not possible. As a consequence, the acquirers were subsequently "blindsided" by problems they were ill-equipped to solve.

Premerger Profitability

Tender-offer acquisitions in our data sample also appeared to differ from voluntary mergers in another important respect: the companies acquired were less profitable, providing some support for the hypothesis that inferior performance may have been one spur to acquisition. Our research advanced beyond previous studies of target company premerger profitability, which were confined to the relatively small population of targets whose shares were publicly traded on securities exchanges.

By tapping a much broader-range data source, we discovered that the average company acquired through a "friendly" merger in the late 1960s and early 1970s was extraordinarily profitable. The average operating income-to-assets ratio for these firms was 20.2 percent, nearly twice the value for all companies in similar industries covered by the Federal Trade Commission's *Quarterly Financial Report* series. Profit rates were significantly lower for large acquired companies than for small firms but even the largest targets reported above-average returns.

In contrast, ninety-five companies absorbed into our Line-of-Business data sample and subjected to tender offers which led directly or indirectly to acquisition had less impressive records. Their pre-tender profitability averaged 3.5 percent below all-manufacturing norms (i.e., 11.08 percent vs. 11.49 percent) and a statistically significant 8.1 percent below the averages for the two-digit industries to which they belonged (i.e., 11.08 percent vs. 12.06 percent). It is interesting to note that the tender-offer targets compared less favorably to their home industries, which tended to be of above-average profitability, than to all manufacturers. However, the average shortfall for tender-offer targets was not so large as to suggest that incumbent management was extremely inept.

Postmerger Performance

Our analysis of postmerger performance uses data broken down to the operating unit level for the Federal Trade Commission's 1975, 1976, and 1977 Line-of-Business samples. The manufacturing "lines of business" or "LBs" were typically defined at the three- or four-digit Standard Industrial Classification level, allowing a close matching of operating unit records to merger histories and careful control for variables that influenced industry-wide profit levels. On average, we examined profits nine years after the merger occurred although there was considerable variation in this lag. Thus, ours is preponderantly an analysis of what happened in the long run following a merger.

Two quite different accounting methods, purchase and pooling-of-interests, have been used with roughly equal historical frequency to account for assets put on a parent company's books through merger. Under pooling accounting, assets are recorded at premerger book values. Under purchase accounting, they are adjusted to reflect the premiums usually paid above book values. In analyzing postmerger profitability, it is important to control for these differences in accounting treatment. We have done so in all our postmerger profitability studies.

On average, the lines of business in our sample having a tender-offer history had postmerger 1975-77 operating income/assets ratios that were 6.0 percentage points *below* control group levels. This difference was statistically significant. This difference included a 3.1 percentage point negative deviation associated with the use of purchase accounting. There was no statistically significant difference in the postmerger performance of LBs acquired in hostile tender offers, as distinguished from "white knight" acquisitions and tender-offer acquisitions uncontested by incumbent management.

Further analysis revealed that the postmerger performance deficiency (as measured by operating income-to-asset ratios) of tender-offer LBs resulted largely from the step-up of asset values associated with the use of purchase accounting in conjunction with the payment of takeover prices above premerger book values. When accounting revaluations are stripped away by analyzing the ratio of cash flow (before deduction of depreciation charges) to sales, lines with a tender-offer history were found to have an average performance deficiency of 1.6 percentage points, or 15.8 percent below the all-sample cash flow to sales percentage of 10.1 percent. The relative size of this posttakeover performance deficiency was similar to the size of the pretakeover performance deficiency observed in our studies of premerger profitability.

Thus, our analysis suggests that acquirers failed to significantly improve the operating performance of their acquisitions, but paid substantial premiums for the privilege of trying. This result is more closely consistent with hubris, empire building, tax avoidance, or bargain theories of takeover motivation than with synergy or inefficient management displacement theories.

"Voluntary" mergers had a rather different postmerger performance history. Whereas tender-offer takeovers were followed by neither degradation nor improvement of operating performance, once accounting effects were controlled, the much more numerous "normal" mergers showed definite signs of postmerger performance deterioration. For the mergers consummated under pooling-of-interests accounting, premerger operating income-to-asset ratios averaged more than ten percentage points above peer industry averages. Postmerger values of the same performance indicator for 100 percent pooling merger lines were 1.3 percentage points above, 1.6 percentage points below, and 3.4 percentage points above peer industry norms controlling also for market share for 1975, 1976, and 1977 respectively. For the three years together, pooling merger lines surpassed their peer industries by 0.4 percentage points. This represented a sharp drop from premerger performance.

Similarly, for purchase-accounting acquisitions, cash flow to sales percentages (stripped of merger revaluation effects) were 1.2 percentage points below 1975-77 control group values. This difference is statistically significant. Before merger, profitability of firms acquired in purchase accounting transactions was insignificantly different from peer-group averages.

An exactly matched pre- and postmerger sample confirmed the conclusion that profitability dropped sharply after the merger occurred. In addition, this sample was compared for the same time period to nonacquired companies with similar size and above-average profitability characteristics. The nonacquired companies maintained 40 percent of their supranormal profits, while the acquired companies kept only 10 percent. The difference between the acquired and nonacquired profit declines was statistically significant.

Purely conglomerate acquisitions incurred the greatest drop in profitability presumably because the acquiring corporations had little managerial experience in these lines of business. Postmerger sell-off rates were also highest for purely conglomerate mergers. Even horizontal acquisitions, however, appear to have experienced a deterioration in postmerger profitability. These results provide even less support than the tender-offer sample results for the synergy and inefficient management displacement hypotheses. Our findings once again appear much more consistent with hubris, and speculative and empire-building motivational theories.

Research and Development

Another efficiency argument for mergers is that, by blending small, innovative enterprises into larger corporations with strong financial backing, they permit the intensification of research and development (R&D) efforts. Our analysis of 2,955 lines of business for the year 1977 provides no support for this hypothesis. Lines of business originating from mergers had significantly lower company-financed R&D to sales ratios than product lines with similar market shares in the same industries, but without a merger history. The merger-linked R&D shortfalls which were in the range of 5 to 8.5 percent, appear to have been more severe for conglomerate than horizontal mergers, although the differences between these two categories were not statistically significant.

Conclusion

Do mergers and takeovers lead to long-run performance improvements? Analysis of the short-run stock market reactions to merger announcements suggests that they may. The exact causes of the short-run stock price gains remain unclear, however, and analysis of stock prices two or three years after a merger casts doubt as to whether the combined returns to acquired and acquiring company shareholders remain positive.

To clarify these ambiguities, we have undertaken a broad-ranging study of three merger performance dimensions: survival, profitability, and R&D intensity. Our results provide little support for the hypothesis that the average merger or takeover yields significant improvements in efficiency and operating unit performance. To be sure, there are exceptions. Yet, one must be concerned when the average tendency is no change in performance (as for tender offer targets) or poorer performance (for the characteristically small firms acquired in the typical voluntary merger of the 1960s and early 1970s). In order to secure sufficient data for a long-run perspective, our analysis has been avowedly historical. It is possible that managers have learned their lessons from the merger failures of the 1960s and 1970s and that the long-run performance of 1980s-vintage mergers will be better. But a once-burned public has yet to be shown that the new mergers will in fact lead to more efficient firms.

Notes

The views stated are those of the authors and not necessarily those of the FTC. The findings presented in this paper were taken from public research reports which have been reviewed to ensure that individual company line-of-business data were not disclosed.

1. Robin Marris, "A Model of the 'Managerial' Enterprise," *Quarterly Journal of Economics*, vol. 77 (May 1963), pp. 185–209; and Henry G. Manne, "Mergers and the Market for Corporate Control," *Journal of Political Economy*, vol. 73 (April 1965), pp. 110–20.

2. Gershon Mandelker, ''Risk and Return: The Case of Merging Firms,'' *Journal of Financial Economics*, vol. 1 (December 1974), pp. 303–35.
3. For a survey citing more than fifty such studies, see Michael C. Jensen and Richard S. Ruback, ''The Market for Corporate Control: The Scientific Evidence,'' *Journal of Financial Economics*, vol. 11 (1983), pp. 5–50.
4. Fischer Black, ''Noise,'' *Journal of Finance*, vol. 41 (July 1986), pp. 529–34.
5. Our research reveals that ''mergers of equals'' tend to be more profitable than mergers among firms of widely disparate sizes.
6. Ellen B. Magenheim and Dennis C. Mueller, ''On Measuring the Effect of Acquisitions on Acquiring Firm Shareholders,'' forthcoming in John Coffee et al., ed., *Knights, Raiders, and Targets: The Impact of the Hostile Takeover* (Oxford University Press, 1987).
7. ''The Market for Corporate Control,'' p. 20.
8. Details of our work are contained in David J. Ravenscraft and F. M. Scherer, *Mergers, Sell-offs, and Economic Efficiency* (Brookings: Washington, 1987).
9. W. T. Grimm & Co., *Mergerstat Review: 1985* (Chicago: 1986), p. 92.

4

Leveraged Buyouts: Wealth Created or Wealth Redistributed?

Kenneth Lehn and Annette Poulsen

Public controversy concerning corporate takeovers now proceeds from an almost universal recognition that these transactions create substantial wealth for shareholders of target companies. Numerous studies have documented this fact, including a recent Securities and Exchange Commission (SEC) analysis which found that approximately $40 billion in premiums were paid to target shareholders in corporate takeovers during 1980-85.[1] Although the takeover debate persists, it no longer involves serious controversy about the plight of target shareholders in these transactions.

The current dispute centers around the question of whether shareholder value also represents the social value created by corporate takeovers. Defenders of corporate takeovers generally argue that the premiums paid in these transactions reflect increases in social wealth resulting from more efficient resource allocation. Although little is known about the source of this increased value, the defenders often suggest that takeovers create wealth because of economies of scale, synergistic gains, or replacement of inefficient management. In contrast, many critics argue that takeover premiums do not reflect newly-created wealth. These premiums, it is argued, consist almost exclusively of existing wealth that is redistributed from other claimants on the firm's assets, including bondholders, taxpayers, employees, and local communities.

The "wealth creation" versus "wealth redistribution" controversy pertains not only to hostile takeovers, but also to highly leveraged, going-private transactions. In going-private transactions, shareholders of a publicly-held corporation are bought out, typically at a large premium, by a bidder who wishes to take a concentrated ownership position in the reconstituted, privately-held firm. Frequently, these transactions are referred to as "management buyouts," because incumbent management is often the bidder, or "leveraged buyouts,'' because these transactions usually are financed heavily by debt. Hereafter, we refer to going-private transactions as leveraged buyouts.

During the past several years, both the number and dollar value of leveraged buyouts have substantially increased. Table 1 lists the annual number, mean equity value, and total equity value of these transactions during 1980-84. This sample will be described more fully later. For now, note that both the number and average size of leveraged buyouts increased steadily during this period. Eight leveraged buyouts were consummated in 1980 involving firms with a pretransaction mean equity value of approximately $24.5 million. In 1984, the corresponding numbers were 35 transactions and a mean equity value of about $156.8 million. Hence, the total equity value of firms that went private during this period increased from $195.8 million in 1980 to $5,488.6 million in 1984, a 27-fold increase. Since 1984, several Fortune 500 companies have gone private via a leveraged buyout, including Uniroyal, Levi Strauss, RH Macy, Beatrice Companies, and Jack Eckerd.

The premiums paid in leveraged buyouts have evoked conflicting interpretations. Defenders of these transactions generally argue that the premiums derive from a socially desirable reorganization of the firm that results in better alignment of managerial incentives. Critics argue that the premiums come largely at the expense of bondholders and taxpayers. This paper empirically examines a sample of leveraged buyouts during 1980-84 in hopes of contributing to this debate. Before addressing these issues, we first describe leveraged buyouts in more detail.

Structure of Leveraged Buyouts

Leveraged buyouts can be structured in several ways. Typically, the investor group wishing to take the firm private, hereafter referred to as the bidder, forms a shell corporation that becomes the legal entity making the acquisition. In reverse mergers, the shell corporation is merged into the target firm; in forward mergers, the target firm is merged into the shell corporation. Shareholder approval of mergers generally is required under state law, with the minimum percentage approval varying by state. Some states have short-form merger statutes that allow the owners of a ''large'' percentage of the outstanding shares of a corporation to enter into a merger without the approval of the other shareholders. As an alternative to a merger, the shell corporation can make a tender offer for the target firm's shares, or it can simply buy the target firm's assets and issue a liquidating dividend to the target firm's shareholders. However the transaction is structured, shareholders in the target firm receive cash, debt securities, or some combination of the two in exchange for their shares.

Typically, the financing of a leveraged buyout entails the use of senior

TABLE 1
Number and Size of Leveraged Buyouts
(1980-84)

Year	No.		Mean Equity Value ($000)	Total Equity Value ($000)	
1980	8	(7.5%)	$ 24.5 million	$ 195.8 million	(1.8%)
1981	9	(8.5%)	80.5 million	724.5 million	(6.6%)
1982	22	(20.8%)	71.5 million	1,572.4 million	(14.4%)
1983	32	(30.2%)	91.3 million	2,922.4 million	(26.8%)
1984	35	(33.0%)	156.8 million	5,488.6 million	(50.3%)
	106*	(100.0%)	$102.9 million**	$10,903.7 million	(100.0%)

*Relevant COMPUSTAT data missing for two firms.
**Mean Value for Entire Sample.

debt, subordinated debt, and common equity. The proportions of each type of security vary, but usually senior debt accounts for the largest proportion of financing in these transactions. The senior debt typically is advanced by a commercial bank, insurance company, leasing company, or limited partnership that specializes in venture capital investments and leveraged buyouts. Frequently, commercial banks enter into a revolving-credit agreement with the going-private firm and secure their loans against the firm's accounts receivables, plant and equipment, and inventories. Senior debt held by insurance companies and leasing companies typically is secured against the firm's fixed assets and has a fixed repayment schedule, usually five to seven years.

Subordinated debt, referred to as "mezzanine money," is provided most frequently by pension funds, insurance companies, venture-capital/leveraged-buyout limited partnerships, venture-capital subsidiaries of commercial banks, and foundations and endowments. Three legal changes have fostered the growth in this type of financing of going-privates and are considered to be important in explaining the recent increase in leveraged buyouts. First, the 1978 change in capital gains tax that encouraged the formation of venture-capital limited partnerships led to the creation and expansion of numerous

TABLE 2
Average Long-term Debt, Shareholders' Equity, and Debt-Equity Ratio,
Before and After a Leveraged Buyout
(for 58 LBOs, 1980-84)

	Before - LBO	After - LBO	Percentage Change
Avg. Long-Term Debt	$45.6 million	$165.1 million	262%
Avg. Shareholders' Equity	99.7 million	29.9 million	-70%
Avg. Debt-Equity Ratio	0.457	5.524	1109%

TABLE 3
Number and Size of Leveraged Buyouts by Industry

	No.	Mean Equity Value ($000)	Total Equity Value ($000)	Percent of Total Equity
Apparel	7	(6.6)	$ 67.4 million	$ 471.6 million	(4.3%)
Bottled & Canned					
Soft Drinks	5	(4.7)	153.3 million	766.7 million	(7.0%)
Food	9	(8.5)	50.9 million	458.3 million	(4.2%)
Publishing	3	(2.8)	231.8 million	695.4 million	(6.4%)
Retail	16	(15.1)	90.5 million	1,447.9 million	(13.3%)
Rubber & Misc.					
Plastics	5	(4.7)	22.0 million	110.2 million	(1.0%)
Textiles	12	(11.3)	163.7 million	1,965.2 million	(18.0%)
Other	49	(46.2)	101.8 million	4,988.4 million	(45.7%)
	106	(100.0)	$102.9 million	$10,903.7 million	(100.0%)

funds that specialize in leveraged buyouts. These funds have become the principal vehicle by which pension funds, insurance companies, and foundations and endowments have invested in leveraged buyouts. Second, the U.S. Department of Labor, by its authority under the Employee Retirement Income Security Act of 1974 (ERISA), has promulgated regulations that classify leveraged buyout investments as "prudent" and thus eligible for investment by pension funds. This decision, along with the substantial growth of pension funds, undoubtedly facilitated the financing of leveraged buyouts. Third, a 1984 change in the U.S. tax code encouraged the use of employee stock-ownership plans (ESOPs), which supposedly has accounted for a significant percentage of financing in post-1984 leveraged buyouts.

The equity capital used in leveraged buyouts is most often provided by the managers of the target firm and/or the outside investor group that provides some of the debt financing. Inevitably, the common equity in all leveraged buyout firms is more tightly held after the transaction than it was before.

Table 2 contains data that illustrates the dramatic change in capital structure that results from leveraged buyouts. These data were obtained from proxy statements filed with the SEC for fifty-eight firms in our sample. These firms were selected because pro forma data on the change in capital structure were included in the proxy filing. The average book value of long-term debt in the quarter preceding the leveraged buyout proposal was approximately $45.6 million and the corresponding book value of shareholders' equity was approximately $99.7 million, resulting in an average debt-to-equity ratio of 0.457. The pro forma statements revealed that following the leveraged buyout the average book value of long-term debt would increase by 262 percent to $165.1 million, the average book value of shareholders' equity would contract by 70 percent to $29.9 million, and that the average debt-equity ratio would increase by more than eleven-fold to 5.524. The average sum of long-term debt and shareholders' equity increased 34 percent from $145.3 million before the leveraged buyout to $195 million after the leveraged buyout.

Wealth Creation or Wealth Redistribution?

Wealth-Creation Hypothesis

Proponents of the wealth-creation hypothesis frequently argue that leveraged buyouts create value by realigning managerial incentives in a way that enhances the productive efficiency of the firm. Economists and legal scholars have long recognized that a potential conflict exists between managerial incentives and shareholder interests in publicly-traded companies that are characterized by diffuse ownership structures and relatively small shareholdings of corporate managers. This potential conflict derives from the fact that managers in these firms do not bear the full wealth consequences of their decisions; their decisions affect the value of all outstanding equity, yet they own relatively little equity. If the "outside" (i.e., nonmanagement) equity is held diffusely, then monitoring by outside shareholders is "incomplete," because no individual shareholder receives the full value created by his or her costly monitoring activity.

Some scholars argue that the principal reason for leveraged buyouts is to reconstitute the firm's capital structure in order to mitigate managerial incentive problems. Since management buyouts result in concentration of most, if not all, of the firm's equity in the hands of management, the wealth consequences of their decisions are more effectively internalized. In nonmanagement buyouts, the equity will be tightly held by a specialist who presumably will closely monitor managerial performance, efficiently structure executive compensation, and thereby improve the productive efficiency of the firm. According to the wealth-creation hypothesis, the premiums paid in leveraged buyouts largely reflect the minimum amount by which the bidder expects to increase the value of the firm (i.e., the discounted value of future cash flows) through improved managerial efficiency.

Jensen (1986) has extended the wealth-creation hypothesis by elevating the role played by debt in mitigating managerial incentive problems.[2] A frequent characteristic of leveraged buyout candidates, Jensen argues, is the simultaneous presence of low-growth prospects and substantial cash flow. Jensen says:[3]

> Free cash flow is cash flow in excess of that required to fund all projects that have positive net present values when discounted at the relevant cost of capital. Conflicts of interest between shareholders and managers over payout policies are especially severe when the organization generates substantial cash flow. The problem is how to motivate managers to disgorge the cash rather than investing it at below the cost of capital or wasting it on organization inefficiencies.

Low-growth prospects suggest that opportunities to reinvest the cash flow profitably in the firms' current lines of business are limited. If the firm's management is specialized in its current lines of business, then it is unprofitable to invest the cash flow in acquisition of new lines of business. Leveraged buyouts effectively result in the "disgorging" of cash flow to the firm's securityholders, which Jensen contends is the value-maximizing use of this cash flow. The substantial debt resulting from leveraged buyouts serves as a bonding device; management is committed to pay out a substantial portion of the cash flow in the form of coupon payments on the debt, rather than reinvest it unprofitably. Since the penalty for defaulting on a coupon payment is presumably greater than the penalty for reducing dividend payments, debt more effectively compels management to pay free-cash flow to the firms' securityholders.

Empirical results. Casual inspection of the frequency distribution of leveraged buyouts by industry confirms Jensen's observation that these firms typically operate in "mature" industries with apparently limited growth opportunities. Table 3 lists the number and size of leveraged buyouts by industry for a sample of 106 leveraged buyouts. (This sample was collected from three sources: COMPUSTAT; Drexel, Burnham, Lambert; and Thomas H. Lee Co.) Sixteen of the firms, or 15.1 percent of the sample, were in the retail industry, accounting for $1.5 billion, or 13.3 percent of the value of the firms that went private via a leveraged buyout. Twelve firms, or 11.3 percent of the sample, were textile firms, accounting for approximately $2 billion, or 18.0 percent, of the value of leveraged buyouts. Also represented heavily in the sample were food processing firms (8.5 percent of the sample accounting for 4.2 percent of the value), apparel firms (6.6 percent and 4.3 percent, respectively), and bottled and canned soft drinks (4.7 percent and 7.0 percent, respectively). These five industries account collectively for 46.2 percent of the sample and 46.8 percent of the value of the leveraged buyouts.

Table 4 shows the average cumulative abnormal returns associated with the first announcement of a leveraged buyout proposal in the *Wall Street Journal* for ninety-two leveraged buyouts in our sample. The announcements vary from contemplating a leveraged buyout proposal to a board of directors' approval of a leveraged buyout proposal. Conventional event-study methodology was used to extract market-induced effects from the firms' stock price movements on the event date. The average net of market stock price reaction to these announcements is 20.10 percent when measured over a period of twenty days before the announcement to twenty days after the announcement. The cumulative t-statistic is 12.8, which indicates that the cumulative abnormal returns are significantly different from zero. Measured over a "twenty day window," that is, ten days before the announcement through ten days after the announcement, the average net of market stock price reaction is 20.76 percent, with a t-statistic of 18.5. Measured over a two day window—

TABLE 4
Cumulative Daily Abnormal Returns Associated with First Announcement of a Leveraged-Buyout Proposal for 92 Leveraged Buyouts
(t-statistics in parentheses)

Number of Trading Days (before, and after) Announcement	Cumulative Daily Abnormal Return
(−20,20)	20.10%
	(12.8)
(−10,10)	20.76%
	(18.5)
(−1,0)	13.93%
	(41.1)

Where possible, all daily stock returns were obtained from CRSP (Center for Research in Securities Prices) tapes. For stocks that are traded over the counter, returns were obtained from the ISL (Investment Statistical Listing) tapes of Interactive Data Services, New York. The stock returns of eighty-two firms in our sample were contained on the CRSP tape and the stock returns of twenty firms in our sample were contained on the ISL tape. The stock returns of six firms were not contained on either tape. Nine additional firms were dropped due to insufficient returns data.

one day before the announcement through the day of the announcement—the average net of market stock price reaction is 13.93 percent with a cumulative t-statistic of 41.1. Although these results are somewhat less dramatic than results that DeAngelo, DeAngelo and Rice (1984) found for a sample of going-private transactions in the 1970s,[4] they nonetheless indicate that shareholders benefited greatly from leveraged buyouts during 1980-84.

Table 5 contains summary statistics on the premiums paid in leveraged buyouts. The row in this table labeled "Cash Premium Offered" provides statistics for the difference between the offer price and the market price of the firm's common stock twenty trading days prior to the first announcement of the leveraged buyout, divided by the latter price. The average value of the offered premium is 41 percent and it ranges from 2 percent to 120 percent. This variable was calculated only for the seventy-two leveraged buyouts in the

TABLE 5
Premiums Paid in Leveraged Buyouts, 1980-84

	Number of LBOs	Mean	Std. Deviation	Minimum	Maximum
Cash Premium Offered	72	41.0%	23.2%	2.0%	120.0%
Market-valued premiums	89	39.5%	23.2%	1.7%	120.0%

sample that were all-cash offers, since no direct measure of the market value of non-cash offers was available.

A good approximation of the value of cash and non-cash offers can be obtained, however, from the final price at which the firm's common equity traded before it became private. Hence, we calculated a second measure of the premiums paid in leveraged buyouts—the "Market-valued Premium." This premium is the difference between the final price at which the company's equity traded and its market price 20 days prior to the first going-private announcement, divided by the latter price. The average value of the market-valued premium for the eighty-nine firms in the sample for which we obtained these data was 39.5 percent, ranging from 1.7 percent to 120.0 percent. Since the market-valued premium can be calculated for more firms, we use this measure in the analysis that follows.

To empirically probe Jensen's hypothesis, we collected COMPUSTAT data on the cash flow for sixty-six firms in the sample. These firms represent all firms in the sample for which COMPUSTAT had data on both earnings and depreciation expense for the year preceding the leveraged buyout. We created two measures of cash flow: the ratio of operating income plus depreciation expense to the market value of equity $[(CF/EQ)_1]$ and the ratio of income before extraordinary items, plus depreciation expense to market value of equity $[(CF/EQ)_2]$. Although these are not proxies for "free" cash flow, because we have not yet proxied the firms' growth prospects, we posit that a direct relationship between each of these measures of cash flow and premiums is consistent with Jensen's hypothesis.

The data reveal a direct and significant relationship between the two cash flow measures and the market-valued premiums paid. Table 6 contains the mean premium for firms with low and high ratios of cash flow to equity. Shareholders in the thirty-three firms with the lowest values of $(CF/EQ)_1$ received an average premium of 33.4 percent, whereas shareholders in the thirty-three firms with the highest values of $(CF/EQ)_1$ received an average premium of 49.0 percent, a difference that is significant at the 0.99 level. The average premiums increase from 31.0 percent for the twenty-two firms with the lowest values of $(CF/EQ)_1$, to 39.5 percent for the twenty-two firms with the median values of $(CF/EQ)_1$, to 53.1 percent for the twenty-two firms with the highest values of $(CF/EQ)_1$.

The same regularities characterize the relationship between the second measure of cash flow $(CF/EQ)_2$, and premiums. The average premium for the thirty-three firms with the lowest values of $(CF/EQ)_2$ was 33.8 percent, whereas the average premium was 48.6 percent for firms with the highest values. The average premium increases steadily with $(CF/EQ)_2$, from an average of 33.2 percent for the twenty-two firms with the lowest values, to 38.8

TABLE 6
Mean Cash Flow to Equity Ratio (CF/EQ) and Mean Market-valued Premiums for Firms with Low Cash Flow-to-Equity Ratios and High Cash Flow-to-Equity Ratios

Sample	Number of Firms	Mean Cash Flow-Equity	Mean Market-valued Premiums
A. *Cash Flow = Operating Income & Depreciation Expense (CF/EQ)$_1$*			
50% Lowest (CF/EQ)$_1$	33	0.291	33.4%
50% Highest (CF/EQ)$_1$	33	0.637	49.0%
33% Lowest (CF/EQ)$_1$	22	0.250	31.0%
33% Median (CF/EQ)$_1$	22	0.399	39.5%
33% Highest (CF/EQ)$_1$	22	0.727	53.1%
B. *Cash Flow = Income Before Extraordinary Items & Depreciation Expense (CF/EQ)$_2$*			
50% Lowest (CF/EQ)$_2$	33	0.137	33.8%
50% Highest (CF/EQ)$_2$	33	0.303	48.6%
33% Lowest (CF/EQ)$_2$	22	0.117	33.2%
33% Median (CF/EQ)$_2$	22	0.190	38.8%
33% Highest (CF/EQ)$_2$	22	0.341	51.6%

percent for the twenty-two firms with the median values, to 51.6 percent for the twenty-two firms with the highest values of (CF/EQ)$_2$.

Table 7 contains estimates from an ordinary least squares regression in which premium is regressed on each of the two measures of cash flow. When entered separately, the coefficient estimates on (CF/EQ)$_1$ and (CF/EQ)$_2$ are 0.473 and 0.888, respectively, and both of these estimates are statistically significant (t-statistics of 3.9 and 3.5, respectively). (CF/EQ)$_1$ alone explains more than 19 percent of the variation in premiums and (CF/EQ)$_2$ alone explains more than 16 percent of the variation in premiums.

To standardize for firm size, the ordinary least squares regression was run with the market value of equity (EQUITY) also included as an independent variable. When equity value is included, the coefficient estimate on (CF/EQ)$_1$ actually increases to 0.558 and its t-statistic increases to 4.1. Similarly, the coefficient estimate on (CF/EQ)$_2$ increases to 0.962 and its t-statistic increases marginally. The coefficient estimate on EQUITY was not significant in either equation.

Although we have not yet controlled for growth prospects, the data contained in Tables 6 and 7 are consistent with the wealth-creation hypothesis and more specifically with Jensen's version of this hypothesis.

TABLE 7
Ordinary Least Squares Estimates of Market-valued Premiums
as a Function of Cash Flow-to-Equity Measures and
as a Function of Equity Value (t-statistics in parentheses)

Intercept	0.192	0.119	0.212	0.177
	(3.1)	(1.5)	(3.4)	(2.2)
(CF/EQ)$_1$	0.473	0.558		
	(3.9)	(4.1)		
(CF/EQ)$_2$			0.888	0.962
			(3.5)	(3.5)
EQUITY		0.0000002		0.0000001
		(1.4)		(0.7)
Number in the sample	66	66	66	66
R^2	0.193	0.216	0.161	0.168
F-statistic	15.3	8.7	12.3	6.4

Wealth-Redistribution Hypotheses

Critics of the view that leveraged buyouts create wealth argue that the payment of premiums in hostile takeovers and leveraged buyouts does not necessarily imply increased social efficiency. Indeed, some argue that it is even incorrect to infer that firm value, let alone social value, is increased simply because premiums are paid to target shareholders in these transactions.

An alternative explanation offered by some critics is the wealth-redistribution hypothesis. They suggest that because these transactions are so highly leveraged, it is likely that at least part, and possibly all, of the increased value in common equity will be offset by a reduction in the value of the firms' outstanding bonds and preferred equity. Empirical support for this hypothesis is found in an article by Masulis (1980), who found that the announcement of a debt-for-common stock exchange offer generally results in diminution in the value of the issuer's outstanding non-convertible bonds.[5]

Redistribution from Bondholders and Preferred Stockholders

The argument that the shareholder wealth created by leveraged buyouts consists largely of redistribution from bondholders and preferred stockholders has appeared frequently in law articles and the popular press. In a supplement to his article in The Business Lawyer (1986), Morey McDaniel wrote:[6]

> The bondholder ripoff has become front-page news. For a vivid account of how stockholders in leveraged takeovers have profited at bondholder expense see . . . "Merger Wave: How Stocks and Bonds Fare," N.Y. Times, Jan. 7, 1986

> . . . "shareholders of the acquired company do great," said Michael S. Hyman, managing director of First Boston Corporation. "Bondholders on both sides are often left holding the bag. It's horrible." . . . *Business Week* has discovered the bondholder ripoff, too. "The takeover and leveraged buyout craze may be a boon for shareholders, but it is slaughtering owners of high grade corporate bonds" [states] Farrell, "Takeovers and Buyouts Clobber Blue Chip Bondholders, *Business Week*, November 11, 1985. . . . Barron's also has reported on the bondholder's plight. "Takeovers, mergers, stock repurchases, and leveraged buyouts are a good news-bad news story." Good news for stockholders as share prices soar. Bad news for bondholders whose bonds are "turned instantly from gems to junk by the swelling of debt taken on to finance the transactions," [states] Forsyth. "Bad Grades: Takeovers Teach a Costly Lesson to Bondholders," *Barron's*, February 24, 1986.

If the central tendency of leveraged takeovers is to diminish bondholders' and preferred stockholders' wealth by the degree suggested in the articles quoted above, then potentially these transactions could leave firm value unaffected, or they could actually diminish firm value.

This version of the "wealth-redistribution" hypothesis, even if empirically valid, suffers from a conceptual weakness that attenuates its importance for public policy. A market for bondholder (and, presumably, preferred stockholder) protection exists in the form of covenants that provide bondholders with protection in the event of changes in control, debt issues, and so forth. Presumably, bondholders pay a price for this protection in the form of lower coupon rates. Bondholders who forgo this protection presumably receive a premium in exchange for bearing some increased risk that their wealth may be expropriated by managerial decisions, or a change in control. McDaniel notes that the market for bondholder protection is adapting to the new takeover environment:[7]

> Bond investors are beginning to demand protection against the ravages of the takeover wars. "Industrial corporations are finally becoming aware that their bonds aren't attractive without protections for bondholders against takeovers," says William Gross, managing director of Pacific Investment Management Co., which runs a $9.5 billion bond portfolio.

Unless significant transaction costs exist that impair the efficiency of the market for bondholder protection, it is difficult to provide an economic justification for a public policy remedy to this supposed problem.

Empirical results. Inspection of the data suggests that although bondholders and preferred stockholders have suffered wealth losses in some leveraged buyouts, this does not appear to be the central tendency. To examine the effect of leveraged buyouts on the wealth of bondholders and preferred stockholders, we consulted *Moody's Bond Record* for a list of firms in our sample that had bonds or preferred stock listed on the New York Stock Exchange or the American Stock Exchange. After compiling this list, we recorded the daily prices of the bonds and preferred stock over a 20-day window centered on the date of the first *Wall Street Journal* announcement of the leveraged buyout, the same date used in examining the common-stock price reaction to the leveraged-buyout announcement. Bond prices were obtained from daily editions of the *Wall Street Journal,* and preferred stock prices were obtained from Standard & Poor's *Daily Stock Price Record* for the New York Stock Exchange, American Stock Exchange, and the Over-the-Counter market.

It should be noted that the inferences which can be drawn from these bond price data are quite limited, since only "odd-lot" trades (i.e., trades of nine bonds or fewer) must be executed through the exchanges. Nonetheless, if the central tendency of leveraged buyouts is to redistribute wealth from bondholders to common stockholders, some evidence of this should be found in these reported bond-price data.

The data refute the hypothesis that leveraged buyouts result in significant redistribution of wealth from bondholders and preferred stockholders to common stockholders. In fact, for the sample of ninety-two LBOs that we studied, sixty-eight firms, or nearly three-quarters of the sample, did not have any listed bonds outstanding; eighty-five firms, or 92.4 percent of the sample, did not have any listed preferred stock outstanding. Twenty-four firms in our sample had thirty-seven listed bonds outstanding and seven firms had ten listed preferred stock issues outstanding.

Table 8 contains price data for the listed bonds and listed preferred-stock around the date of the LBO announcement. Thirteen of the thirty-seven listed bonds traded on the exchange during the 20-day period centered on the LBO announcement date. The average bond price declined 1.42 percent from $83.375 to $82.192 during this period. The average price of the nine nonconvertible bonds decreased by 2.46 percent during this period, from $77.694 to

TABLE 8
Bond and Preferred Stock Price Reaction to
Announcement of Leveraged Buyout

	Average Price 10 Days Prior to Announcement	Average Price 10 Days After Announcement	Average Pct. Change in Price
13 Bonds Traded	$83.375	$82.192	−1.42%
9 Non-convertible Bonds	77.694	75.778	−2.46%
4 Convertible Bonds	96.156	96.625	0.49%
Bond Index	69.815	64.778	−7.21%
10 Preferred Issues Traded	48.288	59.575	23.37%
3 Nonconvertible Preferred	42.417	59.667	40.67%
7 Convertible Preferred	50.804	55.250	8.75%

$75.778. The average price of the four convertible bonds increased by 0.49 percent.

Although the relatively few bonds that traded on the exchange during the period declined in price, this decline was considerably smaller than the average decline in the 20-bond index reported daily in the *Wall Street Journal*. This index declined from an average of $69.815 to an average of $64.778, a decline of 7.21 percent, over this same period. Hence, the data strongly suggest that there was no "net-of-market" decline in the value of the thirteen bonds. These results are consistent with results found by Dennis and McConnell for a sample of ninety-four takeovers during 1962-80.[8]

Price data on the ten preferred stock issues that traded during the period surrounding the leveraged buyout announcement also refute the hypothesis that leveraged buyouts entail considerable wealth redistribution from preferred stockholders to common stockholders. The average price of the ten issues increased by 23.37 percent from $48.288 to $59.575. The seven convertible preferred issues increased in value by 8.75 percent from $50.804 to $55.250. The three nonconvertible preferred issues that traded on the exchange increased in value by 40.67 percent, from $42.417 to $59.667. Although these numbers are not market adjusted, they strongly suggest that preferred stockholders have generally not suffered wealth losses in leveraged buyouts.

Redistribution from Taxpayers

Some scholars have argued that the principal source of premiums paid in leveraged buyouts are tax benefits that accrue at both the corporate and personal level. For example, Lowenstein (1985) has written:[9]

> How can managers and their buying consortia pay so much? Until recently, we could only speculate as to the answer, because once a company went private, a veil dropped. A small but growing number of these firms, however, have returned to the public market. What emerges from the study of one such firm, Fred Meyer, Inc., and of twenty-seven recent buyout proposals is that the single most important factor explaining the pricing of these deals, though not their existence, is taxes. Management often can, with suitable backing, purchase the business from the public and finance the premium portion of the purchase price entirely out of tax generated cash flows.

If leveraged-buyout premiums are financed exclusively by reduction in the firm's tax liability, then leveraged buyouts may increase the value of the firm. But this increase in firm value also diminishes social wealth, assuming that the costs of arranging these transactions are nonzero. The after-tax cash flows of the firm increase under this scenario, but the leveraged buyout indirectly raises the tax liability of other taxpayers.

In this paper, we ignore the personal tax benefits associated with leveraged buyouts. The two most frequently cited corporate tax incentives for leveraged buyouts are the tax deductibility of interest expense and the "step up" of assets to take advantage of liberalized accelerated depreciation deductions permitted by the 1981 change in federal tax law. The U.S. tax code encourages corporate debt financing by allowing interest payments on debt to be deducted from taxable income, while dividend income is taxed at both the corporate and personal level. According to many critics of leveraged buyouts, the premiums paid in these transactions are largely financed by the tax savings associated with the dramatic change in capital structure.

Some scholars have argued that the principal source of premiums in leveraged buyouts is the ability of firms to take advantage of a tax change in 1981 that simplified rules for "stepping up" assets and liberalized the accelerated depreciation schedule, both of which created an incentive for some firms to step up the value of their assets. In order to increase the value of a firm's assets that is used for deducting depreciation expenses from the firm's tax liability, a transaction that establishes the market value of the assets is necessary. Because of recapture taxes, this incentive is greatest for firms that have assets whose tax basis is significantly below their market value and that are relatively undepreciated.

In leveraged buyouts, the Internal Revenue Service allows assets to be stepped up only when certain acquisition techniques are employed. Step-ups are disallowed when a one-tier reverse cash merger is employed, that is, when the bidding shell corporation is merged directly into the target firm. In these mergers, the assets have a carryover tax basis since the IRS considers the corporate identity of the acquired firm to be unchanged. These mergers are treated as recapitalizations, however, which do confer personal tax benefits to managers in management buyouts. Sometimes step-ups are permitted in two-tier reverse cash mergers, which are mergers in which a subsidiary of the shell corporation is merged into the target firm, and then the target firm is merged into the shell corporation. Step-ups are permitted in these mergers, provided that at least 80 percent of the target firm's stock is acquired by the investor group making the merger proposal.

Step-ups also are permitted in leveraged buyouts that are structured as forward mergers or sales of assets. In sales of assets, the target firm either issues a liquidating dividend to its shareholders, or it remains in existence as a registered closed-end investment company. The latter course is chosen only when the assets are sold below tax basis, that is, below the value used for tax purposes. This provides target shareholders, including, of course, the managers, with a tax-free sale of assets and an opportunity to invest the proceeds of this sale in tax-exempt securities, which generally are exempt from corporate taxation as well as personal taxation. To accomplish this, the target firm must have more than 100 shareholders after both the sale of the assets and a self-tender offer designed to take the firm private.

Empirical results. To examine the tax benefits argument, we estimate a linear regression model in which LBO premiums were regressed on the firms' pretransaction tax liability. If tax benefits are a significant factor in leveraged buyouts, then these transactions should be most valuable for firms with relatively high-tax liability. To test this, we collected tax data from the COMPUSTAT tape; tax data were available for eighty-seven firms in the sample. Since premiums represent a percentage change in the value of the common equity, we expressed pretransaction tax liability as the ratio of corporate income tax to market value of equity in the year immediately preceding the leveraged buyout.

The evidence strongly suggests that tax benefits do play a significant role in leveraged buyouts. Table 9 lists the mean tax-equity ratio (T/EQ) and mean premium for firms with low-tax liability and firms with high-tax liability. The average premium for the forty-three firms with the lowest tax-equity ratio was 32.1 percent; the corresponding average for the forty-three firms with the highest tax-equity ratio was 47.7 percent, a difference that is statistically significant. Similarly, the average premium increases from 32.1 percent for the twenty-nine firms with the lowest tax-equity ratio to 36.8 percent for the twenty-eight firms with the median tax-equity rates.

Table 10 contains a set of regression estimates of premiums as a function of both the ratio of cash flow to equity and the ratio of tax to equity, with and without the market value of equity also included as an independent variable. When entered simultaneously, both the cash-flow measures and the tax measure continue to enter the equation with positive and statistically significant coefficient estimates. $(CF/EQ)_1$ and (T/EQ) together explain almost 24 percent of the variation in premiums; $(CF/EQ)_2$ and (T/EQ) together explain more than 21 percent of the variation in premiums. When "equity" is added

TABLE 9
**Mean Tax-to-equity Ratio and Mean Offered Market-valued Premium
for Firms with Low Tax-to-equity Ratios and High Tax-to-equity Ratios**

Sample	N	Mean Tax-equity	Mean Market-valued Premium
50% Lowest Tax-equity	43	0.040	32.1%
50% Highest Tax-equity	43	0.137	47.7%
33% Lowest Tax-equity	29	0.022	32.1%
33% Median Tax-equity	28	0.086	36.8%
33% Highest Tax-equity	29	0.157	50.7%

*The t-statistic corresponding to the difference in the mean premiums for the two subsamples is 3.3. This difference is significant at the 0.99 level.

TABLE 10
Ordinary Least Squares Estimates of Market-valued Premium as a
Function of $(CF/EQ)_1$, $(CF/EQ)_2$, T/EQ, and EQUITY
(t-statistics in parentheses)

Intercept	0.169	0.087	0.184	0.137
	(2.7)	(1.1)	(2.9)	(1.7)
$(CF/EQ)_1$	0.401	0.490	0.739	0.829
	(3.2)	(3.6)	(2.9)	(3.0)
$(CF/EQ)_2$				
T/EQ	0.656	0.691	0.710	0.745
	(2.0)	(2.1)	(2.1)	(2.2)
EQUITY		0.0000002		
		(1.5)		
Sample size	66	66	66	66
R^2	0.239	0.267	0.216	0.228
F-statistic	9.9	7.5	8.7	6.1

as an independent variable, the R^2s increase slightly, and both the cash-flow measures and the tax measure continue to enter with positive and statistically significant coefficient estimates.

Conclusion

Inspection of leveraged buyout premiums has revealed support for both the wealth-creation and the wealth-redistribution hypotheses, two hypotheses that are not, of course, mutually exclusive. Premiums are directly related to pretransaction cash flow, a result that is consistent with Jensen's version of the wealth-creation hypothesis. Premiums are also directly related to pretransaction tax liability, which supports Lowenstein's version of the wealth-redistribution hypothesis. However, no support was found for the argument that premiums in leveraged buyouts come largely at the expense of bondholders and preferred stockholders.

Future research will consist of further testing of these hypotheses. To examine the relationship between "free" cash flow and LBO premiums, several measures of the firms' growth prospects will be calculated and incorporated into the empirical analysis. Furthermore, the relationship between free-cash flow and LBO premiums will be examined for two subsamples of firms: those in which managers owned a substantial percentage of equity in the firm before the LBO proposal, and those in which managers owned little equity in the firm before the LBO proposal. It would seem that the free-cash-flow theory of leveraged buyouts would predict a stronger relationship between free-cash flows and LBO premiums for the latter subsample than for the former subsample.

To further test the effect of LBO announcements on the value of the sample's outstanding bonds, data on bond rating changes will be collected. If a significant proportion of the sample sustained a decline in bond rating during the period surrounding the LBO announcement, then it is likely that the reported bond price data is masking a more significant effect on bond values. Finally, our present tax variable is a reported tax rate, not an "effective" tax rate. Although we have no reason to suspect that our present tax variable is biased, in the future we shall examine the relationship between effective tax rates and LBO premiums.

Notes

The SEC, of a matter of policy, disclaims responsibility for any private publication or statement by any of its employees. The views expressed herein are those of the authors and do not necessarily reflect the views of the Commission.

1. Office of the Chief Economist, U.S. SEC.
2. Michael C. Jensen, "Agency Costs of Free Cash Flow, Corporate Finance and Takeovers," *American Economic Review* (May 1986), pp. 323–29.
3. Ibid, p. 323.
4. Harry DeAngelo, Linda DeAngelo, and Edward M. Rice, "Going Private: Minority Freezeouts and Stockholder Wealth," *Journal of Law and Economics* (October 1984), pp. 367–402.
5. Ronald Masulis, "The Effect of Capital Structure Change on Security Prices: A Study of Exchange Offers," 8 *Journal of Financial Economics* 139 (1980).
6. Morey W. McDaniel, "Bondholders and Corporate Governance—A Supplement," manuscript, 10 March 1986.
7. Ibid, p. 36.
8. Debra K. Dennis and John J. McConnell, "Corporate Mergers and Security Returns," manuscript, 27 March 1985.
9. Louis Lowenstein, "Management Buyouts," 85 *Columbia Law Review* (1985), pp. 730–31.

5

Impacts of Takeovers on Financial Markets

Murray L. Weidenbaum and Richard E. Cook

In the view of many observers, credit markets are negatively affected by "non-productive" merger activity. Speaking for the Federal Reserve System, Chairman Paul Volcker says, "I . . . have concerns about the potential risks associated with mergers and takeovers when these transactions involve unusual amounts of leveraging." After acknowledging that many, but not all, mergers may have positive social effects, Volcker warns that "these potential benefits clearly are diminished if the mergers are accompanied by more fragile balance sheets or more precarious loan portfolios."[1]

Private-sector financial executives use even stronger language. In talking about the takeover boom, Thomas S. Johnson, president of the Chemical Bank, states, "I'm worried about what this leveraging up will do. . . . I'm worried that the aggregate of all these things, including leveraged buyouts, is simply a perverse result of greed and not a logical, rational thing. I don't know how all this debt will be serviced."[2]

Felix Rohatyn of Lazard Freres uses more colorful language to describe the financing of corporate takeovers: "It says something about where we are in our financial system when impeccable institutions buy something that calls itself 'junk' up front."[3]

By no means do these expressions of *macro* financial concerns exhaust the criticism of the current trend in highly leveraged takeovers. Takeovers are seen by others as draining resources from longer-term investment and growth-enhancing activities. In the event of default on high-yield, high-risk *junk* bonds, many financial institutions—especially state-chartered savings and loan associations—may be adversely affected. Takeover activity is also criticized because of large transaction costs benefiting lawyers, investment bankers, accountants, and printing and advertising firms.

The responses to these arguments take many forms. The concern over transaction costs is put into perspective; their large absolute size (in millions of dollars) is dwarfed by the billions of dollars involved in the financing process—although not necessarily by the annual profits of the companies involved. To the critics of junk bonds, the rejoinder is that the risk/reward ratio of these securities is in line with the economics of the market and basic principles of financial analysis. One risks more in order to earn more. Moreover, the credit is not used up, but recycled in the economy. In any event, credit to finance the equity purchases in the largest takeovers in 1984 amounted to only 1 to 1.5 percent of the domestic debt.[4]

Some analysts note that the takeover business is the most lucrative market currently available to the banks. The commitment and syndication fees and high interest rates offset in part the many problem loans in agriculture, energy, commercial real estate, and overseas investments. In any event, the impacts of takeovers on financial markets deserve special attention.

The Role of Mergers

Macroeconomic Impacts

In recent years, the pace of mergers has increased noticeably. In 1985, 2,991 companies were acquired—more than double the total for any year in the 1970s (see Table 1). These transactions amounted to $138 billion, a tenfold increase from the general level a decade earlier.

Although many knowledgeable observers have voiced concerns over the rising debt in the United States, this worry is apparently not caused by takeover activity, per se. The staff of the Federal Reserve System keeps track of debt issued in connection with acquisitions and mergers of $1 billion or more (see Table 2). Such large deals account for only 1 percent of all mergers and acquisitions, and less than half of the total amount spent for these purposes.[5]

Likewise, bank lending for takeovers does not seem to cause great concern. Merger-related loans for 1984 totaled $32 billion, including $25 billion from American banks. This may seem large, but it was only about 2 percent of the total loans outstanding at U.S. banks in December 1984.

Moreover, many merger-related bank loans are paid down fairly quickly with funds raised by sales of assets or with proceeds from the sale of commercial paper or of long-term securities. For example, about two-thirds of the bank loans extended in 1984 for larger mergers were repaid by the beginning of May 1985.

TABLE 1
Mergers and Acquisitions of U.S. Corporations[1]

| | COMPLETED TRANSACTIONS[2] | | ANNOUNCED TRANSACTIONS[3] | |
	Number	Dollar Volume ($ billions)	Number	Dollar Volume ($ billions)
1967	1,800	$15.0	2,975	n.a.
1968	2,440	28.0	4,462	$43.6
1969	3,012	n.a.	6,107	23.7
1970	1,318	n.a.	5,152	16.4
1971	1,269	n.a.	4,608	12.6
1972	1,263	n.a.	4,801	16.7
1973	1,064	n.a.	4,040	16.7
1974	1,088	n.a.	2,861	12.5
1975	859	n.a.	2,297	11.8
1976	1,058	n.a.	2,276	20.0
1977	1,139	n.a.	2,224	21.9
1978	1,364	n.a.	2,106	34.2
1979	1,420	n.a.	2,128	43.5
1980	1,470	34.7	1,889	44.3
1981	2,231	72.4	2,395	82.6
1982	2,182	65.1	2,346	53.8
1983	2,191	50.5	2,533	73.1
1984	2,915	123.2	2,543	122.2
1985	2,991	138.0	3,001	179.6
1986 - 1st half	1,546	79.6	n.a.	n.a.

n.a.—not available.
1. Purchases of U.S. corporations by other U.S. companies and by foreign companies. Divestitures or sales of subsidiaries, divisions, or product lines also are included.
2. Data from *Mergers and Acquisitions* magazine. Includes transactions valued at $1 million or more in cash, market value of capital stock exchanged, or debt securities. Partial acquisitions of 5 percent or more of a company's capital stock are included if the size requirement is met. Data shown for the number of transactions completed in the years 1970-79 exclude divestitures and foreign acquisitions.
3. Data published by W. T. Grimm. Data represent announcement of transactions, some of which were not actually completed. The series records announcements of any transfer of ownership of at least 10 percent of a company's assets or equity. Foreign acquisitions of U.S. companies are also included.

Some commentators have expressed concern over the use of low-grade (junk) bonds to finance mergers. In 1985, $6.2 billion worth of junk bonds were issued for mergers. However, that was only 5 percent of acquisition activity for that year. This suggests that the rise of junk bonds is not a driving force behind the current wave of mergers. Moreover, $10 billion of junk bonds were used for purposes unrelated to takeovers, an amount greater than the total issue of these bonds in any year prior to 1984.[6] Clearly, junk bonds

TABLE 2
Largest Merger and Acquisition Transactions of U.S. Companies[1]
(in millions)

Acquiring Company	Acquired Company	Price Paid
1984		
Chevron	Gulf	$13,300
Texaco	Getty Oil	10,120
Mobil	Superior Oil	5,700
Royal Dutch/Shell	Shell Oil	5,670
KMI Continental[2]	Continental Group	2,750
Beatrice	Esmark	2,725
General Motors	Electronic Data Systems	2,500
Champion Int'l.	St. Regis	1,840
Dun & Bradstreet	A.C. Nielsen	1,300
IBM	Rolm	1,260
PACE Industries[2]	City Investing	1,250
American Stores	Jewel Cos.	1,150
JWK Acquisition[2]	Metromedia	1,130
Texas Eastern	Petrolane	1,040
Total		$51,735
1985		
General Electric	RCA	$6,300
Philip Morris	General Foods	5,628
General Motors	Hughes Aircraft	5,025
Allied Corporation	Signal Companies	4,851
R. J. Reynolds	Nabisco	4,905
Baxter Travenol	American Hospital Supply	3,703
Capital Cities Communications	ABC	3,500
Nestlé	Carnation	2,894
Monsanto	G. D. Searle	2,717
Coastal Corporation	American Natural Resources	2,454
KKR[3]	Storer Communications	1,497
Internorth	Houston Natural Gas	2,260
Pantry Pride	Revlon	1,700
KKR[3]	Union Texas Petroleum	1,700
Rockwell Int'l.	Allen-Bradley	1,651
Procter & Gamble	Richardson-Vicks	1,246
Rupert Murdoch	Metromedia	1,400
Textron	AVCO	1,380
Cooper Industries	McGraw-Edison	1,377
Farley Industries	Northwest Industries	1,158
Chesebrough-Pond's	Stauffer Chemical	1,218
Cox Enterprises	Cox Communications	1,265
Mid-Con Corp.	United Energy Resources	1,242
Haas Family	Levi Strauss	1,110
BASF	Inmont Corporation	1,000
Wickes Companies	Gulf & Western (part)	1,073
Management Group	MGIC Investment	1,000
Total		$65,254

TABLE 2 (*Continued*)

Acquiring Company	Acquired Company	Price Paid
1986		
KKR[3]	Beatrice Companies	$6,250
Occidental Petroleum Corp.	Mid-Con Corp.	3,762
Capital Cities Communications	American Broadcasting Co.	3,530
U.S. Steel Corp.	Texas Oil & Gas Co.	2,997
News Corp. Ltd.	7 TV Stations (from Metromedia Inc.)	1,990
Multiple Acquirers	Group W Cable Inc.	1,700
Aancor Holdings Inc.	National Gypsum Co.	1,600
Eckerd Holdings Inc.	Jack Eckerd Corp.	1,582
Turner Broadcasting System	MGM/UA Entertainment Co.	1,507
Ralston Purina Co.	Union Carbide Corp.-Battery Div.	1,415
Wells Fargo & Co.	Crocker National Corp.	1,072
Total		$26,131

1. Shares in U.S. companies totaling $1.0 billion and over. Divestitures are excluded. Data are based on public information.
2. Leveraged buyout.
3. Kohlberg, Kravis, Roberts (buyout).
Source: Federal Reserve System and *Mergers & Acquisitions* magazine.

are not simply a device for acquiring companies cheaply. Nor do junk bonds play a major financing role in hostile takeovers. In 1984, for example, only 2 percent of hostile takeovers were financed with junk bonds.[7]

Furthermore, the increased risk associated with these bonds is no secret. Preston Martin, former vice chairman of the Federal Reserve System, noted:[8]

> Most of the purchasers of these so-called "junk bonds" . . . are large, sophisticated investors who should be aware of the risks involved in holding such investments.

The higher rates paid on these bonds suggest that the investors who buy them are fully aware of the added risk, although the adequacy of the risk premiums involved has not yet been tested by adversity. Table 3 shows that the defaults to date have not been significant. Approximately 3.4 percent of the speculative-grade bonds managed by sixteen major investment bankers went into default during the period 1 January 1980-11 September 1986. In any event, the cumulative defaults of junk bonds came to less than $3 billion in a period of almost seven years, or less than $500 million a year.

Likewise, takeovers, per se, are a small part of an overall wave of corporate restructuring. In the 18 months from January 1984 to mid-1985, nearly 400 of

TABLE 3
Default Experience for Junk Bonds,
1 January 1980 - 11 September 1986

Lead Manager	Speculative Grade Bonds Sold (in $ millions)	Amount Defaulted (in $ millions)	Percent Defaulted
Drexel Burnham	$44,927	$845	1.9%
Merrill Lynch	8,964	896	10.0
Salomon Bros.	4,652	25	0.5
Shearson Lehman	4,450	0	0.0
First Boston	3,875	290	7.5
Goldman Sachs	3,301	0	0.0
Morgan Stanley	3,089	25	0.8
Bear Stearns	2,945	169	5.7
E. F. Hutton	2,343	84	3.6
Prudential-Bache	2,308	230	10.0
Kidder Peabody	1,791	0	0.0
L. F. Rothschild	1,456	150	9.2
Smith Barney	1,220	53	4.3
Paine Webber	1,364	0	0.0
Donaldson Lufkin	958	160	17.0
Total	$86,043	$2,927	3.4%

1. Excludes investment-grade issues later downgraded.
2. Defaults are issues which at any time received a D rating from Standard & Poor's Corp.
Source: IDD Information Service; Edward Altman, New York University; Wall Street Journal, 29 September 1986.

the 850 largest corporations underwent some type of restructuring—acquisition, divestiture, spinoff, or stock buyback. Yet only 52 of these moves—or about one-eighth—were either direct or indirect results of takeover threats.[9] Of course, it is likely that some of the others were in response to more general fears brought on by the high level of takeover activity.

Impacts on Individual Firms (Micro Effects)

A different view emerges from the balance sheets of certain companies. Many firms, especially those that have fought off unsolicited takeover efforts, have greatly increased their debt loads. This has caused a surge in corporate-debt downgrades. According to Standard and Poor's, 31 percent of the downgrades in 1985 resulted from corporate restructurings.[10] Shown here are four extreme examples of the changing pattern of indebtedness before and after repelling unwanted suitors.[11]

Total Debt & Preferred Stock as
Percent of Total Capitalization

	Before	After
Phillips Petroleum	39%	84%
Unocal	21	78
CBS	20	76
Union Carbide	35	88

Source: Lazard Freres & Co.

A. Gilbert Heebner, the economist for Core States Financial Corporation, cautions against arbitrarily declaring highly leveraged balance sheets to be unhealthy in all cases. For example, the managers of a company who acquire ownership interest through a leveraged buyout may be more motivated and effective.

However, some companies are bound to suffer because of increased debt. Heebner suspects that some firms may find their capital cushions to be inadequate during the next recession, that "many companies which have replaced capital with debt will not survive when the current business expansion ends."[12] Gerald A. Pollack, an economist formerly on the staff of Exxon, points out that in recession we can expect debt/equity ratios based on market values to rise, interest rates to fall, cash flow to be reduced, and the rate of bankruptcies to grow. He cautions that many companies that recently have gone private are so highly leveraged that a recession might well threaten them with bankruptcy.[13]

Heebner also believes that the large amounts of debt will likely make the next recession more severe. The economy as a whole has been "leveraged up" and thus has a thinner cushion to withstand a severe jolt.[14] A related concern is that policymakers eventually may decide to relieve the pressure on debtors by turning to easy money policies, which could lead to a new round of inflation.

Rising Indebtedness in the U.S. Economy

Every major part of the American economy has been going deeper into debt in recent years. *Time* magazine has described the aggregate of business, government, and consumer borrowing as making the United States "a buy-now, pay-later nation."[15] Considerable statistical support is available for that dramatic statement. Total outstanding debt in the United States rose 2-1/2 times between 1977 and 1984, increasing from $3.3 trillion to $8.2 trillion over that seven year period. A more restrictive measure, total domestic, nonfinancial debt, tripled during the past decade, rising from $2.3 trillion at the end of 1975 to $7.0 trillion in early 1986.[16]

It is clear that the aggregate debt load of both the public and the private sectors of the United States has been expanding at unprecedented rates in recent years. That is a dramatic shift from the 1960s and 1970s, when the ratio of total nonfinancial debt to GNP was stable, fluctuating around 1.4. The total debt of all domestic, nonfinancial sectors rose at an annual rate of 19 percent from the end of 1982 to early 1986. By the first quarter of 1986, the ratio of debt to GNP had risen from 1.4 to 1.7.[17]

According to Paul Volcker, the rapid growth of debt has "disturbing implications for the fragility of the financial system over time." He noted in April 1986 testimony to a House Subcommittee that the debt problem is particularly worrisome now "when certain groups of borrowers are already under severe financial stress."[18]

Yet it is important to note that there is nothing especially significant about one or another ratio of debt to income. The degree of financial intermediation has been changing. Many "nonfinancial" firms now both lend and borrow. Thus, from one point of view, the data on debt contain some double counting. Moreover, the willingness to take on large volumes of additional debt certainly has not impeded economic expansion. To some degree, the high levels of borrowing have helped support the spending needed to keep the economy growing, although the higher debt burden may increase the risk of failure in the next recession.

The federal government has increased its indebtedness dramatically. The public debt rose from $572 billion in 1977 to $1.6 trillion at the end of the first quarter of 1986. But during the same period, nonfinancial business firms in the United States expanded their indebtedness by a larger sum, although not at quite the same rapid rate. Total business indebtedness rose from $1.0 trillion in 1977 to $2.4 trillion on 31 March 1986, more than doubling in absolute magnitude. The indebtedness of all three major sectors—government, business, and households—has been expanding faster than the GNP.[19]

Many authorities view these trends with caution. In the fall of 1985, Chairman Volcker wrote to Senator William Proxmire the following:[20]

> The speed of debt growth does concern me. So far, the debt burdens have not in any clear way proven an obstacle to the overall expansion of the economy, but I don't believe current trends are compatible over time with economic and financial stability.

Simultaneously, the equity base supporting business debt seems, on the surface, to be shrinking. The current wave of mergers and especially the efforts of defending management to deter takeovers have resulted in the retirement of large amounts of corporate stock. In fact, some of the new debt replaces stock that has been retired. For American business as a whole, the value of shares retired exceeded the value of new shares issued in six of the last ten years (see Table 4, column 5). In 1985, for example, the excess of stock retirements was $81.6 billion. This change is without precedent.

However, it now seems that this trend is subsiding. According to Salomon Brothers, cash offerings of new securities in the first eight months of 1986 were running approximately 79 percent over the 1985 rate.[21]

There are other, more basic reasons to believe that this development is not as serious as it appears. The "de-equitization" has been more than offset by the large amount of profits that American corporations have been reinvesting (see Table 4). Even after providing for the replacement of capital consumed in production (measured by straight-line depreciation), $126 billion of economic profits were retained by nonfinancial businesses in the United States in 1985, and that rate continued in the first three months of 1986. Moreover, the de-equitization of American corporations may, on occasion, mean no more than that some firms are going private. Professor Alfred Chandler sees advantages in this development: "It can again make long-term thinking possible, if the new owners really want to manage."[22]

How heavy then has the expanded debt load of American business become in comparison to the total ability to carry it? One basic measure, the debt/

TABLE 4
Increases in Corporate Equity
Nonfinancial Corporate Business, Excluding Farms
(in $ billions)

Year	Total Internal Funds[1]	− Depreciation =	Retained "Economic" Profits	+	Net New Equity Issues	=	Net Increase in Equity
1975	119.7	93.8	25.9		9.9		35.8
1976	134.2	103.8	30.4		10.5		40.9
1977	157.4	114.3	43.1		2.7		45.8
1978	175.7	129.2	46.5		−0.1		46.4
1979	188.8	147.7	41.1		−7.8		33.3
1980	189.5	167.8	21.7		12.9		34.6
1981	230.4	189.5	40.9		−11.5		29.4
1982	234.3	207.1	27.2		11.4		38.6
1983	280.5	215.2	65.3		28.3		93.6
1984	334.8	228.5	106.3		−77.0		29.3
1985	378.5	252.1	126.4		−81.6		44.8
1986-IQ[2]	396.8	259.5	136.3		−60.0		76.3

1. Includes inventory valuation adjustment.
2. Seasonally adjusted annual rates.
Source: Flow of Funds Accounts, Federal Reserve System.

equity ratio, shows a significant rise—from about .7 in the early 1970s to over 1.0 at the present time. However, when the data are converted from book to current market values, the ratio of debt to equity remains well below the peak of 1.3 reached in the middle 1970s (see Figure 1). Moreover, a far more positive picture is revealed when corporate debt is related to total net worth; that ratio remains below 1.0.

Alternatively, with debt valued at par and book net worth adjusted to reflect the replacement cost of tangible assets, the debt-to-net-worth ratio remains well below 1.0, although it has risen from 0.4 in 1982 to 0.5 in the third quarter of 1985. This level is significantly below that of the 1960s and especially the peak of 0.7 reached in 1970.

Another standard measure of debt burden is interest coverage, defined as the ratio of funds available for interest payments to net interest expense. In the third quarter of 1985, aggregate interest coverage stood at 4.3, approximately midway between the past decade's high and low (5.5 in 1977 and 1978 and 2.8 in 1982).[23] Funds available for interest are before-tax profits plus interest expense plus the inevitable adjustment items.

Perhaps the most relevant measure from the viewpoint of economic analysis is the relationship between corporate indebtedness and the productive assets that it finances. To cast some light on this matter, Table 5 compares the increase in net long-term investment plus working capital (presumably mainly associated with inventory changes) with the total rise in debt over the same period. It is clear that over the last decade, as well as in the most recent periods, the increase in physical assets has been larger than the rise in corporate indebtedness. It seems, therefore, that there is real value behind the rising debt load of American business. However, cynics might suggest that valuations of physical assets are far less durable than the assets themselves, depending heavily on their anticipated use and future profitability.

In any event, the rising indebtedness of U.S. business has been accompanied by substantial downgrading of corporate debt. Standard and Poor's, for example, reduced the ratings of 976 debt issues between 1980 and 1985, while upgrading only 546. The percentage of issues rated AAA (the highest category) has declined from 5.2 percent in 1980 to 2.7 percent in 1984. Meanwhile, the portion rated B (speculative) has risen from 14.4 percent to 19.2 percent over the same period.[24]

Yet in an analysis prepared in November 1985, the staff of the Federal Reserve Board concluded, "Despite the rapid accumulation of debt, market indicators do not reveal generalized concerns about credit quality."[25] The Fed staff developed Figure 2 to make the point. It can be seen that total domestic debt (excluding financial institutions to avoid double counting) has experienced only a moderately rising ratio to GNP over the past thirty years.

It is especially interesting to note that the big swings in the two major com-

FIGURE 1
Debt/Equity Ratios,
Nonfinancial Nonfarm Corporations

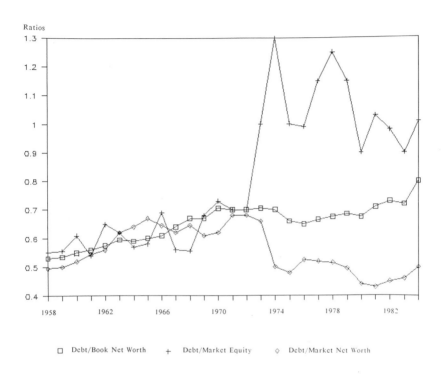

□ Debt/Book Net Worth   + Debt/Market Equity   ◊ Debt/Market Net Worth

Source: Unpublished study by Gerald A. Pollack, based on data from the Federal
           Reserve System.

ponents occurred prior to 1970—with a major relative decline in federal indebtedness offset by a rapid rise in private borrowing. Of current interest is
the fact that, in the last several years, both public and private borrowing has
been rising faster than the economy as a whole, driving the debt-to-GNP ratio
to a new high.

The Fed staff goes on to point out agriculture as an obvious problem area.
Farming, however, is a sector of the economy relatively untouched by mer-

TABLE 5
Increases in Productive Assets Compared with Increases in Debt
Nonfinancial Corporate Business, Excluding Farms
(in $ billions)

	1975	1976	1977	1978	1979	1980	1981	1982	1983	1984	1985
Fixed investment	117.7	131.5	152.7	176.3	205.8	219.3	249.4	244.0	251.7	313.5	353.0
− Straightline depreciation	93.8	103.6	114.3	129.2	147.7	167.8	189.5	207.1	215.2	228.5	252.1
= Net fixed investment	23.9	27.9	38.4	47.1	58.1	51.5	59.9	36.9	36.5	85.0	100.9
+ Direct investment abroad	14.0	11.6	11.5	15.7	26.6	21.9	13.0	4.7	9.3	7.8	(6.1)
= Net long-term investment	37.9	39.5	49.9	62.8	84.7	73.4	72.9	41.6	45.8	92.8	94.8
+ Net working capital	25.3	51.4	66.4	70.5	93.5	76.5	66.9	22.7	70.3	95.1	84.0
= Total increase in assets	63.2	90.9	116.3	133.3	178.2	149.9	139.8	64.3	116.1	187.9	178.8
Increased debt	20.9	44.2	69.7	80.6	96.0	80.4	103.4	71.9	54.6	181.7	156.0
Ratio: Increased assets/ Increased debt	3.0	2.1	1.7	1.7	1.9	1.9	1.4	0.9	2.1	1.0	1.1

Source: Unpublished study by Gerald A. Pollack, based on data from the Federal Reserve System.

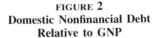

FIGURE 2
Domestic Nonfinancial Debt
Relative to GNP

Ratios

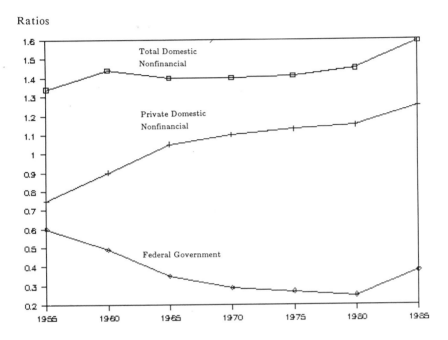

Source: Federal Reserve System.

---

gers or takeover threats. Another area of potential weakness not shown in these ratios is the shift, for many U.S. companies, from long-term to short-term debt. For all non-financial corporations, the portion of debt that is short term has risen from 35 percent in 1971 to over 50 percent in 1985.

Some Observations

Acquisitions, and especially hostile takeovers, generate much press and public attention. For many individual firms, these changes in corporate control are traumatic. This surely can be true for the shareholders, executives, employees, customers, suppliers, and surrounding communities involved. But for the United States as a whole, it does not seem that merger efforts, friendly or hostile, have yet had a significant impact on the overall level of financial activity.

Moreover, some experts expect the pace of takeover activity to fall, although no sign of a decline has yet appeared. "Takeovers come in waves, and this wave seems to be coming to an end," concludes Dean Richard West of the New York University Graduate School of Business.[26] Several reasons for a falloff have been cited.

A major factor expected to slow the takeover boom is the rise in stock prices during 1986. In 1985, in contrast, undervalued assets and large cash flows made many companies attractive takeover targets. Also, the continued uncertainty about the effects of recent changes in federal tax law may cause potential bidders to postpone attempts. It would be ironic if public concern with the merger phenomenon accelerates just as the phenomenon itself is peaking. In that event, any congressional action in this area would be dealing with a fading concern.

Meanwhile, the Federal Reserve Board has promulgated serious restraints on the use of high-yield junk bonds, which now cannot make up more than half of the financing of certain types of hostile tender offers. At the same time, the bellwether Delaware Supreme Court has approved the use of strong antitakeover defenses (so-called poison pills) by potential target firms.

Hostile takeover attempts may be further restrained by Unocal's success in fending off the unwanted bid by T. Boone Pickens, although the SEC is currently studying proposals to limit the use of this particular defensive tactic. Nevertheless, in the first four months of 1986, hostile suitors won nearly 90 percent of unfriendly takeover bids above $250 million.[27] In part, this departure from prior experience reflects recent court decisions that stress the responsibility of directors to sell to the highest bidder when a company is up for sale.

Conclusion

Corporate takeovers exert an ambivalent impact on financial markets:

1. In terms of the effect on the overall economy (macroeconomic impacts), the role of takeovers in U.S. financial markets is extremely modest, although overall indebtedness in the American economy is rising markedly.

2. At the microeconomic level, the financial condition of some individual firms has become more precarious, although the financial condition of most American businesses remains fundamentally sound.

A word of caution is in order. It is clear that the takeover movement does reinforce—albeit only to a minor degree—a worrisome trend toward greater indebtedness in the American economy generally.

Notes

1. Paul A. Volcker, Chairman, Board of Governors of the Federal Reserve System, letter to Senator William Proxmire, dated 8 November 1985 plus attachments.
2. Preston Martin, *Statement before House Committee on Banking, Finance and Urban Affairs*, Washington, D.C., Board of Governors of the Federal Reserve System, 3 May 1985, p. 2.
3. "The Great Takeover Debate," *Time*, 22 April 1985, p. 46.
4. Quoted in Leonard Silk, "The Peril Behind the Takeover Boom," *New York Times*, 29 December 1985, p. 1F.
5. Telephone conversation with Pat Lawlor, Federal Reserve Board of Governors, Washington, D.C., 14 August 1986.
6. "Junk Bond Funding for M & A," *Mergers & Acquisitions*, Vol. 21, No. 1, July/August 1986, p. 50.
7. James Balog, *Financing and Restructuring for a Competitive World*, an address to the Valley National Bank Investment Management Forum, October 1985, p. 4.
8. Martin, *op. cit.*, p. 6.
9. Balog, *op. cit.*, p. 4.
10. Standard & Poor's, *Creditweek*, 27 January 1986, p. 13.
11. Louis Perlmutter, *Takeovers: The Current Outlook*, a presentation to the Economic Club of Chicago, Chicago, Illinois, 3 March 1986, p. 13.
12. A. Gilbert Heebner, *Debt—A Cloud Over the U.S. Economy*, remarks to the Economic Club of Pittsburgh, Pa., 18 February 1986, p. 12.
13. Gerald A. Pollack, *The "De-Equitization" of American Industry: How Serious A Problem?*, unpublished paper, 13 December 1985, p. 2.
14. Heebner, *op. cit.*, p. 12.
15. Charles P. Alexander, "Let's Make a Deal," *Time*, 23 December 1985, p. 43.
16. "Flow of Funds Summary Statistics," *Federal Reserve Statistical Release*, 10 March 1986.
17. *Ibid.*
18. Paul A. Volcker, *Statement before the Subcommittee on Telecommunications, Consumer Protection and Finance of the Committee on Energy and Commerce*, Washington, D.C., 23 April 1986, p. 4.
19. "Flow of Funds," *op. cit.*
20. Volcker, letter dated 8 November 1985, *op. cit.*, p. 1.
21. Henry Kaufman, *Comments on Credit* (New York: Salomon Brothers, Inc., 19 September 1986), p. 4.
22. Alfred D. Chandler, Jr., "How the Heirs of Sloan and DuPont are Faring," *Across the Board*, May 1986, p. 34.
23. Pollack, *op. cit.*, p. 2.
24. "Corporate Downgrades Set Record," *Standard & Poor's Creditweek*, 27 January 1986, pp. 13–14.
25. *Recent Debt Growth* (Federal Reserve Board Staff Memorandum attached to Paul A. Volcker letter of 8 November 1985 to Senator William Proxmire), p. 5.
26. Quoted in John C. Perham, "It's a New Game in Mergers," *Dun's Business Month*, April 1986, p. 28.
27. Data compiled by Erick Gleacher, Morgan Stanley & Co., cited in Daniel Hertzberg, "Takeover Activity Slows as Stocks Surge," *Wall Street Journal*, 25 April 1986, p. 6.

6

Tender Offer Regulation and the Federalization of State Corporate Law

Robert B. Thompson

The current wave of corporate takeovers has opened a new front in the long-running debate over the federalization of state corporation law.[1] State law traditionally has regulated the relationship between shareholders and directors within a corporation. Federal securities laws affect that relationship through required disclosure and prohibitions against fraud but have not disturbed the primacy of state control. The Supreme Court's landmark decision in *Santa Fe Industries, Inc.* v. *Green*[2] confirmed this federal/state balance when it rejected efforts to interpret fraud in the federal securities laws as including shareholder complaints of management misconduct. The court based its decision, in part, on a reluctance to federalize a substantial part of state corporation law.

Some recent judicial decisions interpreting the Williams Act, the federal government's 1968 legislation on tender offers, present a different vision of the appropriate role of state and federal regulation. These courts see the Williams Act (and the commerce clause of the Constitution) as a mandate to protect the ''market for corporate control''[3] against state interference. In particular, they read the federal law as preserving for shareholders the right to use a tender offer to oust corporate management. This broad vision of the federal government's role initially developed in contexts which did not threaten the primacy of state regulation of the shareholder-director relationship. The state takeover laws that were declared unconstitutional addressed only a bidder's responsibilities in seeking to buy the shares of a target company shareholder.

However, in the wake of these failed statutes, states passed new takeover laws, frequently termed ''second generation'' statutes, that sought to regulate takeovers as part of the corporations code, modifying the relative rights of shareholders and directors in ways that often made takeovers more difficult.

Attacks on these statutes, therefore, more directly question the extent to which the federal securities laws supplant state corporate law.

In the 1986 term, the Supreme Court heard a case challenging the constitutionality of a second generation state takeover statute.[4] The Reagan administration and the Congress also struggled with this issue, particularly whether there should be new federal law on "poison pills," "greenmail," or "golden parachutes," defensive tactics to hostile takeovers which currently are regulated under state law. This extended battleground intensifies the need to identify the principles that define the appropriate realm of federal and state law.

This paper suggests that the division of state and federal responsibility for tender offers can best be understood by distinguishing regulation of economic activity occurring across markets from regulation of economic activity within a firm.[5]

State corporate law traditionally has governed activity within a firm. Each state's corporation code and its judicially-applied common law of fiduciary duty determine the legal relationship between directors and shareholders. The proxy, periodic disclosure, and antifraud provisions of the federal Securities Exchange Act of 1934 assist shareholders in monitoring the performance of their managers and thereby affect the shareholder-director relationship. But these federal provisions do not purport to change the substance of the relationship between shareholders and their managers that has been created by state law.

States may differ in the extent to which they provide shareholders with protection against action by their directors. For example, California tends to give more protection to shareholder interests, while Delaware's corporation act gives more freedom and flexibility to corporate managers. In theory, leaving the governance of these relationships to state law permits the states to compete for corporate charters, each acting as a laboratory within our federal system to develop legal rules for corporate governance that best facilitate raising capital.[6] If a state designs its corporate code to favor hometown management at the expense of shareholders, that state's corporations will be seen as less attractive investment vehicles and the state will lose incorporations to other states.

For discrete market transactions occurring outside the corporate form, the federal government's role is substantially greater. State blue-sky laws regulate the sale of securities, but these individual state laws are limited to sales within each state. The key regulation of interstate issuances of securities is federal law, the Securities Act of 1933. It was passed in the first hundred days of the New Deal, in part because of the inability of the states to regulate national distributions involving stock sales in various states.[7]

Regulation of tender offers inevitably combines the two types of regulation just discussed. Tender offers involve discrete market transactions between a bidder and target company shareholders who may be located in all fifty states, transactions for which a federal rule would be appropriate. The legislative history of the Williams Act reflects efforts to combat bidder coercion of shareholders' tender-offer decisions. In addition, tender offers dramatically affect the relationship between shareholders and their managers, matters which Congress usually has left to state law. In this respect, tender offers are an alternative to derivative suits, proxy fights, or other voting mechanisms by which shareholders can monitor their managers pursuant to state law.

The state and federal functions are clearly interrelated. The possibility of a tender offer in the marketplace makes shareholder rights against management under state law more effective. Conversely, if shareholder rights against management under state law are ineffective, there may be less incentive for a bidder to seek control by a tender offer. This interrelationship illustrates the complexity of tender offer regulation but it does not necessarily require a different division of federal and state responsibility from that which has existed for the last half century. States should still be left free to set the rules for corporations chartered under their law, even if those rules have some effect on tender offers. Federal law should continue in its supplemental disclosure role for the shareholder-director relationship and the primary regulatory role for discrete market transactions between bidders and target company shareholders.

This paper analyzes the appropriate federal and state roles for corporation law by first analyzing the incomplete view of federal-state relations found in current case law. Subsequent sections discuss in detail the methods by which states now seek to regulate takeovers and the degree to which these state methods are consistent with federal law.

The Conflicting and Incomplete View of Federalism in Current Case Law

Hostile takeovers have produced more case law and commentary in recent years than any other corporate law topic. Yet the cases and the commentary present a confused and often inconsistent view of the appropriate role of the federal and state government in regulating takeovers. This confusion can be seen for example in the report of the Securities and Exchange Commission's Advisory Committee on Tender Offers which recommended the continued preeminence of state corporation law governing a target's management response to a tender offer while at the same time proposing a number of new federal regulations that would restrict state interference with tender offers.[8] Similar confusion is evident in two groups of cases interpreting the Williams Act which are the focus of this paper. Cases ruling on whether state takeover laws are unconstitutional by and large reflect more restrictive views about state regulation than those cases interpreting the validity of private defensive tactics.

Edgar v. MITE Corporation and Other Cases Ruling on State Takeover Statutes

After the passage of the Williams Act in 1968, states enacted their own takeover statutes. By the time of the Supreme Court's 1982 decision in *Edgar v. MITE Corp.*,[9] there were thirty-seven such state statutes. In many respects, these statutes were patterned after the Williams Act as disclosure-oriented regulation of the bidder and the bidder's transactions with the shareholders of the target company. Many states, in an apparent effort to help local companies fend off unwanted takeovers, exceeded the Williams Act and provided additional investor "protection" such as hearings by state officials on the fairness of the tender offer. Since these statutes usually applied to tender offers for companies with only minimal contacts with the state, such as having assets or shareholders within the state, there was a strong likelihood that a takeover bid involving shareholders across the country would be subject to conflicting state requirements.

In *MITE*, the Supreme Court invalidated the Illinois takeover statute as an impermissible indirect regulation of interstate commerce because its burdens on interstate commerce outweighed the benefits to Illinois. A plurality of the court would have invalidated the statute as a direct regulation of interstate commerce and as such, is preempted by the Williams Act. Since *MITE*, lower courts have used all three arguments to strike down state statutes.

Preemption and the supremacy clause. Under Article VI, clause 2 of the United States Constitution, state law must yield when it conflicts with federal law. State takeover laws usually are written so that it is physically possible to comply with the provisions of both the federal and state acts, thereby avoiding direct conflict. But clear precedent also holds that a state law is invalid if it "stands as an obstacle to the accomplishment and execution of the full purposes and objectives of Congress."[10] The breadth of the Williams Act's purpose obviously becomes the key determinant of the role for state law.

There seems to be general agreement in the case law that Congress sought to protect investors by providing them with the necessary information to make a decision when confronted with a tender offer. A state law that interfered with that disclosure clearly would be preempted. More ambiguity exists concerning the extent to which the Act tries to create or maintain neutrality between the takeover bidder and the target management.

Some history about the development of the Williams Act is helpful on this point. The bill originally introduced by Senator Williams in 1965 proposed to regulate the bidder more severely than did the final legislation. Changes in the bill, such as deletion of a requirement for precommencement notification of a tender offer to the target company, apparently reflected an awareness that too much regulation would discourage takeovers and prevent them from being a check on "entrenched" management. Thus, Congress disclaimed any "intention to provide a weapon for management to discourage takeover bids."[11]

The courts and commentators have debated the breadth of this "neutrality" objective. Those narrowly interpreting neutrality hold that Congress decided not to go as far as the original bill in order to prevent unnecessary interference with the existing shareholder-management relationship. Under this view, the bill simply sought to keep federal regulation of bidder-shareholder transactions from making matters worse for the shareholders vis-a-vis their management; it expressed no judgment on other actions (e.g., state law, bylaw, or charter amendments) that might interfere with the shareholder-management relationship.

A broader view of the neutrality objective holds that Congress established the desired balance between bidder and management, and between shareholder and management which the states cannot change. Among those who view Congress as having acted to establish a balance, further division is possible between: 1) those who read the legislative declaration to prevent any upset of that balance whether by state or private action, and 2) those who suggest that the 1968 balance may be upset, so long as it is not by new state legislation. The latter interpretation would appear to permit private action upsetting the balance, including defensive tactics taken by directors pursuant to the broad authority in longstanding provisions of state corporation codes and traditional common law.

The three justices who made up the plurality in *MITE* seemed to interpret neutrality broadly. Justice White said "[I]t is also crystal clear that a major aspect of the effort to protect the investor was to avoid favoring either management or the takeover bidder." He agreed with the Court of Appeals that Congress "sought to protect the investor not only by furnishing him with the necessary information but also by withholding from management or the bidder any undue advantage that could frustrate the exercise of an informed choice."

Thus, the plurality justices concluded that the Illinois act was preempted insofar as it provided for a hearing that created the potential for delay and thereby "upset the balance struck by Congress by favoring management at the expense of stockholders." The Illinois provision permitting its secretary of state to decide the fairness of a tender offer would also be preempted in the view of the plurality justices because it "offers investor protection at the expense of investor autonomy—an approach quite in conflict with that adopted by Congress."

Two justices dissented from the plurality view. Justice Stevens did not see

Congressional efforts to be neutral in its own legislation as "tantamount to a federal prohibition against state legislation designed to provide special protection for incumbent management." Justice Powell noted that, "the Williams Act's neutrality policy does not necessarily imply a congressional intent to prohibit state legislation designed to assure—at least in some circumstances—greater protection to interests that include but often are broader than those of incumbent management."

For the most part, subsequent judicial decisions have followed the plurality, even occasionally making it into a holding of the Supreme Court. Some decisions suggest that the federal policy of permitting investors to make their own decisions casts doubt on barriers that might prevent a shareholder selling in a market influenced by the presence of a bidder.

There are others, however, with lingering doubts. For example, Judge Posner of the U.S. Seventh Circuit Court of Appeals has written: "Most courts have agreed that the Williams Act strikes a balance between target management and tender offeror that the states may not upset. . . . Of course it is a big leap from saying that the Williams Act does not itself exhibit much hostility to tender offers to saying that it implicitly forbids states to adopt more hostile regulations, but this leap was taken by the Supreme Court plurality and us in *MITE* and by every court to consider the question since."[12]

Direct regulation of interstate commerce. Article I, Section 8, clause 3 of the United States Constitution gives Congress the power to regulate interstate commerce. The clause may prevent state regulation of interstate commerce even if Congress has not specifically spoken. Justice White found the Illinois statute to be an impermissible state regulation of interstate commerce for both its direct and indirect effects. Only three other justices joined in the part of the opinion invalidating the Illinois Act as an impermissible direct regulation on interstate commerce but it, too, has been followed by several lower courts. Justice White particularly criticized the fact that the Illinois Act purported to regulate commerce wholly outside the state and that many states could impose similar regulations such that "interstate commerce in securities transactions generated by tender offers would be thoroughly stifled." This emphasis on "extraterritorial" regulation may mean that this "direct regulation" argument will be applied less often to second generation statutes which do not purport to regulate corporations not chartered in that particular state and, thus, do not raise the possibility of multiple states regulating the same transaction.

Indirect regulation of interstate commerce. The only part of Justice White's opinion to command a majority found the Illinois Act unconstitutional under the test of *Pike* v. *Bruce Church, Inc.*[13] which held that where a state statute "regulates interstate commerce indirectly, the burden imposed on that commerce must not be excessive in relation to the local interest served by the statute."

Three points in the majority's opinion recur in subsequent court decisions and have implications for the application of *MITE*'s reasoning to state corporation law. First, the court describes as "substantial" the effect of allowing Illinois to block a nationwide tender offer. The court was concerned that depriving shareholders of the opportunity to sell their shares at a premium hinders the "reallocation of economic resources to their highest valued use, a process which can improve efficiency and competition." This unqualified praise of tender offers has implications for other state corporation laws which similarly can reduce "the incentive the tender offer mechanism provides incumbent management to perform well."

In addition, the *MITE* opinion discounted both of the local interests claimed by Illinois. The language used in that opinion was broad enough to apply to many other state statutes. The Court said, "[W]hile protecting local investors is plainly a legitimate state objective, the State has no legitimate interest in protecting nonresident shareholders. Insofar as the Illinois law burdens out-of-state transactions, there is nothing to be weighed in the balance to sustain the law." Based on this language, other courts have held that there is no interest in protecting nonresident shareholders, even if they own stock in a local corporation. According to this theory, if Delaware's corporation statute were subjected to an interstate commerce balancing test, Delaware would have little or no interest in protecting out-of-state shareholders of Delaware corporations.

Finally, the Court gave scant value to the internal affairs doctrine as a justification for state regulation of a corporation incorporated under its law. As defined by the court, "[t]he internal affairs doctrine is a conflict of laws principle which recognizes that only one State should have the authority to regulate . . . matters peculiar to the relationships among or between the corporation and its current officers, directors and shareholders—because otherwise a corporation could be faced with conflicting demands." The Court stated that tender offers which contemplate a transfer of stock "do not themselves implicate the internal affairs of the target company."

A subsequent lower court decision extends this point to conclude that "[r]egulation of *shareholders*—and those who would become shareholders—is not the same as regulating the corporation itself."[14] This ruling overlooks the fact that one of the major effects of state law "regulating the corporation" is to define the rights of shareholders against management within that corporation. Indeed almost all courts following *Edgar* v. *MITE* fail to acknowledge that federal law regulates tender offers in part because of their effects on the shareholder-management relationship, but in a way that complements, without supplanting, the existing state substantive regulation of that relationship.

Similarly several courts have opined that the Williams Act reflects a choice of a market approach over a fiduciary approach without recognizing the intended interaction of the Williams Act with longstanding state and common law fiduciary duties used for regulating shareholder-management relations.[15] In these contexts, the courts' broad statement of the federal legislative purposes and narrow recognition of state interests has the effect of federalizing a large portion of state corporation law.

In one sense, the conclusions in this section are overstated. Most of the judicial statements cited here occurred in decisions interpreting "first generation" statutes like the Illinois statute that really do not involve the more difficult questions about the division of federal and state responsibility. In those statutes, the states sought to regulate market transactions between bidders and target shareholders, the exact transaction which Congress had regulated by the Williams Act, and an area in which there was no history of state regulation nor any indication of Congressional intent to preserve this area for state regulation. In addition, the broad extraterritorial reach of these statutes and the possibility of many states regulating the same transactions raised substantial interstate commerce objections. But the judicial notions of a broad purpose for the Williams Act and a broad reach for the interstate commerce clause have gained a powerful momentum that has begun to affect statutes where there is a more direct conflict between the Williams Act and traditional state regulation of corporations.

Schreiber v. Burlington Northern, Inc. and Other Cases Ruling on Private Defense Tactics

In contrast to the *MITE* line of cases, another body of case law recognizes that the Williams Act was superimposed over existing state regulation of corporations in a way which left substantial room for state law. Many of these cases acknowledge the influence of *Santa Fe Industries, Inc. v. Green,* the Supreme Court's leading decision on the relationship of federal securities law to state corporation law.

In this line of cases, litigation frequently originated in a challenge to defensive tactics implemented by target management to ward off an unwanted tender offer. The plaintiff, who sometimes was a competing bidder, argued that the management moves were manipulative acts prohibited by §14(e) of the Williams Act. In *Mobil* v. *Marathon Oil,* the U.S. Sixth Circuit Court of Appeals held that the target management's sale of its most valuable asset to one of two bidders competing for the target's shares was a manipulative act that artificially capped the market for shares and harmed shareholders.[16]

Three other circuit courts of appeal and the U.S. Supreme Court in *Schreiber* v. *Burlington Northern, Inc.*[17] have roundly rejected the approach of the Sixth Circuit. The narrow holding of these cases is that "manipulation" requires misrepresentation or nondisclosure, a view consistent with earlier Supreme Court definitions of that term. The more interesting aspect of these cases for current discussion is their view of the role for state and federal law which provides the basis for the courts' narrow definition of manipulation.

These cases emphasize that the focus of federal regulation in the Williams Act is primarily that of disclosure. They reject the plaintiffs' efforts to bring under the Williams Act actions which essentially are shareholder claims of management breaches of fiduciary duty. The facts in *Schreiber* ,for example, involved the cancellation of a tender offer by a bidder that suggested that the target board of directors might have benefited at the expense of their shareholders. In *Mobil,* and other circuit court cases, the target board granted an option to one of two bidders or otherwise locked up the target's assets.

The Eighth Circuit said simply, "Where the claim is breach of fiduciary duty without more, the plaintiff's remedy lies under state law."[18] The Third Circuit decision which was affirmed by the Supreme Court in *Schreiber* expressly declined to follow *Mobil* because of the Supreme Court's reluctance, expressed in *Santa Fe,* to federalize state corporation law.

A 1983 district court decision, *Data Probe Acquisition Corp.* v. *Datatab, Inc.,*[19] tried to reconcile *MITE* and *Santa Fe.* In ruling on whether a target board's defensive tactic violates §14(e), Judge Sofaer wrote that Congress imposed two duties on tender offer participants: "first, to provide shareholders the required information; and second, to refrain from any conduct that unduly impedes the shareholders' exercise of the decision-making prerogative guaranteed to them by Congress. . . . Congress indeed meant for the federal courts to prevent tender offer participants from interfering with the informed investor choice that the Act sought to assure." Indeed, Judge Sofaer argued that *Edgar* v. *MITE* "(written by the Justice who authored *Santa Fe),* is strong evidence that the Court will recognize that the Williams Act has federally enforceable objectives, beyond mere disclosure."

Yet, the district court's effort to reconcile *MITE* and *Santa Fe* did not survive appeal. The Second Circuit found the claim to be a breach of fiduciary duty, which if entertained "would unquestionably embark us on a course leading to a federal common law of fiduciary obligations." The court noted that under existing federal legislation it is not free to condemn a breach of fiduciary duty.

The division of regulatory responsibility between the federal law's emphasis on disclosure and state law regulation of fiduciary duty tracks closely the accommodation of state and federal regulation worked out in cases applying Rule 10b-5 to allegations of corporate mismanagement.[20] In cases alleging that directors have breached their fiduciary duty to shareholders by causing the corporation to engage in a securities transaction favorable to the directors personally but unfavorable to the corporation, courts have had to confront the intersection of federal securities regulation of the purchase and sale transaction and state law regulation of the intracorporate relationship between shareholders and directors. In *Santa Fe*, the Supreme Court ruled that, absent express authorization from Congress, the Court would not interpret Rule 10b-5 to federalize the large body of corporate law that involves transactions in securities.

Several of the *Schreiber* cases cite *Santa Fe*, in effect holding that the Williams Act does not federalize all of state corporation law that affects tender offers. These cases have let state law decide whether a board can take particular defensive action that has the effect of depriving shareholders of the opportunity to accept a tender offer. This deference ought to have some effect on judicial interpretations of "second generation" takeover statutes that frame the takeover regulation in the form of traditional regulation of internal corporate affairs.

Second-Generation Statutes and Constitutional Challenges to Private Defensive Tactics

The Overlap of Second-Generation Statutes and Private Defensive Tactics

Neither the *MITE* nor *Schreiber* lines of cases discuss in detail the conflicting approaches of the other cases. Either the issue was not raised, or the court summarily disposed of the issue with conclusory statements that the constitutional prohibitions of the supremacy clause and the interstate commerce clause apply only to state, not private actors.

The incompleteness of the analysis in these cases has become more obvious as state legislatures have changed their method of regulating takeovers. Instead of free-standing statutes labeled as regulation of securities transactions, states are now putting their takeover legislation within their corporation code and emphasizing the similarity of this new legislation to traditional state regulation of corporate internal affairs. In effect, these new statutes are changing the substantive relationship between shareholders and managers, usually with the effect of making managers less vulnerable to challenges from their shareholders. Challenges to these new statutes, therefore, may also apply to the many other provisions of state corporation codes which also regulate the shareholder-management relationship.

As takeover statutes have become more like corporation codes and written to regulate intrafirm relationships, it has become more difficult to distinguish their barriers to interstate commerce and to the broadly interpreted purposes of the Williams Act from the barriers thrown up by directors of target corporations pursuant to existing authority in the corporation codes. Indeed, to some extent statutes have copied defensive tactics pioneered by target firms providing a type of standardized contract for firms incorporated in that state.

The interrelationship of the two lines of cases becomes more obvious after considering the variety of methods by which states have sought to protect target managers from unwanted takeover bids and the inability to make much of a rational distinction between them. Consider the following strategies found in current state law:

Revised first-generation statutes require bidders to give disclosure to target shareholders and provide for enforcement of violations beyond the enforcement provided by the Williams Act. Several states revised their first-generation statutes after *MITE,* removing the extraterritoriality and the hearing or precommencement notice provisions criticized by the Supreme Court. Federal courts have upheld provisions of this sort in the Minnesota and Massachusetts statutes.

Control share acquisition statutes condition the right to vote shares obtained in a tender offer on a majority vote of all shareholders. These statutes extend the analogy made by the Williams Act which sought to subject all types of changes in control to parallel federal regulation. The control share acquisition statutes seek to subject different types of changes of control to parallel state regulation. Just as mergers have traditionally required the approval of shareholders, these statutes would condition change of control through a tender offer on a majority vote of the shareholders. Five of these statutes (Ohio, Indiana, Hawaii, Missouri, and Minnesota) have been held unconstitutional in federal court, perhaps because they regulate the intrafirm relationship by directly regulating the market transaction.

Reduced vote statutes limit the voting power of a shareholder who owns more than 20 percent of the company to 10 percent of those shares unless the holders of a majority of shares vote to restore full voting rights at a meeting called for that purpose. Wisconsin passed this variation of a control share acquisition statute in 1986.

Appraisal statutes give individual shareholders a right to have their shares redeemed by the corporation under specified circumstances such as the acquisition by another shareholder of a majority (or some smaller portion) of the target company's stock. Almost all state corporation statutes provide appraisal rights to minority shareholders who dissent from fundamental corporate changes such as mergers. These takeover statutes, such as Pennsylvania's law, extend that right to shareholders in a tender offer. These new statutes copy the general appraisal procedure but the definition of "fair value" to be paid for the shares sometimes is different (and more favorable to shareholders) in the takeover statutes.

Second-step/five-year delay statutes forbid second-step mergers and other similar transactions for five years following any tender offer that does not have the prior approval of the target company's board of directors. New York passed such legislation in 1985, and it has been followed by Kentucky,

Indiana, and Missouri. These statutes impose a potentially severe time penalty on bidders who avoid the board and take their offer directly to shareholders.

Second-step/supermajority-fair price statutes condition a second-step merger or other similar transaction following a tender offer on a supermajority vote or paying the remaining shareholders a statutorily defined fair price. These statutes, pioneered by Maryland, have the appearance of being less restrictive than the New York statute because there is no absolute time limit. But the definitions of fair price are sometimes written in a way so favorable to remaining shareholders that the second-step merger is extremely expensive. These statutes also encourage bidders to negotiate with the target board of directors since the onerous provisions often are waived for transactions approved by a majority of the preexisting board.

Fiduciary duty statutes codify a definition of the fiduciary duty of directors broader than the definition of that term in a state's common law. A statute of this type might, for example, authorize directors of a target company responding to a tender offer to consider a variety of interests beyond those of shareholders.

Traditional corporation statutes in states without specific takeover laws contain provisions that grant boards of directors broad permissive powers to manage the corporation. The similarity of this approach to those previously mentioned becomes more obvious in states such as Delaware, where state courts have interpreted traditional corporate law to authorize boards of directors to take steps similar to defensive tactics that other states have implemented by special statute.

Even this list does not exhaust the various approaches. But it provides enough of a glimpse of the potential for state regulation to aid our discussion of the appropriate role of state and federal law.

Application of MITE *Theories to Second-Generation Statutes*

The preemption and interstate commerce theories of *MITE* have been used to challenge "first generation" state regulation of tender offers and a much broader realm of state legislation, including those just described.

Preemption and the broad purpose of the Williams Act. A recurring argument is that the Williams Act mandates a market for corporate control unfettered by state law. The legislative history contains several references to providing investors with information so they may make their own choices. Both courts and commentators have viewed this purpose as protecting the shareholders' right to decide, or protecting the shareholders' right to freely sell their shares into a market where there are tender offerors. Management defense tactics that remove the tender-offer decision from the shareholder arguably frustrate the shareholder choice that Congress sought to protect or frustrates the Congressional intention that securities markets be free and open. It is only a short step to say that the Williams Act, therefore, limits defensive tactics that preclude shareholder consideration of tender offers.

A frequent corollary drawn is that Congress intended the shareholders to be the actual decision-makers and not some other group—a state commissioner, the target board of directors, or even the shareholders collectively rather than individually. A variation of this theme was sounded by Judge Wilson in the Fifth Circuit's decision in *Great Western United Corp.* v. *Kidwell.* He argued that Congress chose a "market approach" over what he labeled the "fiduciary approach" of an Idaho law that sought to give the target board of directors an opportunity to respond to a takeover.[21]

This view can be used to attack several state statutes. The control share acquisition statutes effectively put the decision about a tender offer into the hands of the shareholders as a group. Several courts have struck down these statutes on this basis.

The second-step/five-year delay statutes, such as the one in New York, place the tender offer decision in the hands of the directors unless the bidder is willing to wait five years for a second-step merger. The Maryland second-step/supermajority fair price statute also puts the decision in the hands of the directors unless the bidder wants to attempt to get the supermajority vote or pay the statutory price. These second-step statutes are more indirect in providing directors with decision-making powers, but they raise the costs of a tender offer, thereby reducing the number of tender offers and limiting the opportunity for shareholders to sell their shares into a market which includes potential tender offerors.

The fiduciary duty statutes can also be attacked as taking the decision out of the hands of shareholders if they sanction director action which can block a tender offer. Even the appraisal statutes could be vulnerable to similar arguments. If a nonmajority group seeks appraisal and raises the bidder's takeover cost, thus possibly deterring the offer, the statute can be read as putting the decision in the hands of this small group contrary to the shareholder-decision approach of the Williams Act.

Interstate commerce. The heightened concern about state regulation of interstate commerce, illustrated in the *MITE* line of cases, also has potentially broad implications for state takeover legislation and state corporation laws. Many of the cases, including the *MITE* plurality, seem to equate interference with the market for corporate control to interference with interstate commerce. Ruling on an Indiana law, Judge Posner wrote that, "the efficiency with which [a corporation's tangible assets] are employed and the proportions in which the earnings they generate are divided between management and shareholders depends on the market for corporate control—an interstate, indeed international, market that the State of Indiana is not authorized to opt out of, as in effect it has done in this statute."[22]

If this is so, a variety of laws and defensive tactics can be subjected to interstate commerce challenge:

- The control share acquisition statutes have been held to impair the bidder's ability to deal with the target shareholders.
- The New York and other second-step statutes that impede the tender offer process also interfere with the ability of a bidder to do business with target shareholders, even if somewhat more indirectly.
- State blue sky laws have been ruled invalid if they interfere with the timing of an interstate tender offer and, thus, decrease its chances of success.
- Any state corporation statute (e.g., permitting cumulative voting, staggered terms for directors, no removal of directors without cause prior to the end of a term, authorizing issuance of "poison pill" stock) which makes it more difficult for a tender offer to be made similarly interferes with the market for corporate control.
- State common law could be challenged on similar grounds. Judicial adoption of an "equal opportunity rule," entitling all shareholders to share in a control premium might run afoul of the prohibitions in the commerce clause.[23]
- Even such apparently unrelated laws as those requiring a bond to appeal a judgment are vulnerable to this challenge. Texaco, Inc. argued in its case against Getty Oil that Texas bond requirements impermissibly interfered with the market for corporate control and were, therefore, invalid. The court did not rule on that issue but it could flow logically from previous holdings.

This broad connection of interference with the market for corporate control and interference with interstate commerce only addresses the "burdens" side of the balancing equation used for indirect interferences with interstate commerce. The *MITE* decision and those which follow it suggest that this burden will occur in many of the examples previously cited and that it will be "substantial."

On the benefits side of the equation, *MITE* and subsequent courts ascribe very little weight to state regulation of corporations chartered under its law. *MITE* characterized the internal affairs doctrine, which looks to the state of incorporation for the rule governing internal corporate affairs, as a conflict of laws doctrine "of little use to the State in this context." Other courts have found the doctrine of little use to the state in other contexts.[24] Delaware, with many national corporations and few resident shareholders, will have to persuade a court that the benefits to its state treasury and to its local citizenry from being a center of incorporations outweigh the burden on interstate commerce from its state laws which impede tender offers.

States might have more success in convincing courts that benefits to *resident* shareholders outweigh the costs where a state takeover law is limited to locally incorporated enterprises and the great majority of shareholders in the target corporation are state residents. Courts have upheld laws against interstate commerce challenges in two such cases.[25]

On the other hand, just limiting the reach of the law to local residents was not enough for the Sixth Circuit which found that the shares held by Michigan shareholders were instrumental to obtaining a majority in a nationwide tender offer so that a state procedure excluding the offer for Michigan residents would interfere with the national tender offer and thereby burden interstate commerce.[26]

As a result of the preemption and interstate commerce rulings seeking to protect the market for corporate control, there may be a substantial federalization of the law of shareholder-management relations. This matter was never expressly debated by Congress in passing the Williams Act, even though federalization of state law has been vigorously debated in a variety of other areas.

Reconciling *MITE* and Schreiber: Principles That Define the Appropriate Realms of State and Federal Regulation

This section examines policies which could provide a basis for reconciling *MITE* with the policies of *Santa Fe* as set forth in the *Schreiber* line of cases and thereby define federal and state roles.

Distinguishing State from Private Conduct

There is little direct conflict between the *MITE* and *Schreiber* lines of cases if activities in the *Schreiber* cases may be characterized as private actions to which the constitutional prohibitions of the supremacy clause and the commerce clause do not apply. This, in fact, has been the argument used by the first courts to address the issue of whether *MITE*'s constitutional principles apply to defensive tactics in a tender offer fight. The Delaware Supreme Court in *Moran* v. *Household International*,[27] a decision upholding a poison pill defense under Delaware law, relied on the accepted constitutional principle that only state action can violate the commerce or supremacy clauses. The court ruled that statutory authorization of private conduct is an insufficient nexus.

That holding seems inconsistent with other cases in which preempted state law has not been so narrowly defined. For example, in *San Diego Building Trades Council* v. *Gannon*, the Supreme Court held that state common law could not be applied in a way that frustrates federal labor policy.[28]

There is also precedent for a broader preemption when the overlap is between federal securities laws and state corporate regulation. In a recent Sixth Circuit case, *In Re General Tire and Rubber Securities Litigation*,[29] shareholders challenged the dismissal of a derivative suit by the corporation's directors acting pursuant to directors' authority under state law to manage the corporation. Under Ohio common law, it seemed likely that the board's decision would be protected from judicial review by the business judgment rule, a common law judicial principle by which courts defer to business decisions of authorized management absent self-dealing or some other disability. Plaintiffs claimed this application of state common law would frustrate federal policy underlying the proxy provisions.

The Sixth Circuit acknowledged that it would preempt application of the Ohio business judgment rule if the rule frustrated the federal proxy laws but declined to do so in this case because it saw no causal connection between the plaintiff's claims and the transactions authorized by shareholders through the proxy process. Still, the court left no doubt that in other situations federal policy can overrule the business judgment rule. Using similar reasoning, the business judgment rule would not protect defensive tactics authorized under state law if it conflicted with the Williams Act.

The result of the *General Tire and Rubber* case is consistent with the Supreme Court's decision in *Burks* v. *Lasker* which also involved a challenge to a director dismissal of a derivative suit as conflicting with federal law. The Court rejected the claim, not because the director action was "private" but because federal policy was not broad enough to supplant authorization of director action found in state law. In language which has bearing on the Williams Act, the Court said, "in this field congressional legislation is generally enacted against the background of existing state law; Congress has never indicated that the entire corpus of state corporation law is to be replaced simply because a plaintiff's cause of action is based upon a federal statute."[30]

The cited cases provide ample precedent for preempting director conduct authorized by state law if federal policy would thereby be frustrated. Courts, therefore, should focus on the purpose of the federal law rather than the state/private distinction. If the purposes of the Williams Act are interpreted in light of the *MITE* plurality to maintain neutrality in the broader sense of that term, then many director actions can be found to be preempted by the Williams Act.

This focus on Congressional purpose provides a second method by which a court has avoided the constitutional issue regarding private defensive tactics. The Second Circuit in *Data Probe Acquisition Corp.* v. *Datatab, Inc.* suggested that the Williams Act was more concerned about some state laws (special takeover statutes) than other state laws (corporate statutes or common law authorizing director conduct). In *Data Probe* the district court had ruled, "[t]he notion that the reasoning in *Edgar* v. *MITE Corp.* can be distinguished as inapplicable to private suits seems unsound." The Second Circuit declined to follow such reasoning. Without discussion, the Second Circuit held the commerce clause inapplicable to a challenge to director conduct. It disposed of the supremacy clause objection by interpreting the Williams Act to bar only "legislative regulation of the tender offer process, including administrative review of the fairness or unfairness of the offer.'' In a footnote, Judge Winter noted that *MITE* did not involve "the application of fiduciary obligations of a contractual nature imposed by state law," suggesting that this second type of state regulation, the kind involved in *Data Probe,* would not be preempted.

Under this view, the *MITE* and *Schreiber* lines of cases can be reconciled if the Williams Act reflects a policy choice to override positive state regulation of tender offers but not state regulation achieved by imposing fiduciary obligations of a contractual nature or by common law applications of the business judgment rule which enable directors of target companies to implement defensive tactics. This focus on the form of state regulation, however, produces an awkward policy result. Interference with the market for corporate control would be banned if written into a specific state takeover law but permitted if accomplished by directors under a more general state law which in effect authorizes the private parties to do what the state cannot. The Delaware legislature and judiciary would be permitted to foster and encourage a system that enables corporations to hire expensive lawyers to erect barriers to takeovers which interfere with the market for corporate control. Yet, other states would be seen as intruding on federal regulation or interfering with interstate commerce when they seek to assist their corporations by providing a standardized takeover barrier.

Interference with the market for corporate control cannot be so easily separated. Indeed, the SEC's Advisory Committee on Tender Offers lumped together harm to the economy from defensive tactics provided by takeover statutes and from action instituted by private parties acting pursuant to state law. The elusive nature of such a distinction becomes apparent upon consideration of the various ways that state governments have chosen to structure their corporation laws to help directors. Delaware's broad grant of authority to directors may well be a more effective means of aiding managers against shareholders. Practically, it removes the need for a separate takeover statute to protect its corporations.

It is not self-evident that Delaware's approach to shareholder-management relations should be treated differently from Ohio's control-share acquisitions statute. Moreover, it is difficult to distinguish fiduciary duty, appraisal, and second-step statutes from the Delaware or Ohio statutes. All of these laws appear to interfere with the market for corporate control to some extent, and all appear to reflect a conscious state policy about the relative positions of shareholders and managers within a corporation. These new statutes suggest that division based on state versus private conduct or positive state legislation versus state law imposing fiduciary obligations is not going to produce a consistent theory to differentiate the role for state and federal law in regulating takeovers.

Protectionism and Interstate Commerce Jurisprudence

Questions about the meaning of the commerce clause have occupied a significant place in the deliberations of the Supreme Court since the Court's earliest days, spawning a variety of theories and constant litigation. A recurring theme is a basic hostility to protectionist state legislation that blatantly discriminates against out-of-state economic interests. Certainly judges in the *MITE* line of cases have ascribed this type of motive to state statutes that appear designed to prevent the takeover of local firms, even if the acquiring firm may make more efficient use of the assets.

In a corporate setting, courts may be tempted to apply this principle too frequently. The in-state/out-of-state division which provides a necessary factual foundation for a finding of state protectionism substantially overlaps in corporate cases with a management/shareholder division. For many large American corporations, managers will reside in the state of incorporation (or that state is likely to identify with management) and the great majority of shareholders are likely to reside in other states. Any state law regulating internal corporate affairs that favors the interests of management over laws favoring shareholders, including laws which make takeovers more difficult, may adversely affect interstate commerce by transferring the costs of the regulation (including the lost benefit of an advantageous takeover) to out-of-state shareholders. In this situation, a court will have a difficult time separating management provisions that discriminate against out-of-state interests from many other management provisions in the corporation code. Application of this theory may lead to the federalization of large parts of corporation law.

A court's effort to determine if an entire state corporation code impermissibly regulates interstate commerce is eased by the constitutional principle that Congress may explicitly or implicitly redefine the extent to which states may regulate interstate commerce. In corporate governance, Congress clearly has left a broad area of shareholder-management relations to state law. A state may use its authority over corporations to prefer managers over shareholders in a way that unduly harms out-of-state interests but that tendency will be checked to some extent by the competition between states for corporate charters.

Against this background, courts should reserve invalidation for commerce clause reasons only for those cases where the state statute blatantly discriminates against out-of-state interests. Where the alleged discrimination cannot be easily distinguished from shareholder-management conflicts, courts should not use the commerce clause to stifle state policy debates or the debate over federalization of corporation law.[31]

Regulation of the Market for Corporate Control as Distinguished from Regulation of Capital Markets

Judge Ralph Winter, the author of the Second Circuit's *Data Probe* decision, had previously suggested an alternative theory that would distinguish the appropriate realms of state and federal regulation. In an article written while he was on the Yale Law School faculty, Winter preferred state law governance of corporations. He argued that the competition between states for charters would facilitate development of rules most appropriate for the capital market.[32] A state corporation code that reduces the yield to shareholders will spawn corporations that are less attractive as investment opportunities than comparable corporations chartered in other states or countries and less attractive than bonds, savings accounts, land and other investments. Only managers wanting a "one-shot-take-the-money-and-run-raid" would be attracted. Winter, however, exempts regulation of the market for corporate control from this system of preferred state regulation because of a concern that competition among the states will provide inadequate protection in this situation.

If state regulation of the market for corporate control is less effective than state regulation of other aspects of intrafirm relationships, the proper scope for federal and state law can be defined based on that principle. Yet a significant part of Winter's argument turns on the extraterritoriality of early takeover laws which could operate outside of the competition between state legal systems for corporate charters. Now that state laws regulating takeovers have been rewritten to apply only to locally incorporated corporations,[33] the competition for charters may be more effective.

Even if there is a need for a federal law to prevail over state law in regulating the market for corporate control, it is not at all clear that Congress intended this displacement in passing the Williams Act. The tender offer is not the only means by which the market for corporate control operates, although it well may be the most effective. Other mechanisms such as a proxy fight perform a similar function, and they were already federally regulated when the Williams Act was enacted. Congress sought to fill a gap in the federal regulatory scheme by covering this newly popular method of acquiring control. There is no evidence that this new regulation of tender offers was intended to regulate the shareholder-director relationship differently from previous federal regulation.

Federal Recognition of State Regulation of Economic Activity within the Firm

The theories discussed thus far fail to reconcile federal intervention in tender offers permitted in the *MITE* cases with the respect for state law found in the *Schreiber/Santa Fe* cases. The best explanation for the division of responsibility between federal and state government views state law as providing the primary regulation of the rights among participants within the corporation and federal law as facilitating the exercise of these state-provided rights but not creating additional substantive rights. The Williams Act's regulation of market transactions between a bidder and a target company shareholder aids shareholders in monitoring management but it should not be read as altering existing substantive rights of shareholders against those of their managers.

This is not to say that federal law is not concerned with regulating economic activity within a firm. A variety of provisions in the Securities Exchange Act of 1934 are intended to affect the intrafirm relationship:

- Proxy rules aim to "prevent management or others from obtaining authorization for corporate action by means of deceptive or inadequate disclosure."[34]
- Periodic disclosures required by §13 of the 1934 Act similarly aid shareholders in evaluating the performance of their managers and making decisions concerning the exercise of their rights against managers.
- Antifraud provisions back up the specific disclosure obligations in accomplishing the desired protection for shareholders.

Apart from assisting shareholder monitoring of management performance, both the disclosure requirements and the antifraud provisions protect investors in the specific transactions in which they buy and sell securities. Similarly the Williams Act has two interrelated effects, first on the market transactions between the bidder and the target shareholders and second on the intrafirm relationship. The Congressional decision to include substantive regulation of the market transaction between the target shareholder and the bidder (by including requirements on pro rata acceptances of tenders and withdrawal rights for shareholders who tender) should not necessarily imply congressional intent to provide new substantive rights for shareholders against managers when that approach is contrary to almost all previous federal regulation of intrafirm activity.

Other parts of the federal securities laws specifically regulate changes in corporate control and this federal regulation is nonsubstantive. For example, in friendly acquisitions such as a merger, federal law mandates disclosure if proxies are solicited from shareholders in order to obtain the necessary approval required by state law. Similarly, federal disclosure is required if the acquisition takes the form of a sale of assets, but only if state law requires a shareholder vote. If the particular state permits directors to take action without shareholder approval (e.g., short form mergers in most states) the shareholders will not receive the benefit of the federal disclosures.

In hostile takeovers which take the form of a proxy fight for the election of directors, federal law mandates disclosure while state law provides election rules. If a hostile group seeks control by offering a share-for-share exchange, federal law again requires disclosure. Tender offers were continually compared to these transactions during consideration of the Williams Act. The new Act was designed to fill a gap in existing regulation and to do so in a way parallel to existing regulation.[35] In these pre-existing areas of federal regulation, the federal role does not extend to substantive rights of shareholders vis-à-vis management.

Tender offers are not the first area in which a dispute over federal regulation of intrafirm relationships has arisen. Indeed, the previous debates should provide guidance in interpreting the Williams Act.

For proxy regulation, the most instructive case is *SEC* v. *Transamerica Corporation*,[36] a 1947 decision by the Third Circuit ruling on whether a corporation's proxy solicitation must include proposals made by shareholders. One of the SEC's rules required management's proxy statement to include any shareholder's proposal concerning subjects about which state corporation law permits shareholders to act. Transamerica's management asserted that a by-law (implemented pursuant to the corporation's charter and the provisions of Delaware's corporations code) authorized them to act "as a block or strainer to prevent any proposal to amend the bylaws, which it may deem unsuitable, from reaching a vote at an annual meeting of stockholders."

The Court ruled that the corporation's position was "overnice" and "untenable" apparently as a matter of management's rights under Delaware law. But then, perhaps as Professor Louis Loss has noted, "because the court realized that it did not have the last word in interpreting the state law,"[37] it added an alternative holding or obiter:

> But assuming arguendo that this was not so we think that we have demonstrated that Gilbert's proposals are within the reach of security-holder action were it not for the insulation afforded management by the notice provision of By-Law 47. If this minor provision may be employed as Transamerica seeks to employ it, it will serve to circumvent the intent of Congress in enacting the Securities Exchange Act of 1934. It was the intent of Congress to require fair opportunity for the operation of corporate suffrage. The control of great corporations by a very few persons was the abuse at which Congress struck in enacting Section 14(a). We entertain no doubt that Proxy Rule X-14A-7 represents a proper exercise of the authority conferred by Congress on the Commission under Section 14(a). This seems to us to end the matter. The power conferred upon the Commission by Congress cannot be frustrated by a corporate by-law.

The Court's finding of a Congressional intent to require fair opportunity for corporate suffrage parallels similar findings by more recent courts requiring the relatively unfettered operation of the market for corporate control.[38] But that may be reading Congressional intent too broadly. In the proxy area, the SEC in 1954 amended its shareholder proposal rule (now Rule 14a-8) to require inclusion only of shareholder proposals which are "a proper subject for action for security holders" under "the laws of the issuer's domicile." As Professor Loss has observed, "the Commission probably has little choice under the statute. When the state law is clear that a particular matter is for the directors alone, that would seem to be decisive. If Congress had intended to give the Commission power to reallocate functions between the two corporate organs, so revolutionary a federal intervention would presumably have been more clearly expressed."[39] He added in a footnote the observation that, "This would approach federal incorporation in all but name."

A similar debate concerning possible federal substantive regulation of intrafirm relationships has arisen in connection with Rule 10b-5, which prohibits fraudulent or deceptive devices in connection with the purchase or sale of securities. During the 1960s and 1970s, some federal courts interpreted this rule to cover not just misrepresentations but also fraud in the broader sense of unfair conduct by corporate fiduciaries. In *Santa Fe Industries, Inc.* v. *Green,* a 1977 decision written by Justice White, the author of the *MITE* decision, the Supreme Court squashed such an expansive reading by requiring that a plaintiff show a deceptive or manipulative act (not just unfairness) in order to invoke section 10(b).

In what is perhaps its clearest indication to date of the interrelationship of federal securities law and state corporation law, the Court said:[40]

> Absent a clear indication of Congressional intent we are reluctant to federalize the substantial portion of the law of corporations that deals with transactions in securities. . . . "Corporations are creatures of state law and investors commit their funds to corporate directors on the understanding that except where federal law *expressly* requires certain responsibilities of directors with respect to stockholders, state law will govern the internal affairs of the corporation."

Since *Santa Fe* several federal courts of appeals have broadly interpreted "deception" so as to give a federal remedy to shareholders who were mistreated by their managers.[41] These courts interpret *Santa Fe* to exclude from Rule 10b-5 only those cases that have both deficiencies present in *Santa Fe*— that is, they deal with corporate mismanagement and lack any deception. If corporate mismanagement is accomplished by deception, a federal remedy accrues. If the challenged transaction involves an act by a corporation—e.g. the managers cause the corporation to sell corporate stock to themselves or their friends for too low a price—the necessary deception is that of the corporation. Courts have found material deception of the corporation where those who caused the corporation to act had a conflict of interest and they did not disclose the true facts to shareholders.

These cases have been vigorously criticized by some judges and commentators as inconsistent with the Supreme Court's decision in *Santa Fe*. Their effect is to provide a federal remedy to a shareholder who has been harmed by a faithless fiduciary. But even as so extended, the federal 10b-5 cause action depends on the shareholder-manager relationship created by state law. If state law provides no substantive right against the directors, then there is no federal disclosure obligation. A federal remedy exists only if there is a state remedy. In effect, these courts interpret the disclosure provisions of the federal securities laws as intended to supplement and safeguard shareholder rights against directors provided by state law.

The tender-offer cases go further by establishing substantive rights for shareholders against their managers. For example, Judge Sofaer in the district court decision in *Data Probe*, held that Congress imposed two duties on tender offer participants. The first duty is disclosure and the second, "to refrain from any conduct that unduly impedes the shareholders' exercise of the decision-making prerogative guaranteed to them by Congress."[42] In finding prerogatives granted by Congress instead of state law, the judge seems to be ruling that there is a substantive federal right. The reasoning is similar to that used in the *Transamerica* case—why would Congress require disclosure if it did not intend for shareholders to be able to effectively use that disclosure? Yet in both the proxy and Rule 10b-5 areas, Congress and the courts have recognized that these federal rights were facilitating shareholder rights derived from state law, but not displacing the relationship as determined by state law.

A third area where federal law has affected shareholder rights against management, albeit to a lesser extent than the two areas previously mentioned, is derivative suits. Such litigation occurs when a shareholder sues on behalf of the corporation after the board has refused to sue. Often the defendants in such suits are insiders who would be unlikely to cause the corporation to sue itself. The derivative suits function as a means by which shareholders can monitor their managers, one of a variety of checks in a list which would also include proxy fights and tender offers as well as the discipline provided by outside directors or the market for the corporation's products, or the corporation's participation in the markets for capital and labor. The effectiveness of derivative suits in this regard has been controversial. There have been recurring proposals for change by those who feel the cost of this form of monitoring is too high for the benefits received.

Federal law affects derivative suits, but the federal presence has been limited to procedural rules governing the conduct of such suits in federal court. The federal courts apply state substantive laws regarding the relative rights within the corporation of shareholders and directors. If state law permits directors to terminate derivative suits, federal courts will not interfere unless the dismissal would violate a federal policy. This lack of substantive rules regarding derivative suits is thus consistent with other areas in which the federal law has sought to regulate intrafirm relationships.

These examples of federal restraint in interfering in intrafirm relationships might be less relevant if Congress saw tender offers as having an effect that called for a more intrusive federal approach. Judge Sofaer put the argument this way:[43]

> A different form of protection is necessary under the Williams Act than under the 1934 Act because tender offer battles, even in a context of full disclosure, create extreme pressures and may involve tactics which distort or even abort the investment decision. Furthermore, whereas available state court remedies might be sufficient to warrant refusing to recognize a federal claim for "unfairness" under Section 10(b), a federal, injunctive remedy is a necessary adjunct to the Williams Act goal of preventing abuse of the tender offer procedure *before* they damage shareholders by undermining or aborting the tender offer process.

Yet, it is hard to find evidence in the legislative history of such a dramatic change in the relationship of federal law to state regulation of intrafirm relationships. The House and Senate hearings focused on filling a gap in the federal regulation, not changing the face of federal regulation. Senator Williams' initial bill, introduced in 1965, had been written as an amendment to §10(b) of the 1934 Act but was later moved to §14 after an SEC memorandum suggested the proxy section would be a more appropriate place for tender offer rules.

As further evidence of the more limited reach intended for the Williams Act, the legislative history contains several references to various defensive tactics that management might take. While Congress clearly decided not to impose a new federal law that would delay and benefit management, it did not forbid directors from using their authority under state law to undertake those activities (except in those situations where the defensive tactic involved management initiating a tender offer for its own shares).

Conclusion

Broader federal regulation may be necessary or appropriate to deal with possible harm to shareholders arising from defensive tactics which interfere with the market for corporate control. But concern over the vulnerability of shareholders to improper dealings by their managers has been the traditional concern of state law. Federal law has been involved in this area for at least fifty years, but its presence has always had a due regard not to supplant state regulation of the intrafirm relationships.

In light of this prior history, any change in the role of federal law should not be lightly inferred. Congress, not the courts, should declare any such extension. The substantive regulation of market transactions between a bidder and target company shareholders in the Williams Act does not necessarily imply that Congress also intended to adopt a federal policy giving shareholders new federal substantive protection beyond their rights available under state law. Federalization of corporation law deserves more direct consideration than has appeared so far in judicial decisions applying the Williams Act.

Notes

Research for this chapter was supported in part by a grant from the Center for the Study of American Business, Washington University. Larry Ribstein read an earlier version of this chapter and Kevin Barrett of the Washington University class of 1987 provided research assistance. This chapter departs from some of the formalities of traditional legal scholarship in hopes of providing the reader an uninterrupted flow of thought. Footnotes have been eliminated whenever possible. Almost all substantive content appears in the body of the text. A citation to a decision appears when the decision is first discussed or quoted. Subsequent citations of the case are omitted if the source is obvious to the reader.

 1. Previous debate over federalization of state corporate law centered on proposals for federal chartering of corporations based in part on the perceived inability of states to give appropriate protection to shareholders against possible abuses by managers and others. See, e.g., Cary, "Federalism and Corporate Law: Reflections Upon Delaware," 83 *Yale Law Journal* 663 (1974); Schwartz, "A Case for Federal Chartering of Corporations," 31 *Business Lawyer* 1125 (1976). See also the case law from the early 1970s discussed in the text accompanying note 41, describing some judicial efforts to read Rule 10b-5 to provide a federal remedy for management overreaching of shareholders.

    Similar debates also occurred in earlier areas. See, e.g., Stevens, "Uniform Corporation Laws through Interstate Compacts and Federal Legislation," 34 *Michigan Law Review* 1063 (1936); 69-A "FTC Utility Corporations," S Doc. No. 92, 70th Cong., 1st Sess. (1934).
 2. 430 U.S. 462, 97 S. Ct. 1292, 51 L. Ed.2d 480 (1977).
 3. See, e.g., *Icahn* v. *Blunt*, 612 F. Supp. 1400 (W.D. Mo. 1985); *Fleet Aerospace Corp.* v. *Holderman*, 637 F. Supp. 742 (S.D. Ohio 1986) aff'd 796 F.2d 135 (6th Cir. 1986) and the cases cited in note 14 infra.

    Professor Henry Manne developed the concept of the market for corporate control in the mid-1960s. See Manne, "Some Theoretical Aspects of Share Voting," 64 *Columbia Law Review* 1427 (1964).
 4. *Indiana* v. *Dynamics Corp. of America*, Dkt #86–97, probable juris noted 107 S. Ct. 258 (1986).
 5. Economic theory has distinguished economic activity occurring across markets from economic activity within a firm. See Coase, "The Nature of the Firm," *Economica*, New Series Vol. IV 386, 388 (1937). The exact nature and significance of that distinction, and the reasons for the existence of firms has been much debated. See, e.g., Alchian and Demsetz, "Production, Information Costs, and Economic Organization," 62 *American Economic Review* 777 (1972). Recent economic literature views a corporation as a nexus of contracts which poses the question as to how relationships inside a firm are different from relationships that are outside a firm. See Jensen and Meckling, "Theory of the Firm: Managerial Behavior, Agency Costs and Ownership Structure," 3 *Journal of Financial Economics* 305, 311 (1976). Without attempting a precise articulation of how these

relationships may differ, I argue in this paper that Congressional allocation of federal and state responsibilities in the corporate and securities area reflects this difference in the means chosen by the parties to structure their economic activity and in particular reflects a distinction between regulation of the shareholder/manager relationship and regulation of discrete market transactions, such as the purchase and sale of securities.

6. See, e.g., Winter, "State Law, Shareholder Protection, and the Theory of the Corporation," 6 *Journal of Legal Studies* 251 (1977); Romano, "Law as a Product: Some Pieces of the Incorporation Puzzle," 1 *Journal of Law Economics & Organization* 2 (1985).

7. See L. Loss, *Securities Regulation* 105–07 (2d ed. 1961).

8. For a description of the Advisory Committee's Recommendations and the SEC's response, see Quinn & Martin, "The SEC Advisory Committee on Tender Offers and Its Aftermath—A New Chapter in Change-of-Control Regulation" in Steinberg, ed., *Tender Offers, Developments and Commentaries* (1985).

9. 457 U.S. 624, 102 S. Ct. 2629, 73 L. Ed.2d 269 (1982).

10. *Edgar* v. *MITE Corp.*, 457 U.S. 624, 631 (1982) quoting *Hines* v. *Davidowitz*, 312 U.S. 52, 67, 61 S. Ct. 399, 404, 85 L. Ed. 581 (1941).

11. *Rondeau* v. *Mosinee Paper Corp.*, 422 U.S. 49, 58, 95 S. Ct. 2069, 2075, 45 L. Ed.2d 12 (1975).

12. *Dynamics Corp. of America* v. *CTS Corp.*, 794 F.2d 250, 261–62 (7th Cir. 1986); probable juris noted 107 S. Ct. 258 (1986).

13. 397 U.S. 137, 90 S. Ct. 844, 25 L. Ed.2d 174 (1970).

14. *APL Limited Partnership* v. *Van Dusen Air, Inc.*, 622 F. Supp. 1216, 1223–24 (D. Minn. 1985); *Fleet Aerospace Corp.* v. *Holderman*, 637 F. Supp. 742, 763 (S.D. Ohio 1986) ("so fundamental that it cannot be disregarded") aff'd 796 F.2d 135 (6th Cir. 1986).

15. *Great Western United Corp.* v. *Kidwell*, 577 F.2d 1256, 1279 (5th Cir. 1978), rev'd on other grounds sub nom. *Leroy* v. *Great Western United Corp.*, 443 U.S. 173, 99 S. Ct. 2710, 61 L. Ed.2d 464 (1979). See also cases in notes 22, 24, and 26.

16. 669 F.2d 366, 375 (6th Cir. 1981).

17. See *Schreiber* v. *Burlington Northern, Inc.*, 731 F.2d 163 (3d Cir. 1984) aff'd 105 S. Ct. 2458 (1985); *Feldbaum* v. *Avon Products, Inc.*, 741 F.2d 234 (8th Cir. 1984); *Buffalo Forge Co.* v. *Ogden Corp.*, 717 F.2d 757 (2d Cir) cert. denied 464 U.S. 1018, 104 S. Ct. 550, 78 L. Ed.2d 724 (1983); *Data Probe Acquisition Corp.* v. *Datatab Inc.*, 722 F.2d 1 (2d Cir. 1983) cert. denied 465 U.S. 1052, 104 S. Ct. 1326, 79 L. Ed.2d 722 (1984).

18. *Feldbaum* v. *Avon Products, Inc.*, 741 F.2d 234, 237 (8th Cir. 1984).

19. *Data Probe Acquisition Corp.* v. *Datatab Inc.*, 568 F. Supp. 1538 (S.D.N.Y. 1983) rev'd 722 F.2d 1 (2d Cir. 1983). cert. denied 465 U.S. 1052, 104 S. Ct. 1326, 79 L. Ed.2d 722 (1984).

20. See note 41 infra and accompanying text.

21. *Great Western United Corp.* v. *Kidwell*, 577 F.2d 1256, 1279 (5th Cir. 1978), rev'd on other grounds sub nom. *Leroy* v. *Great Western United Corp.*, 443 U.S. 173, 99 S. Ct. 2710, 61 L. Ed.2d 464 (1979).

22. *Dynamics Corp. of America* v. *CTS Corp.*, 794 F.2d 250, (7th Cir. 1986), probable juris noted 107 S. Ct. 258 (1986).

23. See Levmore, "Interstate Exploitation and Judicial Intervention," 69 *Virginia Law Review* 563, 625 (1983).

24. See, e.g., *APL Limited Partnership* v. *Van Dusen Air, Inc.*, 622 F. Supp. 1216,

1223 (D. Minn. 1985); *Fleet Aerospace Corp.* v. *Holderman*, 637 F. Supp. 742, 763–64 (S.D. Ohio 1986) aff'd 796 F.2d 135 (6th Cir. 1986).
25. See *Cardiff Acquisitions, Inc.* v. *Hatch*, 751 F.2d 906 (8th Cir. 1984); *L.P. Acquisition Co.* v. *Tyson*, 772 F.2d 201 (6th Cir. 1985).
26. *Martin Marietta Corp.* v. *Bendix Corp.*, 690 F.2d 558, 567 (6th Cir. 1982).
27. 500 A.2d 1346 (Del. 1985).
28. 359 U.S. 236 (1959) (tort action for damages resulting from unfair labor practices—picketing and boycotting nonunion employer—preempted by §§ 7–8 of the National Labor Relations Act). See generally *Arkansas Louisiana Gas Co.* v. *Hall*, 453 U.S. 571 (1981) (Natural Gas Act blocked method by which state court calculated damages in a breach of contract action); *Chicago and North Western Transportation Co.* v. *Kalo Brick and Tile Co.*, 450 U.S. 311 (1981) (Interstate Commerce Act precluded common law negligence action based on alleged failure to maintain roadbed and common law tort action for purported interference with contractual relations with customers brought by rail line against regulated rail carrier who sought and obtained ICC approval to abandon railroad line.) Cf. *Silkwood* v. *Kerr-McGee Corp.*, 104 S. Ct. 615 (1984) (punitive damages permitted for state common law action against operator of nuclear power plant despite claim of preemption by federal nuclear power regulation; common law action may be preempted but federal policy in this case found not to extend so far as to require preemption of this action).
29. 726 F.2d 1075 (6th Cir. 1984).
30. *Burks* v. *Lasker*, 441 U.S. 471, 478, 99 S. Ct. 1831, 60 L. Ed.2d 404 (1979). See also *Galef* v. *Alexander*, 615 F.2d 51, 64 (2d Cir. 1980) (federal policy precludes summary dismissal of a well-pleaded claim under § 14(a) pursuant to the business judgment of defendant directors where the claim goes to the disclosures required by the federal act); *Lewis* v. *Anderson*, 615 F.2d 778 (9th Cir. 1980) (federal policy does not preclude dismissal of §§ 10(b) and 14(a) claims by a special litigation committee); *Abramowitz* v. *Posner*, 672 F.2d 1025 (2d Cir. 1982) (same).
31. "The inherent conflicts between managerial autonomy . . . [and] . . . investor protection . . . ought to be worked out at the policy level and not diverted into the unpredictable byways of commerce clause jurisprudence." Anderson, "The Meaning of Federalism: Interpreting the Securities Exchange Act of 1934," 70 *Virginia Law Review* 813, 845 (1984).
32. Winter, "State Law, Shareholder Protection, and the Theory of the Corporation," 6 *Journal of Legal Studies* 251 (1977).
33. All second generation statutes described in this chapter (excluding the revised first generation statutes) have been written to apply only to corporations chartered under that particular state's law and often also require some other connection to the state such as a specified portion of assets or shareholders.
34. *J.I. Case Co.* v. *Borak*, 377 U.S. 426, 431 (1964).
35. See *Senate Report*, No. 550, 90th Cong. 1st Sess. at 3 (1967). See also "Memorandum of the SEC to the Committee on Banking and Currency," *U.S. Senate on S.2731 89th Congress*, reprinted in 112 Cong. Rec. 19003, 19005 (1966). See 113 Cong. Rec. 854 (1967), "The need for such legislation has been caused by the increased use of cash tender offers rather than the regular proxy fight to gain control of publicly owned corporations . . . [t]his legislation will close a significant gap in investor protection under the Federal securities laws . . ." (remarks of Senator Williams).
36. 163 F.2d 511 (3d Cir. 1947) cert. denied 322 U.S. 847.

37. See L. Loss, "Fundamentals of Securities Regulation 537" (1983).
38. See e.g., *Data Probe Acquisition Corp.* v. *Datatab Inc.*, 568 F. Supp. 1538, 1545 (S.D.N.Y. 1983), rev'd 722 F.2d 1 (2d Cir. 1983) cert. denied 465 U.S. 1052, 104 S. Ct. 1326, 79 L. Ed.2d 722 (1984).
39. Loss, supra note 37 at 530 and n.65.
40. 430 U.S. at 479, quoting *Cort* v. *Ash*, 422 U.S. 66, 84 (1975). Section 16b of the Securities Exchange Act of 1934 is an example of an express federal responsibility of directors to shareholders.
41. See, e.g., *Goldberg* v. *Meridor*, 567 F.2d 209 (2d Cir. 1977) cert. denied 434 U.S. 1069 (1978); *Kidwell ex relevant Penfold* v. *Meikle*, 597 F.2d 1273 (9th Cir. 1979); *Healey* v. *Catalyst Recovery of Pa., Inc.*, 616 F.2d 641 (3d Cir. 1981); *Wright* v. *Heizer Corp.*, 560 F.2d 236 (7th Cir. 1977) cert. denied 434 U.S. 1066 (1978); *Alabama Farm Bureau Mutual Life Insurance Co.* v. *American Fidelity Life Insurance Co.*, 606 F.2d 602 (5th Cir. 1979) cert. denied 499 U.S. 820 (1980).
42. *Data Probe Acquisition Corp.* v. *Datatab Inc.*, 568 F. Supp. 1538, 1545 (S.D.N.Y. 1983) rev'd 722 F.2d 1 (2d Cir. 1983) cert. denied 465 U.S. 1052, 104 S. Ct. 1326, 79 L. Ed. 722 (1984).
43. *Data Probe Acquisition Corp.* v. *Datatab Inc.*, 568 F. Supp. 1538, 1544 (S.D.N.Y. 1983) rev'd 722 F.2d 1 (2d Cir. 1983) cert. denied 465 U.S. 1052, 104 S. Ct. 1326, 79 L. Ed.2d 722 (1984).

7

The Antitrust Division as a Regulatory Agency: An Enforcement Policy in Transition

E. Thomas Sullivan

The controversy over corporate control of capital markets escalated in the early to mid-1980s with a tidal wave of mergers, acquisitions, takeovers, and leveraged buyouts.[1] While a number of explanations have been offered for this merger trend, one of the most important factors was the Reagan Administration's eased antitrust standards and review procedures.

The Antitrust Division of the Department of Justice is responsible for challenging mergers that have a reasonable probability of substantially lessening competition or of creating a monopoly. Merger enforcement has not always been consistent, however. It has varied with administration agendas and economic theories. For example, from the inception of the Clayton Act in 1914 until its major revision in 1950, the Department of Justice brought only 16 merger cases. The following decade, only 27 mergers were challenged by the government. The high point was reached in 1968 when the Department filed 24 cases. In the first five years of the Reagan Administration, the Antitrust Division challenged only 26 mergers out of more than 10,000 merger applications. And 13 of those challenged cases resulted in resolution through the entry of consent decrees.

Serious concern has been expressed in several quarters, including the Federal Reserve Board, about the relaxed standards governing antitrust enforcement. But the Antitrust Division's policy, according to U.S. Attorney General Meese, "distinguishes more clearly between procompetitive, efficiency-enhancing mergers on the one hand, and mergers that create a significant probability of increasing prices to consumers, on the other." Although the economic policy employed to interdict corporate takeovers and its distributional effects are obviously important public policy inquiries, equally important, and no less controversial, is the process or procedure by which the Antitrust Division interprets and enforces its statutory mandate.

The Antitrust Division's actual enforcement techniques for resolving merger disputes, rather than the underlying economic policy which favors or disfavors large mergers, are the focus here. The Antitrust Division has evolved from a traditional, litigation-oriented enforcement agency into a regulatory agency. Accepting a negotiational rather than adversarial posture, it avoids lengthy and costly adversarial litigation in exchange for a more efficient resolution of merger issues. This change has important implications for enforcement policy, compliance incentives, and substantive law.

Although the new policy may result in more cost-efficient enforcement, the regulatory role for the Antitrust Division is antithetical to the original intention of the Sherman and Clayton Acts. Nevertheless, the transition has occurred, and at times Congress has sanctioned or ratified it, at least implicitly through inaction. The switch in policy by the Antitrust Division deserves full congressional evaluation.

In attempting to explain the tensions created by the Antitrust Division's regulatory posture, Section I of this chapter reviews the original intention of the drafters of the Sherman and Clayton Acts. Section II identifies classical models of regulation. Section III describes and analyzes the Division's specific procedures and rules. This section demonstrates how the Division has become a de facto regulator, consistent with recognized models of regulation and more recent legislative action. Finally, Section IV analyzes how the Division's review procedures enhance efficiency and clarity in the law and how they are consistent with and supported by the emerging trend of alternative dispute resolution.

Legislative History

The Sherman Act

The first antitrust bills were introduced in Congress in 1888. Senator Sherman, the principal bill's sponsor, argued that Congress could regulate trusts only through its taxing power; later he broadened his argument to include Congress' authority to regulate through the Constitution's commerce clause. After two years of debate, Congress adopted the Sherman Antitrust Act in 1890, including civil and criminal enforcement provisions.

The statute contained only general, substantive principles outlawing restraints of trade and monopolizations. Congress intended the courts to interpret the Sherman Act on a case-by-case basis in accordance with common-law principles and precedents. In an important change, the new legislation gave the federal courts subject-matter jurisdiction. Under common law, if restraints were found unreasonable, they were considered void and unenforceable in the courts. Under the Sherman Act, however, a private suit for treble damages was allowed, and the federal government could bring criminal actions for fines and imprisonment or civil actions for injunctive relief.

Originally, jurisdiction to institute proceedings on behalf of the government rested with the Attorney General's office. From 1903 until 1933, an Assistant Attorney General within the Department of Justice had authority to enforce the antitrust law. (The Antitrust Division was not established until 1933.)

A review of the legislative debates on the Sherman Act indicates that there was little, if any, discussion about the role of the Department of Justice.[2] Debate centered around the issues of constitutionality of the proposed legislation and the dislike for trusts, combinations, and monopolies.

The final bill was drafted in the Senate Judiciary Committee, largely through the work of Senators Edmunds, George, Hoar, and Evarts. It was similar to Senator Sherman's earlier proposal but contained more severe penalties. The public enforcement provisions were the responsibility of the Attorney General. The drafters expressed no doubts that the Attorney General's responsibility was to enforce the law. As Congressman Cannon of Illinois said during the floor debate:[3]

> [The Sherman Act] invokes the equity side, the greatest restraining power of the court, and it makes it the duty of United States district attorneys under the direction of the Attorney General, to go upon the equity side of the court and invoke the strong hand of the chancellor, backed by the whole power of the United States. . . .

But how the law was to be enforced was not widely debated by the Congress. As a retrospective report to the Congress in 1940 observed:[4]

> Nor was there an attempt to devise new machinery of enforcement. In the thought of the nineties the law should be as nearly self-enforcing as possible. The main reliance seems to have been placed upon the private suit. A man knew when he was hurt better than an agency or government above could tell him. Make it worth their while—as the triple-damage clause was intended to do— and injured members could be depended upon to police an industry. If more were needed, the resort was to the usual course of Federal justice. Another duty was added to the overlarge obligations of the Attorney General and of the several district attorneys scattered throughout the land.

As presidential administrations changed, the enforcement of antitrust laws also changed. Certainly in the early years after the adoption of the Sherman Act, public enforcement of the act was directed toward litigation, not regulation.[5] This early policy interpretation is consistent with the scant legislative history on the point, that "The Sherman Act . . . was a method of regulation by lawsuit."[6]

That the Department did not consistently or regularly enforce the statute throughout its early life does not undercut the statute's litigation focus. The irregularity of enforcement was due to enforcement discretion and budget constraints, not lack of authorization or statute clarity. In subsequent years, enforcement mechanisms were strengthened.

Legislative Activity Prior to the Clayton Act

After the turn of the century, President Theodore Roosevelt altered enforcement policy. Although Roosevelt had considered antitrust an important issue as early as 1882, he had no particular antitrust policy when he took office in 1901; only later did he take the lead in advocating strong enforcement.[7] The first case filed by his Department of Justice was *United States* v. *Northern Securities* in 1902. Shortly thereafter, Roosevelt proposed a national regulatory statute: "In the interest of the whole people, the nation should, without interfering with the power of the States in the matter itself, also assume power of supervision and regulation over all corporations doing an interstate business."[8] But Roosevelt did not consider the Department of Justice to be an economic regulator. While he increased Justice Department prosecutions substantially, he also advocated a separate regulatory agency for antitrust actions.

The first regulatory effort was the creation of the Bureau of Corporations in 1903; the Bureau's first investigation was the "Beef Trust" in 1905. Roosevelt wanted it to investigate corporations and report its findings to the administration. Although the Bureau of Corporations was to act as an adjunct to the Department of Justice—and to publicize business conduct—the Bureau and the Department did not consistently cooperate with each other.

Since Roosevelt believed the Department's role was to litigate, he pressed for expanded regulatory authority for the Bureau. "To attempt to control these corporations by lawsuits means to impose upon both the Department of Justice and the courts an impossible burden."[9] Roosevelt, therefore, urged the establishment of an expert commission with supervisory power over firms engaged in interstate commerce—i.e., regulation "by an executive body, and not merely by means of lawsuits."[10] Although a bill to accomplish Roosevelt's objectives was introduced in Congress in 1908, it lost support after long debate.

The matter was important enough to become a campaign issue. During the 1908 presidential campaign, the Democrats proposed, among other changes to the Sherman Act, a federal licensing system, which would require an interstate corporation "to take out a Federal license before it shall be permitted to control as much as twenty-five percent of the product in which it deals."[11] The license was designed to protect the public from watered stock and to prohibit the control by such a corporation of more than 50 percent of the total amount of any product consumed in the United States.[12] President Taft, Roosevelt's successor, proposed a similar form of antitrust regulation.

Instead of proposing to amend the Sherman Act, Taft urged the establishment of compulsory federal incorporation of interstate business. Under the proposal, regulatory powers would be given to the Department of Commerce to regulate stock purchases, to prohibit companies from holding stock in other corporations except upon prior approval, and to require certain disclosures. After the Supreme Court decided *Standard Oil Co.* v. *United States,* Taft amended his federal incorporation proposal to include that supervision should be by "an executive tribunal of the dignity and power of the Comptroller of the Currency or the Interstate Commerce Commission."[13] This idea was supported by Taft's Attorney General, who had negotiated final decrees in major antitrust cases. Said Attorney General Wickersham:[14]

> It is not right that the Attorney General should be subjected to the responsibility of deciding . . . whether or not a proposed plan of disintegration of an individual combination would restore lawful combination. The questions involved are economic; they depend upon information which we can not have in this department; and it was a mere chance that the Bureau of Corporations had investigated, and, therefore, was possessed of facts which enabled it to come to the assistance of the Department of Justice in this particular instance.

The *Standard Oil* decision certainly had a major impact on subsequent legislation, which substantially broadened the Department's enforcement responsibility. In *Standard Oil,* the Supreme Court rejected Taft's interpretation of the coverage of the Sherman Act. As a federal judge deciding *United States* v. *Addyston Pipe & Steel Co.,* Taft had held that the "rule of reason" analysis only applied to ancillary restraints, not to direct restraints such as price fixing, which he characterized as "naked restraints." For Taft, the "reasonableness" of the restraint should not be considered if the restraint was direct; the conduct alone was deemed illegal.

Chief Justice White's opinion in *Standard Oil,* however, adopted a rule of reason analysis significantly broader than Judge Taft's standard. White's majority opinion applied a rule of reason analysis to direct, as well as ancillary, restraints in determining the "reasonableness" of the restraint. Only "unreasonable" or "undue" restraints of trade were illegal under the *Standard Oil* view. When White applied the new standard, the Court found the defendants in *Standard Oil* guilty of engaging in unreasonable restraints of trade. Accordingly, the Court ordered dissolution of Standard Oil.

Immediately after *Standard Oil,* critics charged that White's broader analysis might weaken the statute and broaden the discretion of the judiciary. The new standard was denounced for vagueness. Critics feared that the Sherman Act's effectiveness in controlling trusts, combinations, and monopolies would be diluted. As a result, numerous proposals were drafted in the Congress, some urging the creation of a business court or expert commission that would license the whole range of business decisions from capitalization to business practices. The Sherman Act, with its new standard, was viewed by many as merely a "method of regulation *by lawsuit*" and Bickel wrote that it was too uncertain to be regarded seriously. No congressional consensus emerged on the proposals, however, until after the presidential elections of 1912. The statutory amendments that followed changed the course of the Department of Justice's authority.

The Adoption of the Clayton Act and Direct Control Over Mergers

The debate in Congress in 1911-12 and the political speeches surrounding the campaign of 1912 demonstrated that few people, if any, in positions of authority believed that the Department of Justice's antitrust enforcement authority extended beyond filing lawsuits and litigating cases.[15] After the *Standard Oil* decision, the call became even stronger for supplemental antitrust legislation, the creation of a regulatory agency and the rejection of the idea of federal incorporation. After President Wilson took office in 1912, these proposals soon became reality.

The legislative debates leading to changes in the antitrust laws began in 1913. Senator Cummins presented three proposals.[16] The first two provided for a Bureau of Corporations as a separate administrative agency. The third proposal would have permitted a preclearance approval or disapproval of proposed mergers. The purpose was to facilitate "administrative" ease and efficiency in the enforcement of the antitrust laws. The proposals were offered in the spirit of a system that would regulate competition[17] and aid the Department of Justice in enforcement.[18] A Senate Committee was unable, however, to recommend specific legislation.

President Wilson shared most of Senator Cummins' agenda. Throughout the campaign and in his first year in office, Wilson urged the adoption of supplemental legislation. He proposed a more explicit statute identifying specific prohibited conduct and a new regulatory trade commission. Wilson favored a regulatory commission that would serve as a fact finder and serve to help shape dissolution and divestiture decrees. However, he disapproved of Cummins' proposal to permit a premerger approval or disapproval procedure.[19]

The President believed a premerger, advisory opinion (which had been used twice in the Roosevelt administration) would give the impression that the government was working "with" firms to effect business mergers.[20] Wilson rejected the proposition that the government was or should be in "partnership" with business. He wanted, however, to provide the Department of Justice with "guidance and information" from an administrative body as a "clearing house for information."[21] In fact, the regulatory commission finally approved by Congress had broader powers than Wilson, or his adviser Brandeis, had ever advocated.

Out of compromise in 1914 came two legislative enactments: the Clayton Act and the Federal Trade Commission Act. Each spoke, either explicitly or implicitly, of the role played by the Department of Justice in the merger area.

First, the Clayton Act explicitly prohibited certain practices, including certain mergers. This was a major change from the Sherman Act. Section 7 prohibited stock acquisitions or mergers that may "substantially lessen competition or tend to create a monopoly in any line of commerce."[22] Although this standard was vague and afforded judges little guidance, it was clear from the legislative history that the purpose was "to arrest the creation of trusts . . . in their incipiency and before consummation."[23] Otherwise, the open-endedness of the standard defied specificity and clarity. Even though the House and Senate were aware of textual ambiguities, the spirit of compromise enjoined the membership from being more specific. No provision was made for preclearance of mergers by the Department of Justice or the Federal Trade Commission. Wilson, and not Cummins, had prevailed on this major issue.

The legislative history underlying the creation of the Federal Trade Commission indicates how the Department of Justice was viewed at the time. The debates made clear that a new regulatory commission would introduce new investigative tools and an administrative "body of law" necessary to make antitrust enforcement more effective. The Senate Committee observed that many antitrust problems could have been avoided if a regulatory commission, unlike the Department of Justice, had been established with the enactment of the Sherman Act. The Committee noted that changes in administrations had caused inherent enforcement problems in the Attorney General's office. The Committee favored a separate administrative agency in part because it believed that the public was not ready for a sharp swing in enforcement carried out by the Department of Justice. Thus, while maintaining the Department's law enforcement role under the Sherman Act, the Federal Trade Commission (FTC) was created to establish a regulatory framework over corporations engaged in trade practices in interstate commerce.[24]

In addition to investigative and fact-finding authority, the FTC was empowered to issue cease and desist orders against "unfair methods of competition." The Commission, in the first instances, would define those terms as it enforced the new act. Congress declined to do so; nor did it offer helpful guidance. The Department and the Commission were expected to assess different penalties: criminal penalties by the Department and regulatory penalties for controlling or adjusting markets by the Commission.

Subsequent Amendments of the Antitrust Laws

Section 7 of the Clayton Act was amended by Congress in 1950 to cover assets as well as stock acquisitions. Congress also was influenced because of the difficult burden of proof established in *United States* v. *Columbia Steel Co.* for challenging mergers under the Sherman Act. A review of the Celler-Kefauver debates in the Congress indicates that the enforcement responsibilities of the Antitrust Division were not the subject of debate, although Senator Kefauver inserted in the Congressional Record a reference that recognized the Department's role of "policing business and industry."

In 1955, a special committee set up by the Attorney General published an in-depth study of the antitrust laws. Among the committee's recommendations was the suggestion that Section 7 of the Clayton Act authorize the Department of Justice to use procedures to give prior clearance to proposed mergers. The minority members wanted a strict interpretation of the Department's role as a prosecutorial body with no premerger clearance authority.[25] The committee's recommendations included the possible use of investigatory tools, such as Civil Investigative Demands (CIDs), which the Department had requested to aid in the production of evidence for litigation. The committee distinguished the CID investigatory tool, which it recommended for the Department, from the investigatory subpoena power granted to the FTC. Although the committee wanted the Department to be able to obtain information necessary for its enforcement function and to determine whether to file suit against a corporation, it did not want the Department to be able to enforce such demands through sanctions outside actual judicial proceedings or to create the procedural mechanisms similar to subpoenas authorized by *regulatory* agencies in the performance of their functions. These views were eventually embodied in the 1962 Antitrust Civil Process Act.

The hearings on the Antitrust Improvements Act of 1975 concerning premerger notification illustrate continued concerns about the Department's role. FTC Chairman Lewis Engman said that premerger notification proposed in the Act might lead the Antitrust Division (and the Commission) into "controlling" mergers rather than "maintaining their proper role to enforce the antitrust laws."[26]

In other testimony, the Assistant Attorney General of the Antitrust Division, Thomas Kauper, reaffirmed the notion that the Justice Department primarily enforces the law, characterizing the use of CIDs as "clearly . . . advantageous" in that role. He observed that while the Department is the prosecutor, the FTC is a regulator and "policy maker." However, he pointed out that the Antitrust Division, subject to delegated authority from the Attorney General, had recently become "one of the prime advocates of competition policy before the federal regulatory agencies.'' Kauper added that ''[t]his activity is increasing and becoming ever more important.''[27]

Thus, Congress became aware that the Antitrust Division was becoming more of a public spokesman in the regulatory affairs of other agencies through its competition advocacy program. In addition, Congress knew that the Department's use of preclearance merger procedures might get it more involved in economic regulation.

The debate on the Antitrust Improvements Act carried over into 1976. Again, arguments centered on the boundaries of the Antitrust Division's authority. The minority Committee members opposed the use of CIDs for proposed merger violations because the Department was not considered a regulatory agency; as such, the Department was not subject to the requirements of the Administrative Procedures Act or of congressional oversight, as is the FTC. The minority stated:[28]

> The Department of Justice is not a regulatory agency subject to direct congressional oversight, but is the prosecuting arm of the U.S. Government. There is a vast difference between a prosecutor and a regulator. Conferring the investigatory powers of a regulatory commission on a prosecutor is alien to our legal traditions and contrary to the premise of the fifth amendment, which contemplates that a prosecutor can investigate crime only through the grand jury process.

If CIDs were allowed, the minority argued, the Department would be given ''regulatory'' powers that directly contradicted the original mandate for prosecution of the antitrust laws. The minority characterized the FTC as an investigator and fact-finder with no authority to determine civil or criminal liability and for which ''rigorous protections relevant to criminal prosecutions'' would, therefore, be unnecessary. The minority also distinguished the FTC's inability to intervene before all other government agencies as justification for allowing it broad investigatory powers, while denying such to the Department, which can file ''comments'' with other regulatory bodies. The minority supported its position with the findings of the 1955 Attorney General's Committee Report. Summarizing that Committee's view, the minority felt they too had rejected giving unlimited administrative power to the Department because it is an enforcement agency.

The premerger notification provision was attacked because it assumed mergers are bad per se and that notification was necessary to correct a proposed merger's faulty provisions. The minority thought the Department and the FTC had sufficient powers to stop anticompetitive mergers; the premerger stay provisions would ''indirectly vest in the Department . . . an unjustifiable and destructive regulatory authority.''[29]

Despite these continued, strong warnings, Congress passed, without conference resolution, the Hart-Scott-Rodino Act of 1976. The Act increased CID authority and provided for premerger notification to the Antitrust Division.

In reaction to the minority's criticisms, the Act contained many procedural safeguards against the alleged prosecutorial abuse perceived under the expanded CID authority.[30] It also afforded some protections under the premerger notification to permit speedy resolution of a contemplated transaction while permitting adequate review to ensure compliance with the law and opportunity for effective relief from potential violations.[31]

Congress did not explicitly disagree with the regulatory roles into which the minority cast the FTC and the Department. However, it is not entirely clear whether Congress simply rejected the proposition that the legislation actually altered the roles or whether it was merely satisfied that procedural safeguards in the legislation were adequate protection. Congress was on notice that this legislation would alter the historic enforcement role of the Antitrust Division. The direction was toward that of an economic regulator, especially if one compares the almost identical premerger clearance process approved for and exercised by both the FTC and the Antitrust Division.

Models of Regulation

More than a century has passed since government regulation of industry and private property began in the United States. Regulatory schemes were first sanctioned by the Supreme Court in the 1877 *Munn* v. *Illinois* decision and by Congress with the establishment of the Interstate Commerce Commission. *Munn* set the legal standard for national regulatory intervention in the market: "Property does become clothed with a public interest when used in a manner to make it of public consequence, and affect the community at large. When, therefore, one devotes his property to a use in which the public has an interest, he, in effect, grants to the public an interest in the use, and must submit to be controlled by the public for the common good."[32]

Munn's "affected with public interest" standard is the central principle today for government control of economic activity. It portended broad regulation over business and the establishment of federal regulatory agencies, commencing with the creation of the Interstate Commerce Commission and its regulation over railroads and the enactment of the Sherman Act to control trade practices. Although regulation has taken many forms since the late 19th century, discussion of them can inform contemporary regulatory control at the Antitrust Division.

Changing economic conditions or theories often foster a change in regula tory form or response. Pervasive government regulation reached a high point during the New Deal and Great Society programs. Deregulation, started in the late 1970s, now has reached its crescendo. In certain industries, reregulation is even on the rise. From these regulatory swings, we can describe the forms and purposes of regulation that have evolved.

Regulation has been defined broadly by some commentators to mean government intervention in the market as a means of assuring more competitive performance.[33] Since the *Munn* decision, one of the purposes behind regulation has been government intervention to ensure the more efficient operation of markets. Regardless of the cause of market failure, government intervention has occurred when the perception was that the market was not self-correcting. Frequently, the purpose of intervention has been to redistribute income or wealth or to rehabilitate the economy.

But the purpose or effect of regulation has not always been clear. For example, the "public interest" notion of regulations, which promotes public interest over private gain as justification for market intervention, has been criticized in many quarters. Substantial challenges began in the 1960s, although the origins were much earlier. Political motives of regulation were studied and found, in certain industries and certain eras, to dominate over public interest concerns. Regulation was viewed as purely political, designed to protect those being regulated. As such, regulation is considered a means through which producers or sellers "capture" the industry for private advantage. In addition to political motives, the capture theory is concerned with the economic consequences of regulation: As producers promote regulation and market intervention, increased costs (deadweight losses) are shifted to consumers, competition is discouraged and a redistribution of wealth occurs. Under this theory, regulation is considered anticompetitive. The regulatory framework often may rest on multiple justifications.[34]

Classical models of regulation that have been employed include: (1) cost-of-service ratemaking, (2) reallocation in accordance with the "public interest," (3) standard-setting, (4) historically-based price setting and (5) historically-based allocation. De facto economic regulation also occurs through the use of regulatory controls that preserve competitive markets by imposing: (1) taxes as an incentive or deterrent, (2) a bargaining process through which the regulatory agency bargains with the regulated to achieve consensus, (3) disclosure requirements used for economic purposes, and (4) preclearance (screening) approval procedures. Several of these regulatory paradigms form the basis of the Antitrust Division's present regulatory posture over mergers and acquisitions.[35]

A classical model of regulation is setting standards, which is perhaps the most commonly used technique. The agency first determines the adverse effects and whether they should be eliminated or minimized. After determining the problem and the solution, the agency gathers relevant information necessary to draft a standard. Standards, once promulgated, must of course be enforced. And agency-prescribed regulations that impose rights and obligations must comply with the notice and comment provisions of the Administrative Procedures Act, providing a "concise general statement" of the standard's "basis and purpose."[36]

Another form of regulation is disclosure. Disclosure requirements may be the provision of information to the buying public or be utilized for regulating business activities. In either case, a standard establishing the conditions of disclosure must be set and enforcement mechanisms included. Although similar to standard-setting in many respects, disclosure requirements are narrower. They do not prohibit or prescribe certain products or conduct; they only require disclosure of certain information. Disclosure, when used as a means of economic regulation, can inform regulators of the industry and specific-firm data relevant to competitive market factors. Disclosure requirements are considered less costly and less restrictive than standards set to regulate production, output, or product prices.[37]

A third regulatory control is a preclearance screening process, analogous to standard-setting. Individualized screening occurs when an agency has authority to screen out applicants or applications based on predetermined standards that satisfy regulatory objectives. After a petition for approval is filed, the standards are applied on an ad hoc basis to individual applications. Those not meeting the preclearance standards could be denied or challenged. Preclearance screening is similar to licensing, which implicates allocations or reallocations under public interest standards.

Finally, bargaining is considered an alternative or de facto form of regulation that tries to develop and build a consensus between parties that share similar interests. The process involves trade-offs—each party must determine priorities within certain goals, weigh costs and benefits of each and determine the higher values. Bargaining is more likely to produce voluntary compliance with standards for the least cost. Successful bargaining minimizes enforcement costs as well. The parties are more inclined to voluntarily comply with the standards when they reach a consensus.

But the bargaining process has several inherent shortcomings. First, parties cannot always be forced into agreement. Second, not all parties have equal bargaining power to make the process useful. Third, a final agreement may affect parties not represented at the bargaining process.

These models of regulation have particular application to the Antitrust Division's merger approval process, which the next section describes. In using them, the Department of Justice regulates economic behavior and allocates scarce resources by applying standards and structuring the merged entity to avoid competition problems. The application of these regulatory devices is not typical for a law enforcement agency.

As an example, the Department has issued Merger Guidelines, which set forth a "public interest" standard of competition for market power and collusive practices. As a precondition of review of a proposed merger, the Antitrust Division requires, under the Hart-Scott-Rodino Act of 1976, disclosure of certain economic and financial data of the firms involved. Pursuant to this disclosure, the Division can issue a business review letter setting forth how it intends to enforce "proposed business conduct." This premerger review essentially serves as a preclearance screening process that permits the Division to screen out potentially anticompetitive mergers. If the proposed merger is without objection, the Department issues a business review letter stating it "has no present intention of instituting enforcement proceedings to challenge" the proposed merger. In those instances where the proposal raises antitrust concerns, the Division identifies the anticompetitive effects and bargains or negotiates with the mergering parties to restructure the merger. If the parties fail to reach a consensus on a restructured merger, they can abandon the merger or the Department can file suit to enjoin the proposed merger. The Reagan Administration has used the latter remedy infrequently.

The Antitrust Division as Economic Regulator

The Antitrust Division's transformation from a litigating division to a de facto regulatory agency commenced in the 1960s. The change began with the Division's increased focus on economic analysis of mergers and with the adoption of the 1968 Merger Guidelines.

Merger Guidelines

The 1968 Merger Guidelines expressly set forth the standards, enforcement interpretation, and policy by which the Antitrust Division would determine whether to challenge mergers and acquisitions. They were not considered a substitute for the Division's business review process, which remained the Division's preferred procedure for reviewing individual mergers.

The Guidelines attempted to identify mergers or acquisitions that were likely to facilitate anticompetitive conduct. "Market structure is the focus of the Department's merger policy chiefly because the conduct of the individual firms in a market tends to be controlled by the structure of that market, *i.e.*, by those market conditions which are fairly permanent or subject only to slow change (such as, principally, the number of substantial firms selling in the market, the relative sizes of their respective market shares and the substantiality of barriers to entry of new firms into the market)."[38]

The Guidelines pointed out that in exceptional circumstances the Division could be guided by "a more complex and inclusive evaluation," recognizing that not all proposed mergers might be susceptible to a structure-conduct analysis, especially where the market was in transition. But in the main, the Guidelines centered on identifying acceptable market shares in horizontal mergers,[39] the foreclosure of competition in vertical mergers, the elimination of potential competitors, the creation of reciprocal dealing, and the entrenchment of a dominant firm in a concentrated market.

Despite an attempt to follow the case law, the courts did not regularly adopt the 1968 Guidelines. In the 14-year period following the issuance of the 1968 standards, the Division's philosophy changed, economic analysis refocused, and decisional law developed without adherence to the Guidelines. As a result, a new administration, with an attitude more favorable to larger mergers and market forces, issued new Guidelines in 1982.

The 1982 Guidelines reflected a major change in merger standards. The "law enforcement" philosophy that prevailed at the Antitrust Division when the first Guidelines were issued in 1968 had faded. Indeed, in announcing the new Guidelines, Attorney General William French Smith said the new Guidelines "outline the general principles and specific standards the Department's Antitrust Division uses *in screening* the hundreds of mergers it examines every year."[40] The Department's role as an "enforcement agency" was not mentioned, as it had been in the 1968 Guidelines. He did note that the new standards differed "considerably from the old ones."

First, the 1982 Guidelines centered on preventing mergers that facilitated the exercise of market power—the ability to raise prices above competitive levels without a drop in quality demand—monopolization and cartelization. The emphasis on market power is important because it suggests that the Department is concerned not only with the increased concentration that results from a new merger, but also the potential collusive effects in the industry. The new standards would permit many mergers that would have been challenged under the 1968 Guidelines. This attitude was reflected in the use of a test that concentrated on the horizontal effect of the merger. The Division was allowed greater discretion not to challenge a proposed merger; it insisted on "economic evidence of harm or potential harm to competition before a merger [would] be challenged." The Division's exercise of judgment seemed broader, given the range of economic factors to consider; its discretion not to intervene in capital markets seemed apparent.

> Although they sometimes harm competition, mergers generally play an important role in a free enterprise economy. They can penalize ineffective management and facilitate the efficient flow of investment capital and the redeployment of existing productive assets. While challenging competitively harmful mergers, the Department seeks to avoid unnecessary interference with that larger universe of mergers that are either competitively beneficial or neutral.[41]

This philosophy was largely incorporated in the 1982 Guidelines through the introduction of a more broadly defined market. The new definition reduced the likelihood that a particular merger would raise antitrust concerns. By changing from a four-firm concentration ratio to that of the Herfindahl-Hirschman Index,[42] the Department selected a standard unchartered in merger law and unapproved by the courts. Many antitrust scholars, however, did not believe that a change in definition would lead to different results.

In addition, the 1982 Guidelines explicitly de-emphasized the antitrust importance of vertical and conglomerate mergers. The new Guidelines debunk previous economic theories that feared foreclosure of competition in vertical mergers, the creation of reciprocal dealing or the entrenchment of a dominant firm in a concentrated market. Nonhorizontal mergers are a concern under the 1982 standards if they fall into one of four categories: 1) vertical or conglomerate mergers that eliminate potential competition, 2) vertical mergers that increase barriers to entry by necessitating simultaneous two-level entry, 3) vertical mergers that facilitate collusion, and 4) vertical or conglomerate mergers that facilitate the evasion of rate regulation by a regulated firm.[43] These changes again show that the Department is willing to go beyond the established case law and, through its expanded discretion, regulate mergers by reinterpreting and rearticulating the competition standards of Section 7.

In sum, the 1982 Guidelines expressed a more specifically directed economic policy. The standards were more quantitative in approach and more mathematically precise. They reduced uncertainty and increased predictability of enforcement intentions.[44] As several antitrust commentators with prior Antitrust Division experience have observed, "the guidelines [have] in fact become the general working standard in the field."[45] With the Antitrust Division interpreting its own standards, its approach can be directed more at regulation than law enforcement. The 1982 Guidelines constitute a regulatory standard more pervasive than previous standards, and one open to broad discretion. Negotiated settlements that restructure the merger are implicitly sanctioned. This emerging regulatory philosophy is significant due to the nature and difficulty of private merger litigation. Consequently, if the Department does not challenge a proposed merger, it probably will go unchallenged. The Department's regulatory control through the Guidelines, therefore, is stronger than before.

The Department revised its Merger Guidelines again in 1984. Although only two years had elapsed, clarification and refinement were deemed necessary. Paradoxically, the changes interjected greater uncertainty and decreased predictability into the process. At the same time, the revision increased the Division's interpretive discretion and regulatory nature.

The 1984 standards modified four major considerations found in the 1982 Guidelines: 1) market definitions, 2) treatment of efficiencies as a defense, 3) the inclusion of foreign competition into market definitions, and 4) consideration of failing divisions of healthy firms. The first three of these serve as a basis for understanding the Division's broader regulatory control.

The 1984 Guidelines broaden the test for product and geographic markets. Rather than retain a strict 5 percent price elasticity test,[46] the Division now "may at times postulate a price increase that is much larger or smaller than five percent" over a one year period to determine what products should be included in the product market definition. The range alluded to in this standard is further defined as a "small but significant and non-transitory" price increase. This more ambiguous, subjective test is a return to a broader standard reminiscent of the early case law, one first fully articulated in *United States* v. *E.I. DuPont De Nemours & Co.*

The second major change is the inclusion of foreign competition (and its market share) into the geographic market definition where a foreign film is of competitive significance in the U.S. domestic market. Given the uncertainty in interpreting the data on currency exchange rates, quotas and tariffs, the Division will have to use broad discretion on a case-by-case basis when including or excluding foreign company data in the market definition. This, in turn, will increase the basis for negotiation between the Division and the merging parties, should a question arise whether the Division will challenge the market definition.

In contrast to the 1968 and 1982 Guidelines and prior case law, which rejected efficiency defenses except in extraordinary cases, the 1984 standards embrace efficiency considerations as another factor that the Division will examine. However, the merging parties must provide the Antitrust Division with "clear and convincing" evidence that the claimed efficiencies will result. This significant change is consistent with the new standards' overall textual tone and general philosophy that mergers have the potential to enhance efficiency. The type of data subject to efficiency analysis also is broader than that suggested under the 1982 Guidelines.

In short, the current Guidelines are less precise; they invite a more open-ended balancing analysis, resulting in less rigidity and more discretion. The effect, again, is to introduce greater Division flexibility and control into the screening process. The Guidelines, in large measure, through the standard-setting process, leave the criteria for approving mergers to the discretion of the Antitrust Division.

Premerger Disclosure Requirements

In 1976, Congress passed the Hart-Scott-Rodino Act, which prescribed certain premerger disclosures. The purpose of the Act was to delay or prevent the consummation of mergers until the Department of Justice or the Federal Trade Commission had an appropriate opportunity to analyze the proposed merger. The Act did not change the substantive antitrust law governing mergers. But it did require advance notification and did set forth specific waiting periods, which were designed to give the reviewing agency sufficient time to approve the merger or to proceed expeditiously to seek injunctive relief. The latter procedure would automatically delay or prevent the consummation of the transaction.

Disclosure requirements of the Act are imposed on parties to "very large mergers and acquisitions" in which: 1) either party is engaged in commerce, 2) the net sales or total assets of one of the parties is $10 million or more and the net sales or total assets of the other is $100 million or more, and 3) the acquiring firm, as a result of the acquisition, would hold securities or assets of the other valued at 15 percent of $15 million in value of the voting securities or assets of the acquired firm. The disclosure requirements do not depend on the form of the transaction. Their mandate is pervasive. For example, ordinary acquisition of securities or assets, statutory mergers or consolidations, tender offers, conversion of convertible securities, formation of joint ventures and secondary acquisitions must be reported.

If premerger disclosure is required, the parties must file detailed notification and report forms. The required data include, among other things, the type of transaction, the structure of the merging firms, holdings of the acquiring party in the acquired firm, horizontal overlaps, vertical relationships, and any acquisitions made within the previous 10 years.

The Act empowers the FTC, with the concurrence of the Assistant Attorney General, to issue rules to implement the Act's mandate. In similar fashion, the regulatory authorities have congressionally delegated discretion to exempt certain classes of persons and transactions from compliance with the Act or with any aspect of the notification requirements.

Independently, the Antitrust Division determines the form of notification, receives the filings under the Act, and may extend or terminate the waiting period. In addition, it may ask any person for additional information or documents; such a request extends the waiting period. Finally, the Division may provide the parties to a proposed acquisition with a business review letter, reflecting the Department's opinion regarding the legality of the proposed merger. If it finds that the proposed merger raises anticompetitive concerns, and the merging parties do not agree to a restructured merger, the Division can file an action for injunctive relief in a federal district court.

Business Review Letter

For several decades, the Antitrust Division has been willing, in certain circumstances, to review proposed business conduct and state its enforcement intentions. The early origins of this practice began with the "railroad release" procedure under which the Division would review the proposed business conduct and decide whether it would forego the initiation of criminal proceedings if the proposed conduct were carried out. This was subsequently expanded to include a "merger clearance," in which the Division would state its current enforcement intention and would issue a written statement entitled "Business Review Letter." The procedure is one that gives the Division pretransaction clearance authority to approve or disapprove business conduct that implicates an antitrust environment. It is not a new regulatory concept; the "idea of regulation itself has hinged on the workability of one or another forms of advance advice," says Thomas McCraw in *Prophets of Regulation*.[47] It avoids the adversarial process and is frequently associated with negotiational posturing.

The business review process is initiated with a written request to the Assistant Attorney General. The requesting party must provide the Division with all relevant information and documents that the Division may need. The Division may refuse to consider the request. After examining the business review request, the Division will state its current enforcement intentions, decline to pass on the request, or take such other position as it considers appropriate. The requesting party will be notified accordingly.

At the same time, the Division notifies the requesting party of the Division's action on the business review request. A press release is issued describing the action and attaching a copy of the Division's letter of response. Business review letters state only the enforcement intentions of the Division as of the date of the letter; the Division remains free to bring whatever action or proceeding it subsequently believes is required by the public interest.

Negotiation as a Means to Restructure Mergers

The Antitrust Division initiates further investigation in only a small number of proposed mergers after reviewing the Hart-Scott-Rodino disclosures.[48] When the Division believes a merger will not result in a substantial lessening of competition, further investigation is not undertaken. In those instances where the proposed merger poses a competition problem, the Division has a policy known as "fix it first." This policy rests on a nonadversarial, negotiational approach to dispute resolution. Under the "fix it first" policy, the merging parties are notified by the Division that the proposed merger contains certain anticompetitive problems. The Division informs the parties how these problems might be eliminated. A discussion session frequently is held to see whether the merger can be restructured in order to eliminate the antitrust objection. The Division policy requires that the problems be removed ("fixed") before the merger is consummated. If the problem is eliminated first, the Division will not file an injunction suit to prevent the acquisition. However, if time does not permit the restructuring of a merger before it is consummated, the Division may approve the merger, subject to the entry of a consent decree.

The agreed-upon consent decree will require the resulting company to restructure within a set period of time. As a result of the Division's negotiation efforts, few public enforcement actions are filed today.

The Antitrust Division proposes the restructuring of mergers in several ways. First, and most often, the Division will suggest the acquirer divest a unit or units of either firm, which if retained would cause a lessening of competition. Second, the Division may require the acquiring firm to terminate existing relationships. Third, the Division may require the two parties to enter into a completely different relationship or exercise different roles than those originally negotiated by the parties. Several recent merger restructurings illustrate these methods.

Divestiture. As an example of the first category, where the Division requires that assets be sold off, the Antitrust Division required IBM to divest the mil-spec computer division of Rolm as a precondition to its approval of the merger between IBM and Rolm Corp. The parties' agreement to the Division's suggestions were contained in a curative consent order.

Similarly, when General Electric announced its proposed merger with RCA Corporation, the Division first required General Electric to sell its vidicon tube business. The Division determined, upon review of the Hart-Scott-Rodino filings, that the merging firms accounted for nearly 99 percent of all silicon target vidicon tube sales for military applications in 1985 and 90 percent of all antimony trisulfide target vidicon tube sales. General Electric was a leading producer of silicon and antimony trisulfide target vidicon tubes for military applications, and RCA was the second largest. Because the "sell off" agreement could not be achieved in time, the Antitrust Division filed a complaint and simultaneously filed a consent order setting forth the divestiture agreement of the parties and the Division.

In another merger involving Allied Corporation and Signal Co., the Division required Allied to divest its air turbine starter by the end of 1985. Signal had a market share of over 50 percent and Allied followed in second place. Through the merger they would control more than 70 percent of the noncommunist world market. Without divestiture, the merger would have increased the Herfindahl-Hirschman Index (HHI) by 1975 points, clearly resulting in antitrust problems.

Under the settlement, Allied agreed to sell its air turbine starter business to a buyer that was acceptable to the Antitrust Division. In the event that the sale could not be accomplished by the end of 1985, Allied was required to sell its Bendix Fluid Power division, of which the air turbine starter unit was but a part, by 31 March 1986. The Division believed this forced divestiture would provide a powerful incentive for Allied to locate an acceptable buyer. If the sale of the Bendix Fluid Power division was required, the Division was prepared to request a court-appointed trustee to oversee and execute the sale. The

Allied-Signal merger demonstrates the Division's creative but persuasive regulatory oversight.

One of the most interesting examples of the Antitrust Division's regulatory involvement focused on an entire industry—the beer industry. It was the first time the Reagan Administration challenged a proposed merger. The Justice Department originally became involved in beer mergers during 1981 when Heileman attempted to buy Schlitz.[49] As a result of Justice's challenge, the transaction fell through. Six months later, Stroh made a offer to purchase Schlitz. Justice announced that it would not ask for additional information, but would continue to investigate. Justice's primary concern was in the Southeast, where the merger would increase the HHI by 150 points.[50]

Rather than deciding whether to challenge the merger or to approve it, Justice began negotiating with the parties to produce a solution that would allow the transaction to go through while avoiding any Section 7 problems. A week following its first announcement, Justice announced a proposed consent decree that approved the merger on the condition that Stroh would divest a Schlitz plant in the Southeast. The plant in question could not be sold to anyone but Anheuser-Busch or Miller, the two largest brewers in the country. Eight months later, the consent decree was modified to allow Stroh to trade its Schlitz brewery in Tampa for one of Pabst's breweries in Minnesota, thereby avoiding anticompetitive problems in the Southeast where Schlitz and Stroh both had significant market shares. The Division's involvement in shaping these mergers provides a clear example of its willingness to go beyond mere enforcement and take a proactive role in seeing that mergers are successfully completed.

Another example comes from the brewing industry. Heileman, which was not allowed to intervene in the Justice Department suit involving Stroh and Schlitz, entered an agreement in 1982 to purchase Pabst. The Division announced its intent to challenge the merger because it would result in an increase in the HHI of 112.[51] Six weeks later, the Division challenged an attempt by Heileman to have a third-party nonbrewer purchase Pabst and then sell it to Heileman. Following this challenge, Heileman began negotiating with the Division. This negotiation resulted, four months later, in the Division's securing a proposed consent decree, that allowed Heileman to purchase Pabst under the condition that Heileman would sell 85 percent of Pabst's assets.

Finally, in a controversial merger involving LTV and Republic Steel Corp., the Antitrust Division required LTV to divest certain Republic mills within six months. The Division had determined that the merger implicated competitive concerns in three product markets: hot-rolled carbon and alloy sheet and strip; cold-rolled carbon and alloy sheet and strip; and cold-rolled stainless sheet and strip. The Division required the divestiture of Gradsden mill, cutting the increase in concentration in the carbon and alloy sheet market by one-third. Divestiture of a Massillon mill would eliminate the projected concentration in the stainless steel and strip market. In addition, the Division prohibited LTV from exchanging any data on output or efficiency of its mills with any other competitor or the industry trade association. This unusual precondition seemed unique to the LTV merger. Further, LTV and Republic were enjoined for ten years from acquiring assets or securities from any "substantial" competitor.

Relationship termination. In the second category of cases, the Division has required merging entities to terminate certain relationships if they would create problems for competition. When Signal Companies acquired Wheelabrator-Frye, it had to end its relationship with foreign firms for which both Signal and Wheelabrator-Frye were the U.S. representative. In addition, the Antitrust Division required Wheelabrator-Frye to sell its right to two crude oil processing patents and know-how. This exercise of preclearance discretion was not incorporated in a consent decree, but was negotiated with the parties as part of the Division's "fix it first" policy. The Division, in addition, insisted that Wheelabrator-Frye engage in a bidding process for the sale of crude oil processing patents rather than a bilateral contract "to make sure that the [firm] which ultimately gets it will be the most vigorous and aggressive in the field."[52] The oversight approval of this merger exemplified sweeping regulatory direction and control.

Regulatory "matchmaker." In the third category of mergers, the Division has required certain corporate relationships that had not previously been contemplated by the merging parties. When Alcan Aluminum Ltd. of Canada sought to acquire most of the aluminum-producing assets of Atlantic Richfield Co. (ARCO), it was obvious that ARCO wanted to exit from the industry. Yet the Department's consent order[53] required ARCO to enter into a production joint venture with Alcan in which it would hold 60 percent of the shares and Alcan 40 percent. In the meticulous agreement, the Department required the venture to last for ten years during which no major aluminum producer could acquire the ARCO interest. ARCO, in effect, was prevented from leaving the industry and forced to enter into a corporate marriage.

Procedurally, after the Division conducted its investigation, it opposed the merger. The parties then requested Division officials to "discuss proposals for restructuring the merger."[54] The Department proudly proclaimed that "the use of a production joint venture as a means of settling a [Section] 7 case is . . . an innovation,"[55] although it cautioned that this venture should not be considered a precedent for future cases, "particularly where the challenged acquisition is of an existing rather than prospective competitor."[56]

Consent decrees. Effective relief of civil antitrust violations often can be obtained without going to trial. Under the Antitrust Procedures and Penalties

Act of 1974 ("Tunney Act"), the Antitrust Division has authority to negotiate and enter into consent decrees. Any proposal for a consent judgment submitted by the Antitrust Division in a civil proceeding must be filed with the appropriate district court and published in the Federal Register at least sixty days prior to the effective date of the judgment.

It is the general practice of the Division that the defendants initiate settlement negotiations for a consent decree. The Division frequently files a proposed consent decree at the same time it files a complaint. This procedure recognizes prior negotiation between the Division and the parties. It also is consistent with the Division's "fix it first" policy. The negotiations concerning the restructuring of the transaction often result in an agreement to file a consent decree, which settles the antitrust issues and permits the merger to proceed with modifications in the near future. The entered consent degree can be enforced through subsequent contempt proceedings.

If the Division and the parties can reach a settlement on the language of consent decree, it will be filed with the district court. In addition to the settlement agreement, the Division must file: 1) a competitive impact statement reciting the nature and purpose of the proceeding, 2) a report on the events giving rise to the alleged initiation of the antitrust law, 3) an explanation of the proposal for a consent judgment, 4) a statement of remedies available to the potential private plaintiffs damaged by the alleged violation, 5) a description of the procedures available for modification of such a proposal, and 6) a description and evaluation of alternatives actually considered by the Antitrust Division. Before entering any consent judgment, the court must determine that the entry of such judgment is in the "public interest." In this capacity, the court exercises "an independent check upon the terms of decrees negotiated" by the Department. This review standard is based on those interests or purposes that underlie the antitrust laws.

Competition advocacy program. One of the primary functions of the Antitrust Division is to intervene or participate before administrative agencies that function wholly or partly under regulatory statutes in administrative proceedings. The Antitrust Division examines mergers in regulated industries as they would in any other industry to determine whether the merger is likely to have anticompetitive effects. It considers whether substantial competition between the merging parties will be lessened, and it informs the regulatory agency of its decision.

The Division has been extremely active in the airline industry and transportation regulation. The Division has conducted several investigations of airline mergers—Northwest/Republic, Texas Air/Eastern and TWA/Ozark. In March 1986, the Division urged the Department of Transportation to block Northwest's bid to acquire Republic because competition in the airline industry would be undermined, particularly in the Minneapolis market. It also objected to TWA's acquisition of Ozark because of the resulting concentrated market in St. Louis. The Division also recommended that the Department of Transportation reject Texas Air and Eastern's application for a quick merger approval; it suggested instead "some type of evidence-gathering process" to determine the potential effects in airline competition. However, Texas Air Corporation's offer to sell certain slots and gates to Pan American World Airways resolved the Division's concern. But the Division urged the Department of Transportation to approve People Express, Inc.'s application to acquire Frontier Airlines, Inc. because the transaction would have no anticompetitive effect.

Within the rail transportation area, the Division endorsed a revised plan by Norfolk Southern Corporation, assuring rail competition in connection with its $1.2 billion bid to acquire Conrail. The Division had expressed reservations about the original plan. Appearing before the Interstate Commerce Commission, the Division urged extension of rail deregulation. It advised the Interstate Commerce Commission to allow rates to be set by negotiations between railroads and box car owners.

Although the competitive problems raised in the *regulated* sectors of the economy are complex and varied in number, the Division's increasing advocacy role remains an adjunct to the primary regulator. Yet whenever possible, the current Division promotes reliance on competition rather than on government regulation.

Toward More Efficient Resolution of Merger Conflicts

The preceding sections have demonstrated that the Antitrust Division has become, at least in a de facto sense, an economic regulator of mergers. That such a change has reached its high point during the Reagan Administration is predictable considering the administration's outspoken policy to engage in dispute resolution without litigation. It is hard to discern when this trend evolved, although reasons for the policy shift are evident.

The role of economic regulator paralleled the development of the Economic Policy Office of the Antitrust Division and the use of economic analysis by the Division. That office was established in 1973 by then Assistant Attorney General Thomas Kauper as an outgrowth of the earlier Economic Section of the Antitrust Division. The evidence suggests, however, that the trend toward economic analysis and regulation of mergers began in the mid-1960s, though the Antitrust Division "viewed itself as a litigating agency"[57] through the 1960s. Kauper recently conceded that "by the mid-1960s, economic analysis . . . was a primary factor in the formulation of Division policy."[58]

Indeed, the first Merger Guidelines issued in 1968 represented the first formal policy shift in establishing standards through which the Antitrust Division reinterpreted its enforcement prerogatives and regulated mergers. Throughout the 1970s, efficiency defenses to antitrust were introduced and considered by the Division. The Hart-Scott-Rodino Act was passed in 1976, giving the Division greater supervision of mergers through disclosure requirements. In 1982 and 1984, the Merger Guidelines were reformulated, resulting in merger standards that made challenges to proposed mergers more difficult than the Supreme Court cases suggested.

The operational standards established in these Guidelines were intended to restate "developments in antitrust law and economics, and second, to reduce the uncertainty surrounding the evaluation of mergers and acquisitions by the Department."[59] In practice, the Guidelines serve, together with the disclosure requirements, as preclearance screening devices. The Division either: 1) gives a quasi-license to the proposed merger through interpretation of the standards and negotiation with the parties, or 2) discourages the merger so the proposal fades away without a contest on the merits. Unquestionably, the Guidelines do contain economic policies of the government. The underlying assumptions and distributional effects of those economic policies are not addressed here. The focus is on whether grounds justify this dramatic shift from law enforcement agency to economic planner and regulator. It is this "process" question to which we next turn.

Cost Containment through Preclearance of Mergers

No one doubts the enormous costs associated with litigating antitrust mergers. As a general matter, costs are a dominant concern of litigation today. Public policy is well served if means can be found for reducing the costs of resolving merger disputes. Cost reductions can benefit the public resources of courts and the Antitrust Division, and resources of the merging parties. Containment of litigation costs must be a high priority.

This is particularly true for public enforcement agencies, which, in times of budget restrictions, have to allocate scarce resources efficiently. In antitrust litigation, the Supreme Court has cautioned that efficiency is an important policy rationale, and one that will be enforced. The central question then is whether the current preclearance procedure is a more efficient way to resolve merger issues than traditional litigation. If so, it is in the public interest to continue the Antitrust Division's posture toward merger regulation.

In answering these concerns, we need to inquire whether the Division's alternative means of resolving merger disputes will increase or reduce costs of enforcing Section 7 of the Clayton Act and whether it will reduce enforcement effectiveness. In short, we ask whether the benefits of the present regulatory posture exceed the costs of litigation.

It is well known that the costs of litigation create incentives for the parties and the government to find ways to minimize costs. Alternative means of dispute resolution have increased in importance in reaction to the high costs of litigation. The result is that conflicts are resolved today mainly through alternative means that achieve settlement before full trial. Antitrust litigation is no exception to this trend.

In a recent study on private antitrust litigation, the data showed that settlement was reached before trial in 88 percent of the filed antitrust cases surveyed.[60] Many other antitrust issues were settled before suit was ever commenced. Conflict resolution was achieved because the parties knew that litigation is not costless and that outcomes are not perfectly predictable. For most disputes, the efficient resolution is not the litigated one. Trade-offs result which require the parties and government policymakers to achieve an optimal level of enforcement, one that minimizes costs while maximizing enforcement objectives.[61]

Even if one were to assume that the government's enforcement budget was fixed in real terms, an increase in litigation costs per case yields a decrease in the number of cases that could be brought for adjudication. Consequently, the probability of enforcement decreases and, accordingly, the probability of Section 7 violations increases. The same holds true if the enforcement budget is decreased.

Since we know that litigation is costly, the government policymaker must attempt, in search of the optimal level of enforcement, to calculate costs and benefits of various alternative means of resolving antitrust disputes. Costs are incurred both in the preparation for adjudication and the adjudication itself. The decision to litigate includes an analysis of: (1) the probability of detention and conviction, (2) risk preference, (3) severity and magnitude of judgment, (4) trial versus settlement costs, (5) availability and productivity of each party's resources, and (6) the uncertainty of outcome.[62] In most cases, trade-offs lead parties to use some form of alternative dispute resolution such as negotiated settlement. When this does not occur, the minimum settlement demand of the government (plaintiff) exceeds the maximum settlement demand of the defendant. Efficient case management and resolution of these factors, however, have led the Antitrust Division as a matter of policy to use alternative means for the resolution of merger disputes. That the Antitrust Division has avoided the adversarial process is not necessarily bad as the advantages of its merger resolution process are many.

Although alternative dispute resolution procedures are a current trend, they have existed as long as civilization. They take many forms but essentially include the use of extrajudicial processes, such as negotiations, mediation, arbitration and settlement. In selecting the most effective method of resolution, one needs to consider the general enforcement goals of certainty and clarity of the law, deterrence, resource allocation, case management, justice and legitimacy. These goals, of course, are illustrative rather than exhaustive, and they are not all of equal importance. Moreover, they may not be pursued simultaneously with equal vigor in each case. Public officials pursue those methods of dispute resolution that combine the goals that yield society the greatest utility.[63]

The Antitrust Division's resolution methods achieve many of the principles recognized by these enforcement goals. They also satisfy the underlying arguments favoring alternative dispute resolution. Economic efficiency is the first priority in case management and resource allocation. When we consider the Antitrust Division's process in reaction to a proposed merger—standard setting (Guidelines), disclosure requirements, preclearance screening, negotiation, merger restructure, and consent orders—we see an impressive promptness by government officials. The entire resolution process is substantially shorter, with fewer resources expended, than is traditional, protracted litigation. The relative speed at which the system operates reduces the process costs of each proposed merger and consequently reduces costs for all proposed mergers.

Public confidence in the process is increased as delay is minimized. Court dockets are freed for other important matters, including those few merger cases that cannot be settled. The legitimacy of the system is increased as a result. As legitimacy is maintained, deterrence from the prohibited conduct is encouraged. Deterrence also is fostered by the relative clarity of the merger law as set forth in the Guidelines, compared with the case law ambiguities. To the extent that legal standards are clear, enforced promptly, and backed by adequate deterrence, the efficiency or utility of law is maximized. Efficiency is an important component of any justice-distributing system.

Arguments against Justice's Regulatory Approach

Notwithstanding the efficiency of the present merger process and its use as an alternative means of conflict resolution, not everyone accepts its use. Indeed, opponents of alternative dispute resolution have been quite vocal against any move away from full adjudication. Professor Owen Fiss of Yale, without empirical support, has advanced the most forceful arguments. Fiss criticizes alternative dispute resolution in general and the movement toward settlement specifically by asserting that: (1) the parties may have a relative imbalance of power that may force unfair resolutions, (2) settlements are often reached without authoritative consent because of imperfect representation, (3) lack of a judicial record impairs the settlements' enforcement thereafter, and (4) peace rather than justice is achieved.[64] Although Fiss did not specifically argue against merger settlements, each of his general arguments lacks force when applied to public enforcement of merger regulations.

First, the argument that settlements only achieve justice for the wealthy presupposes disparity in wealth between the disputants. Since the Department of Justice is enforcing the merger laws and large corporations are defending the proposed mergers, the "relative imbalance of power" would not seem to be of substantial public interest, as in the case where indigents might be especially vulnerable. Resources and information regarding the merger are not in short supply for either party.

Second, authoritative consent of the parties also does not seem problematic in this context. Nor, in terms of the general argument, has Fiss advanced any support for his supposition. Corporations have not charged conflicts of interest between themselves and their representatives in the settlement proceedings. Corporations involved in antitrust merger matters generally hire competent experts in the field as counsel. Inside corporate counsel work closely with retained counsel to accomplish the corporate client's desires. The merger teams consist of sophisticated business executives and lawyers who are able to respond quickly to the Division's requests and objections. Therefore, many in the corporate arena advance the fundamental objective that the corporation should avoid litigation.[65] There is no discernable reason why counsel should not pursue alternative means to merger conflicts. The evidence in mergers suggests they are doing just that—negotiating and settling conflicts that do arise.

Third, the lack of a judicial record does not have relevance in the preclearance screening process. The parties are required to submit to the Antitrust Division all relevant financial and economic data required by the Hart-Scott-Rodino disclosure provisions. The Division may set forth its understanding of the conditions and terms of merger in a business review letter. As is frequently the case, the parties can set forth their agreement and understanding in a consent decree. These records can serve as the factual basis for subsequent enforcement actions.

Finally, Fiss asserts that settlements result in peace but not necessarily justice. He opines that adjudication's purposes are broader than establishing peace between the parties: Adjudication is a forum for articulating and effectuating important values "embodied in the substantive law" through the participation of the judge. Although it is true that few public enforcement suits in the merger area are actually filed, the Department of Justice is charged with the responsibility of enforcing the law. To date, no one has argued or documented that the Antitrust Division has established and enforced the Merger Guidelines over an 18-year period in order to withdraw judicial review of mergers or to minimize a perceived "activism" by the judiciary. To be sure, a private cause of action, in addition to public enforcement, exists for challenging illegal mergers. Thus, a judicial forum is available if the Department abrogates its responsibilities or if the parties cannot reach a settlement. Moreover, a negotiated settlement does not inherently inhibit justice from being obtained. In fact, settlements that satisfy both sides may be more just than uncompromising court mandates.

In short, the Antitrust Division's "regulatory judgement" is unquestionably more prompt, less costly and more efficient than full-blown adjudicatory proceedings. The prescreening clearance process is appropriately suited for review of proposed mergers. It avoids the attendant costs of litigation for the merging parties, the Antitrust Division and the courts. From a policy standpoint, the current review process is in most cases a more effective means of resolving merger issues. In this context, the goals of efficiency, justice and legitimacy need not compete; they may each be pursued simultaneously. Efficiency need not diminish the quantity of the justice or the legitimacy of the process.

Conclusion

The Antitrust Division's evolution as an economic regulator is a logical development. At its roots, the legislative history of antitrust shows a nonregulatory concept for the Department of Justice, but it also shows, at least in part, a noneconomic view of the antitrust laws. Thus the early focus on individual behavior was quite appropriate. But when the Department took a more global, economic view of the antitrust philosophy, enforcement became a process of controlling and adjusting the economic aspects of markets. And that is what regulatory agencies traditionally do—tinker with the market. The panoply of merger procedures used by the Antitrust Division facilitates this economic regulation.

The merger review procedures of the Antitrust Division appear more cost-effective than adjudication. The Division regulates mergers through several procedures, including: (1) setting merger standards and guidelines, (2) reviewing market data submitted through required disclosure provisions, (3) establishing a preclearance screening process, (4) suggesting and negotiating merger restructures, and (5) joining in curative or divestment consent orders. The dichotomy lies in the fact that the Antitrust Division has evolved from a traditional, litigation-oriented enforcement agency to a regulatory agency without clear congressional approval or directive.

It is clear that the original intention of Congress, when adopting the Sherman and Clayton Acts, was not to create in the Department of Justice a regulatory agency over mergers. The current regulatory posture permitting preclearance approval of mergers was specifically proposed by Senator Cummins in 1913 and rejected by President Wilson and the 1914 Congress that passed the Clayton Act. Congress subsequently has sanctioned or ratified, at least implicitly, this enforcement transition, although the awareness or impact of this change may not be understood or appreciated by Congress. The change is not merely procedural. It may affect enforcement policy, compliance incentives and the substantive law of mergers. From efficiency and procedural perspectives, however, the gains are many.

Notes

1. The number of acquisitions in 1985 (3,001) was nearly 60 percent greater than the corresponding figure for 1980 (1,889). The 1985 dollar amount was more than quadruple the total value of acquisitions in 1980 ($180 billion versus $44 billion).
2. 21 Cong. Rec. 2456 (1890); 21 Cong. Rec. 3148 (1890).
3. A. Walker, *History of the Sherman Act* 39, 59–60 (1910), *citing* 21 Cong. Rec. 4099 (1890).
4. W. Hamilton and I. Till, Antitrust in Action 10(1940). "Sections 4 and 5 of the Sherman law confer jurisdiction in equity upon the several Circuit Courts of the United States to prevent and restrain violation of the Sherman law in pursuance of petitions presented by the district attorneys of the United States under the direction of the attorney general of the United States on behalf of the United States. Those two sections contain a few special directions for guidance of such proceedings." A. Walker, *supra* note 3 at 59. As one commentator opined twenty years after the statute's enactment: "It therefore follows that whenever it becomes the duty of a particular district attorney of the United States to institute proceedings in equity for the purpose of stopping a particular combination from continuing past violation of Section 1 of the Sherman law, it also becomes the duty of the same district attorney to institute and prosecute proceedings to accomplish the seizure, condemnation and forfeiture of whatever property was the subject of the combination. . . . Moreover, such forfeiture proceedings, under Section 6 of the Sherman law, should always follow or accompany any indictment under Section 1 of that statute." (*id.*, 60–61).
5. W. Letwin, *Law and Economic Policy in America*, 103–42 (1965).
6. A. Bickel, *The Judiciary and Responsible Government 1910–21*, 130 (1984).
7. H.B. Thorelli, *Federal Antitrust Policy*, 412–15 (1955).
8. W. Letwin, *supra* note 5, at 205, 239.
9. *Id.* at 245.
10. *Id.*
11. H.B. Thorelli, *supra* note 7, at 251.
12. H. Thorelli, *The Federal Antitrust Policy*, 551–54 (1954).
13. *Id.*
14. IX A. Bickel, *The Judiciary and Responsible Government* 128 (1984).
15. *Id.* at 129; Letwin, *supra* note 5, at 267–73. Attorney General Harmon, in his report submitted to Congress, strongly supported the use of court litigation as the means of antitrust enforcement, but felt that the detection of possible violations and evidence accumulation should be placed within another bureau. Harmon stressed the need for liberal appropriations and effective organization of prosecutions for Department enforcement of the Sherman Act. *Id.*
16. 49 Cong. Rec. 4126(1913).
17. W. Letwin, *supra* note 5, at 269.
18. 49 Cong. Rec. 4127 (1913). "The Department of Justice will ignore a great many unlawful transactions because there will be doubt as to whether the interference

. . . is direct or indirect. . . . . The committee . . . contents itself now with a statement of its conclusion that there should be further legislation specifically prohibiting certain forms of associations, combinations, or monopoly which admittedly restrain trade and commerce . . . but which may be held by the courts to be indirect or remote interferences." *Id.*

19. 51 Cong. Rec. 1962-63 (1914). "What we are proposing to do, therefore, is, happily, not to hamper or interfere with business as enlightened business men prefer to do it, or in any sense to put it under the ban," Wilson said. "The antagonism between business and government is over. We are now about to give expression to be best business judgment of America, to what we know to be the business conscience and honor of the land. The Government and business men are ready to meet each other halfway in a common effort to square business methods with both public opinion and the law." He later added that "[T]he opinion of the country would not wish to see [a commission] empowered to make terms with monopoly or in any sort to assume control of business, as if the Government made itself responsible." W. Letwin, *Law & Economic Policy in America*, 270–73(1965).

20. *Id.* Cummins, recognizing that such a new agency would hold "quasijudicial" functions and perform a policy role, believed that it could be more efficient than the courts. This proposal was the forerunner to the Department of Justice's premerger notification program in place today.

21. 51 Cong. Rec. 1963 (1914). This was similar to the proposal made by Attorney General Harmon in 1896.

22. 15 U.S.C. 18 (1982).

23. H.R. 15657, 63rd Cong. 2d Sess. 1 (1914).

24. *Id.* at 11083. Senator Newlands, who reported for the Committee on Interstate Commerce, said the regulatory commission was to aid the courts and the Attorney General "in framing and enforcing decrees dissolving corporations," to aid in "the enforcement of the Sherman Act" and to be free from "changing incumbency" of the Attorney General's office. He opined that powers of the new trade commission "are not greatly in excess of those now possessed and for years exercised by the Bureau of Corporations." *Id.* at 10376.

25. Attorney General's National Committee to Study Antitrust Laws of the Department of Justice-3 (1955). In 1914, Senator Cummins had proposed a similar premerger clearance or screening process which failed to reach floor debate.

26. Antitrust Improvements Act of 1975, Hearings Before the Subcommittee on Antitrust and Monopolies of the Commission on Judiciary of the Senate, 94th Cong., 1st Sess. 71 (1975). Engman believed that full investigation of all mergers exceeding the $100 million assets or sales test contained in the bill would be counterproductive. He seemed to believe that the threshold test for which corporations would be required to submit notice might be so low as to: 1) create administrative costs for the Department and FTC to fully investigate as required, and 2) to cause the Department and FTC to scrutinize more business activities and do *not* violate antitrust laws, with the result that the agencies are in fact "controlling" business rather than enforcing laws.

27. *Id.* at 92. 122 Cong. Rec. 15487, 16925–26(1976).

28. *Id.* at 196; 122 Cong. Rec. 15317, 15834, 16485 (1976).

29. *Id.* at 213. *See* 122 Cong. Rec. 16916 (1976).

30. Some of the safeguards against potential CID abuse include: 1) a statement within the CID of the nature of the conduct constituting the alleged violation, 2) protection of confidentiality of CID materials, 3) representation by counsel of any person required to give oral testimony and reservation of legal rights to object to

questions, 4) inability of the Department to compel oral testimony without resort to federal court, 5) nonenforcibility nor penalty for noncompliance with the CID without resort to court, and 6) various grounds of objections to compliance.

31. The premerger notification provisions contained the following "protections" against unwarranted government intrusion into legitimate business transactions: 1) certain types of transfers and acquisitions and exempt, 2) jurisdictional requirements were established regarding size of the parties, amount of voting securities or acquired assets involved to exclude insignificant or trivial transactions, 3) confidentiality of the information was provided, 4) only one extension of the waiting period is permitted to the Department and FTC without a court order, 5) special rules were included for tender offers to speed consideration of such transactions while not needlessly delaying consummation of the offer, and 6) expedited court consideration must be provided when the government seeks injunctive relief.

32. 94 U.S. 113, 126 (1877), *citing de Portibus Maris*, 1 Harg. Law Tracts 78.

33. 1A. Kahn, *The Economics of Regulation* 20 (1970).

34. Robin, Federal Regulation in Historical Perspective 1189, 1252–53 (1986). Wiley, *A Capture Theory of Antitrust Federalism*, 99 Harvard Law Review 713, 723–28 (1986).

35. Several of the classical models of regulation are not relevant to the Antitrust Division's oversight responsibilities on mergers. At least two focus explicitly on price control. For example, cost of service ratemaking generally applies when an agency regulates prices and profits of firms. It has occurred for natural monopolies (public utilities) as well as competitive markets (airlines). The regulator determines the costs and then sets the price or rate structure in order for the firm or industry to receive a "reasonable rate of return."

Historically-based price regulation is an alternative regulatory device used when the regulated firms have disparate costs. Price controls are implemented that allow the firms to charge a price it charged on a particular historical date plus an additional percentage per year. Industry wide price controls (oil prices) have been implemented by use of historically-based price regulation.

Allocation in the public interest applies when there are scarce resources. The regulatory agency will choose a standard under which the scarce resources (television licenses, airline certifications) will be allocated. The agency decides what and how much will be given away, the threshold objective criteria used to judge those qualified, and the duration of the license.

Rather than a public interest standard, a regulator can allocate scarce resources based on historical data. Historically-based allocation has been used when there are short-term scarcities; the oil crisis of 1973 is an example. Allocations are determined on past quantities consumed rather than past prices. As an adjunct to historically-based allocations, price controls or resale restrictions are added in order to prevent those with historical rights in a commodity from earning windfall profits.

Alternative methods to classical regulation in which the Antitrust Division would not normally be involved include setting taxes. In addition to raising revenue, taxes can stimulate or discourage economic behavior and redistribute income (using cost-of-service ratemaking to eliminate windfall profits). Because taxes do not fix prices, they permit the market to allocate the output through normal price system, thereby avoiding allocation through regulation. *See generally* ABA Commission on Law & Economy, Federal Regulation: *Roads to Reform*, 37–40 (1979); S. Breyer, *Regulation and Its Reform*, at 96–119(1982).

36. 5 U.S.C. 553 (1982). Although the Merger Guidelines, discussed hereafter, were issued by the Department of Justice and published in the Federal Register, they are not regulations per se. Distinctions are drawn between promulgated regulations and general statements of policy. Statements of policy are those "issued by an agency to advise the public prospectively of the manner in which the agency proposes to exercise a discretionary power." United States Department of Justice, Attorney General's Manual 30 n.3 (1947) *cited in Brock* v. *Cathedral Bluffs Shale Oil Co., Inc.*, No. 84–1492 (D.C. Cir. 29 July 1986). As the District of Columbia Circuit said in *Brock*, "[a]n agency pronouncement is not deemed a binding regulation merely because it may have 'some substantive impact,' as long as it 'leave[s] the administrator free to exercise his informed discretion'. . . . Federal Register is indication that the statement in question was not meant to be a regulation . . . [but] [t]he real dividing point between regulations and general statements of policy is publication in the Code of Federal Regulations." The Merger Guidelines were not published in the Code of Federal Regulations.

37. ABA Commission on Law and Economy, *Federal Regulation: Roads to Reform* 44 (1979); S. Breyer, *Regulation and Its Reform* 161–64 (1979).

38. 2. Trade Reg. Rep (CCH) 6882 (9 August 1982).

39. The most prominent feature of the 1968 Guidelines horizontal merger analysis was the use of the four-firm concentration ratio. The four-firm concentration ratio examined the premerger market shares of the four largest firms in a market. A concentration ratio of 75 percent indicated a highly concentrated market; it was subject to a more stringent standard of review. This standard was significant because it resulted in lowering the market share combinations which would be challenged in a merger. For instance, in a less highly concentrated market, mergers with firms which had market shares of 5 percent and 5 percent, or 10 percent and 4 percent, or 15 percent and 3 percent were likely to be challenged. In a more highly concentrated market, with a concentration ratio above 75, mergers with shares of 4 percent and 4 percent, or 10 percent and 2 percent, or 15 percent and 1 percent would be challenged. See U.S. Dept. of Justice, Merger Guidelines-1968, paras. 5–6, 2 Trade Reg. Rep. (CCH) at 6683–84; Calkins, *The New Merger Guidelines and the Herfindahl-Hirschman Index*, 71 Calif. L. Rev. 402, 406–07 (1983); *see also Brown Shoe Co.* v. *United States*, 370 U.S. 294 (1962) (use of concentration ratio).

40. U.S. Dept. of Justice, Merger Guidelines-1982, 2 Trade Reg. Rep. (CCH) para. 4500 (4 September 1984) (emphasis added).

41. U.S. Dept. of Justice, Merger Guidelines-1982, paras. 4501, at 6881–87. *See also* Statement by Charles F. Rule, Deputy Assistant Attorney General (1 May 1984), where he characterized the enforcement policy of the 1960s and 1970s as interventionist.

42. The Herfindahl-Hirschman Index (HHI) is calculated by squaring the market share of all the firms in the market and summing the squares. The standard then examines the postmerger HHI number and the change or increase in the HHI caused by the merger. Unconcentrated markets are defined by a HHI below 1,000, moderately concentrated by HHI between 1,000 and 1,800 and highly concentrated by HHI above 1,800. If the postmerger, HHI is below 1,000, the Department is unlikely to challenge the merger; if the postmerger index is between 1,000 and 1,800, the Department is likely to challenge only if the change or increase is more than 100 points; and if the postmerger HHI is above 1,800, the merger is likely to be challenged if the increase is more than 50 points.

43. A merger challenge even in these categories is unlikely unless the HHI of the tar-

get market is over 1,800; if effective collusion is particularly likely a challenge may be made with an HHI lower than 1,800.

44. In 1983, fewer than 2 percent of the mergers required to file Hart-Scott-Rodino disclosures were challenged.

45. Sims and Laude, *supra* note 44.

46. Courts have ruled that product markets should be defined according to a product "interchangeability" standard or the "cross-elasticity of demand" test. The 1982 Guidelines refined this standard by adopting a precise, quantitative test: A market would be recognized for a product and geographic area where a 5 percent price increase would not cause buyers of the product to seek substitutes or would not cause new competitors to enter the product market to compete with the firm that raised the price. If the data demonstrated that a new competitor would enter the market in response to a 5 percent price increase of a product, the product of the outside firm should be included in the market.

47. T. McCraw, Prophets of Regulation 128–30 (1984).

48. For example, the Division conducted expanded investigations as follows: 1978 = 40, 1979 = 102, 1980 = 56, 1981 = 66, 1982 = 56, 1983 = 62.

49. At the time, Heileman was the sixth largest brewer with a 7.5 percent market share, while Schlitz was fourth with an 8.5 percent share.

50. 42 Antitrust and Trade Reg. Rep. (BNA) 769 (15 April 1982). In the Southeast, Schlitz had a market share of 13.4 percent, and Stroh had a market share of 6.9 percent.

51. *Id.* at 1264. Heileman was the nation's fourth largest brewer with 7.6 percent market share and Pabst was fifth with a 7.4 percent market share. Due to the concentration in the brewing industry, any merger that increased the HHI by more than 100 was likely to be challenged.

52. 44 Antitrust Trade Reg. Rep., (BNA) 492 (3 March 1983).

53. Trade Reg. Rep. (CCH) No. 671 at 5 (8 October 1984). The four largest firms in the market account for 87.9 percent of sales. The merger created an HHI rating of 2,300, indicating a "highly concentrated" market.

54. U.S. Dept. of Justice, Press Release, date 5 October 1984 at 3.

55. Trade Reg. Rep. (CCH) no. 671 at 6 (8 October 1984).

56. *Id.* The Antitrust Division's regulating influence is also evident in the application of the "failing company" doctrine to mergers. In *Citizen Publishing Co.* v. *United States,* the Supreme Court approved evidence as a defense to an illegal merger that: 1) the acquired firm was failing, or almost certain to go into bankruptcy with no chance of successful reorganization, and 2) that a no less anticompetitive merger was possible. The "failing company" defense was incorporated into the 1984 Merger Guidelines and expanded to include a "failing division defense." This would permit the acquisition of an unprofitable division of another firm so long as it was on the verge of liquidation.

57. Kauper, 29 Antitrust Bull. 111, 116 (1984).

58. *Id.* at 116-17 (1984).

59. Baxter, *Responding to the Reaction: The Draftsman's View,* 71 California Law Review 618 (1983).

60. Salop and White, *An Economic and Quantitative Analysis of Private Antitrust Litigation,* Georgia Law Journal, (1986).

61. E. Elzinga and W. Breit, *The Antitrust Penalties* 10, 13 (1976). ("The appropriate amount of resources devoted to antitrust activities is . . . determined by the interaction of the marginal social benefit and the marginal social cost curves.")

62. Sullivan and Marks, *The FTC's Deceptive Advertising Policy: A Legal and Economic Analysis*, 64 Oregon Law Review 593, 627–28 (1986). and accompanying footnotes. *See generally* Becker, *Crime and Punishment: An Economic Approach*, 76 Journal Political Economics 169 (1968); Breit and Elzinga, *Antitrust Enforcement and Economic Efficiency: The Uneasy Case for Treble Damage*, 17 Journal of Law and Economics 329 (1974); Clafee and Craswell, *Some Effects of Uncertainty on Compliance with Legal Standards*, 70 Virginia Law Review 965 (1984); Landes, *Optimal Sanctions for Antitrust Violations*, 5 University of Chicago Law Review 622 (1983); Mennell, *A Note on Private Versus Social Incentives to Sue In a Costly Legal System*, 12 Journal Legal Study 41 (1983); Posner, *A Statistical Study of Antitrust Enforcement* 13 Journal Law and Economics 365 (1970); Posner, *An Economic Approach to Legal Procedure and Judicial Administration*, 399 (1972); Schwartz, *An Overview of the Economics of Antitrust Enforcement*, 68 Georgia Law Journal 1075 (1980); Trubek, Sarat, Felstiner, Kritzer, Grossman, *The Cost of Ordinary Litigation*, 31 UCLA Law Review 72 (1983).

63. Bush, *Dispute Resolution Alternatives and the Goals of Civil Justice*, 1984 Wisconsin Law Review 893, 921–62 (1984). Although the evolution of the Antitrust Division's transition to that of an economic regulator can be described, the motivations that drive and shape the Division's policy and procedure have not been widely studied in the political economy literature. *See, e.g.*, J. Wilson, *The Politics of Regulation* 123 (1980). Understanding regulatory behavior and decisionmaking at the Antitrust Division requires an appreciation of the interaction of many contraints.

First, because the Division is within an executive branch department, it is subject to the political agenda and environment set by that administration. Second, statutory and legislative constraints and pressures from congressional oversight committees, especially in the budgetary process, are limitations on the Division's conduct. Third, the Division is subject to checks by the judiciary when it files suit, although it exercises broad prosecutorial discretion whether to sue or not. Fourth, the leadership exercised by the Attorney General and Assistant Attorney General and the strength of opinions held by each influence, to varying decrees, the Division's behavior. Numerous examples of motivating factors are described above, but three seem critical to the present regulatory posture over mergers.

Congressional passage of the Hart-Scott-Rodino Act of 1976 was a major force propelling the Division toward becoming a regulatory authority. Likewise, the "fix it first" policy was motivated by an executive branch desire to reduce the confrontational and adversarial nature of enforcement against business. A desire for less government intervention in capital markets is also another frequent theme. These institutional, political, and operating constraints played a significant role in shaping the Division's perception of the "public welfare" and enforcement. Other commentators have suggested similar constraints and incentives for other agencies. *See generally* K. Clarkson & W. Muvis, *The Federal Trade Commission Since 1970: Economic Regulation and Bureaucratic Behavior* (1981); Weingast, *Regulation, Reregulation and Deregulation: The Political Foundations of Agency Clientele Relationships*, 44 Law and Contemporary Problems 148 (1981); Weingast & Moran, *Bureaucratic Control: Regulation Policy Making By the Federal Trade Commission*, 91 *Journal Political Economics* 765 (1983); R. Katzman, *Regulatory Bureaucracy: The Federal Trade Commission and Antitrust Policy* (1980); Weingast, *The Congressional-Bureaucratic System: A Principal-*

Agent Perspective With Applications to the SEC, (Working Paper No. 86), Center for the Study of American Business, Washington University, St. Louis; Grier, *Congressional Preference and Federal Reserve Policy* (Working Paper No. 95), Center for the Study of American Business, Washington University, St. Louis.

64. Fiss, *Against Settlement,* 93 Yale Law Journal 1073 (1984); Fiss, *Out of Eden,* 94 Yale Law Journal 1669 (1985).

65. See Barnette, *The Importance of Alternative Dispute Resolution Reducing Litigation Costs as a Corporate Objective,* 53 Antitrust Law Journal 277 (1984).

8

Strategies for Responding to Corporate Takeovers

Murray L. Weidenbaum

The process of changing the ownership and control of large American corporations has become an important topic of public debate. Newspapers, magazines, and television news programs are all devoting substantial attention to the new form of business combat known as hostile takeovers. The coverage of these events is dominated by such colorful descriptions as "poison pills," "shark repellents," "junk bonds," "raiders," "white knights," "wolf packs," and "greenmail."

Serious questions of substance are raised about the methods used and the ends achieved. In 1985, more than fifty bills were introduced in the Congress to deal with mergers and acquisitions; more than twenty hearings on the subject were held by nine different committees. However, no single piece of legislation came close to passing. There is hardly a meeting of minds in this controversial area.

My basic point is that good public policy should not choose between "raiders" and "entrenched" management. In my view—based on some experience with companies that are taken over as well as those that do the taking—the focus should be on a neglected third force, the corporation's own board of directors. But before developing that point we need to take a current reading on the status of the debate on takeovers.

We can begin by examining the views of key public and business figures. For example, Lane Kirkland, president of the AFL-CIO, takes the position of the managements who try to fight off unsolicited tender offers. His language is on the forceful side. "I think corporate raids are an outrage and a bloody scandal . . . I see no virtue in it at all." Investor Irwin Jacobs responds: "We're really not a bunch of big, bad wolves. Mergers and acquisitions have created a great deal of value."[1]

Opinions vary sharply on many aspects of corporate takeovers, and especially those made by shareholders who oppose the existing management. Many economists and other scholars welcome the efforts to change the corporate management, contending that this process enhances shareholder value. In striking contrast, executives of these same firms, as well as many other observers, contend that these hostile attempts to change corporate control reduce business productivity and performance. Such efforts are viewed as diverting management attention and corporate resources from the serious business of producing and distributing goods and services. Attorneys and others concerned with the process of governing corporations are frequently aroused by the shortcomings of the procedures used to effect or deter changes in corporate control.

These different reactions to corporate takeovers, especially of the hostile variety, generate fundamentally different responses in terms of what is desirable public policy in the field of corporate governance. Thus, the specific policy proposals follow from the view held on the effects of takeovers.

Effects of Corporate Takeovers

Supporters of greater regulation of corporate takeovers believe that such involuntary changes in corporate control are socially, economically, and financially detrimental. In the words of the investor Warren Buffet, "American industry should not be restructured by the people who can sell the most junk bonds."[2] Hostile takeovers are viewed as leading to forced liquidations or restructuring of viable companies by "raiders" who reap considerable profit. Moreover, the process is supposed to leave the companies in weakened and highly leveraged positions. The groups initiating hostile takeovers are considered to be mere financiers and speculators who are not serious about the operations of the companies, and who are in it solely for quick profits.

In this view, takeover threats force managers to look to the short term in order to keep their stock price high. This diverts attention from longer-term investment potential and growth. Fending off raiders also is seen as forcing management to take time away from managing the business.

Alfred D. Chandler, Jr., the distinguished business historian at the Harvard Business School, worries about the rising trend of unfriendly takeovers: "How can anyone justify it? It provides no productivity, services, or function. . . . While our managers are fighting takeovers, the Japanese are finding it easier to take over their markets."[3]

In this view, short-term changes in share prices are not the appropriate basis for evaluating the costs and benefits of takeovers. The increases in stock prices that frequently accompany the announcement of a hostile tender offer are seen as the ephemeral result of deepened indebtedness. As investment banker Felix Rohatyn puts it, "large corporations can be treated like artichokes and simply torn apart without any regard for employees, communities, or customers, solely in order to pay off speculative debt." Peter Drucker has echoed this theme:[4]

> The new wave of hostile takeovers has already profoundly altered the contours and landmarks of the American economy. It has become a dominant force . . . in the behavior and actions of American managements and, almost certainly, a major factor in the erosion of American competitive and technological leadership.

The standard response of economists is that the stock market's valuation of takeover efforts is very positive. Numerous studies show that the stock of the target goes up quickly on the mere announcement of a tender offer. That of the buyer moves little at all, or it actually declines.

Because markets are considered to be efficient, the run up in stock prices is viewed as reflecting new economic gains in economies of scale, better management and more productive allocation of resources. The very threat of a takeover is supposed to provide a discipline on inefficient management. There may be especially good economic rationales for restructuring in mature industries, where demand has fallen off considerably, overcapacity exists, and research and development and other investment prospects are currently less attractive. In the words of John D. Williams, "IBM isn't a candidate for takeover because it's an exquisitely run company."[5]

The great bulk of the academic literature states that corporate takeovers promote economic efficiency. After all, why else would share prices rise on the mere announcement of a hostile takeover effort? The following are typical statements by scholars and researchers who have written on the subject:

From the *Harvard Business Review:*[6]

Takeover gains come not from the merger's creation of monopoly market power but from its productive economies and synergy. . . . consolidating or altering control of the assets of the companies involved, perhaps because of cost savings from economies of scale or from a highly complementary combination of employees and assets in production and distribution.

From the Federal Reserve Bank of San Francisco:[7]

An alternate description of events underlying takeovers involves the notion of synergy. According to this hypothesis, firms seek to combine in order to exploit complementary productive or financial attributes. Their combined operations presumably would be more economical than that enjoyed by the entities separately.

From the 1985 *Economic Report of the President:*[8]

The evidence is strong that takeovers generate aggregate net benefits to the economy. Although many potential sources of gain from these transactions can be identified, it is difficult to quantify the size of the gain that results from particular sources. . . . Production and distribution economies are one source of gain, particularly in transactions involving firms in related industries. . . . Substantial gains can also result when a takeover causes assets to be shifted to higher valued uses. . . . Improved management is another possible source of gain from mergers and acquisitions. . . . These findings do not establish that all target firms are poorly managed, and they do not suggest that management efficiencies are the primary source of gain from mergers and acquisitions.

From *Regulation:*[9]

Takeovers allow worse managers to be replaced by better, and generate the other sorts of productive efficiencies associated with mergers.

The prevailing school of thought among economists acknowledges that redeploying assets in restructured companies may cause some unemployment and community dislocations, but the assets do not disappear from the economy. The new investors have a strong economic incentive to put them to productive use. Thus, hostile takeovers are seen as creating real value for both bidders' and target companies' shareholders.

The cold, hard reality is, unfortunately, that there is little organized data available to affirm the synergy or efficiency hypothesis. Furthermore, it is difficult to reconcile that hypothesis with the large number of "post-merger divorces"—up to 40 percent of the acquisitions of the 1970s, according to the data published by W. T. Grimm.[10]

F. M. Scherer concludes, after examining the line-of-business data available in corporate annual reports, that tenderers have not managed the businesses they acquired any more profitably than their industry peers. Nor, according to Scherer, have they achieved significant profitability improvements relative to the pretakeover situation.[11]

Some argue that short-term increases in share prices are not the appropriate basis for evaluating the costs and benefits of takeovers. Warren Law of the Harvard Business School points out that a large body of academic work demonstrates that stock prices fluctuate much more than changes in the rationally-formed expectations of shareholders can justify.[12] Moreover, a recent study at the University of Maryland of seventy-eight mergers and takeovers in the period 1976-81 concluded that three years later the price of the acquirers' stock was much lower than if it had continued performing as it had before the acquisition.[13]

An alternative response to the efficient market argument is that, even if there is a gain in the share value of the merged company, the increase does not necessarily prove that expected real operating efficiency increases are responsible. The key factor at work may be a reduction in tax liability.

The Congressional Joint Committee on Taxation discounts the efficiency gains from mergers based on studies showing that stock prices increase substantially after announcement of proposed mergers. One committee staff study notes that it is possible that a large portion of the stock price gain is in fact due to the capitalization of tax benefits arising from the merger.[14] If tax benefits explain the increase in stock price, then it cannot be concluded, from this evidence alone, that mergers increase efficiency.

F. M. Scherer also suggests that the takeover announcement may act as a signaling device spurring investors to revise their expectations concerning underlying earning power. Such revaluations, however, are ruled out by analysts of the efficient market school who believe that markets are constantly factoring in all attainable information affecting security values.[15]

Scherer contends that the conventional wisdom that tender offer targets are characteristically poor performers does not appear to be true on any broad scale. He reports that a sample of seventy-seven tender offer targets during 1950-76 had income/asset ratios of 12.0 percent for the two years preceding the tender offer. In comparison, all manufacturing corporations reported an average of 12.5 percent, not significantly different.[16] A study by the staff of the Federal Reserve Board reported that a large sample of banks acquired by holding companies during 1968-78 did not perform any differently from other banks either before or after acquisition.[17]

Moreover, a study at the Wharton School of fifty-six hostile tender offers initiated during the period 1975-82 found that the targets, as a group, had significantly higher returns on equity than the bidders; thirty-nine had outperformed their bidders over the preceding two years.[18] Another study found that the industrial company targets of hostile takeovers in 1981 had an average return on equity over the prior four years of 16 percent, which is higher than the average for all manufacturing companies.[19]

Scherer also notes some historical evidence that suggests that tenderers have not managed the businesses they acquired any more profitably than their industry peers, nor have they achieved significant profitability improvements. He concludes that the debate needs to be refocused on the fundamental question of what makes for good industrial performance. ''There is a critical need for more solid evidence and less recitation of unsubstantiated 'efficient markets' theology.''[20]

It is intriguing to examine what actually happens to target firms subsequent to acquisition. In the case of the twenty-five major acquisitions of 1965, only thirteen were still part of the acquirers or their successors by early 1986. Ten others were divested, one was dissolved, and still another is up for sale.[21]

To sum up, the controversy about takeovers generates fascinating—and contradictory—conclusions. In general, the shareholders of the target firm usually benefit, especially in the short run, and supposedly because the entrenched management has not been advancing their interests sufficiently to retain their loyalty. However, the shareholders of the acquiring firm rarely benefit. Although this point is downplayed in the literature, it does imply that the takeover effort on the part of the acquiring management must reflect a lack of concern with the interests of their own shareholders.

What then motivates the managements of the raiders? It is hard to believe that they are more concerned with the welfare of the shareholders of the target company than with the owners of their own company. A more credible explanation is that there are large "rents" or extraordinary gains available from control and management of large enterprises, aside from the personal desire for the accretion of greater power. Elsewhere, I have written about the "imperial presidency" of private sector institutions:[22]

> . . . many members of top management of corporations have acquired so-called perks which smack more of the prerogatives of royalty than of the needs of competitive, profit-maximizing professional management.

In order to obtain such special gains, the raiders are willing to offer above-market prices for the shares of the target company. That is, the management of the acquiring firm winds up sharing its new rents with the stockholders of the target firm—but not with the owners of the firm which employs it.

The academic supporters of takeovers tend to look down at the existing managements of target firms because of their supposed lack of concern for their shareholders. To be consistent, it is equally hard to deify the managements of the "sharks," who have little more regard for their own shareholders. This somewhat cynical approach also helps to explain why researchers have found it so difficult to identify the actual improvements in management which are supposed to justify the runup in the market value of the stock of target firms.

Alternate Approaches to Public Policy

Proposed responses to the problems generated by hostile takeovers range from laissez faire to tough new legislation designed to "correct" the perceived market failures. The following are the five key alternate approaches:

No problem exists and therefore no solution is necessary. The prevailing academic view is that the market for corporate control is functioning reasonably well. Given the passive roles of many boards of directors, hostile takeovers are helpful in keeping companies on their toes and in replacing inefficient, entrenched managements. In this view, if there is any role for public policy, it is to prevent existing boards and managements from thwarting the will of the shareholders.

The proponents of freedom for takeovers note that recent legal changes have strengthened the position of existing managements. For example, the Delaware Supreme Court, validated the "poison pill" used by Household International, making it very expensive for a raider to merge with the target company. Also, the Delaware Court upheld Unocal's exclusionary self tender offer to all of its shareholders except the raider T. Boone Pickens, who was to be financed by the issuance of junk bonds.[23]

Several states have enacted legislation to help local companies fend off unwanted bidders. In 1985, New York State enacted an antitakeover law that provides that a bidder who acquires 20 percent or more of the voting power of the target has to obtain the approval of the target company's board of directors or wait five years before merging.[24]

There is a problem with regard to hostile takeovers, but it will cure itself. The substitution of debt for equity and the increasingly short-term orientation of many American corporations are viewed with some concern. These factors are emphasized as a result of the increasingly global context in which U.S. firms compete.

However, those in this second category believe that the hostile takeover phenomenon will cool substantially when the next serious recession reduces the earnings of the highly-leveraged companies. Many corporations that are being restructured to a far riskier mode as a result of leveraged buyouts may go "belly up." It is expected in turn, that these negative experiences will dampen the ardor of other potential hostile suitors and, more pertinent, reduce the funding available to them.

In this second view, the takeover wave will subside as a result of natural causes and hence no change in public policy is warranted. Moreover, the best-intentioned changes, it is contended, will benefit one side of the takeover battles and thus generate pressure for another round of government intervention to even the score.

There is a continuing problem, but it can be handled with further changes in tax policy. Because the tax deductibility of interest is a key element of most hostile takeovers, this group contends that changes need only be made in tax provisions favoring debt over equity.

They point out that interest charges are tax deductible while dividends are taxed twice, once at the corporate level and again at the level of the individual shareholder. The new tax reform legislation removes capital gains advantages for equity financing. However, the reduction in corporate and individual tax rates will reduce tax differentials for debt versus equity overall.

A more direct approach, proposed by some members of the Congress, is to tighten up on tax deductions of interest for designated "unproductive" purposes, such as hostile takeovers.

Additional regulatory devices should be used. One possibility is to tighten the criteria for allowable investments for life insurance companies and pension funds. Also, some favor the SEC investigating trading "abuses," such as manipulation of stock prices via false rumors, leaks, and other sharp arbitrageur practices.

One prominent attorney describes the situation as follows: "We have entered the era of a two-tier, front-end-loaded, bootstrap, bust-up, junk-bond takeover."[25] In this view, the free flow of information has been impeded and the relative economic power of bidders and management has been altered. The use of high-yield, low-rated "junk" bonds to finance acquisition is one such example.

Investment bankers note two current practices that may be considered to be "abuses." One is the ability to commence a takeover without having binding financial commitments in place. Such conditional bids have a headline-grabbing effect and stampede the shares of the company into the hands of arbitrageurs and speculators. The second abuse involves the tactic of putting a company into "play." Seemingly deliberate leaks drive the shares of the company into the hands of the short-term speculators.

The proponents of takeover efforts note that many other abuses arise from the efforts of managements to repel unsolicited overtures. They contend that shareholder value is reduced when companies adopt "poison pills" and other "shark repellents."

The takeover problem is so serious that tough new legislation is required. The aim is to make it more difficult for shareholder groups to make tender offers that are not endorsed by the company's board of directors.

Most of the bills introduced in Congress to regulate corporate acquisitions are designed to protect target companies. The following are some of the proposals contained in those bills:[26]

- Giving outside (nonmanagement) directors of a target company the right to veto a tender offer or the acquisition of a controlling interest, subject to reversal by a vote of the shareholders.
- Requiring tender offerors to file "community impact statements."
- Prohibiting open market purchases by one corporation of more than 20 percent of another's stock.
- Denying successful acquirers a tax deduction for interest on debt incurred to finance their acquisition.

Moving across the spectrum of federal government intervention in corporate governance is no simple matter. Each of the more activist approaches is likely to generate serious and often unexpected side effects—the "government failure" that so frequently accompanies attempts to deal with "market failure."

The available literature on government regulation of business shows that the costs of regulation often exceed the benefits. The real gainers are the regulated firms instead of the people that regulation is designed to protect. In recent years, consumers have generally benefited from substantial deregulation in the airline, trucking, railroad, telecommunications, and energy markets.

Frank Easterbrook and Gregg Jarrell pointed out in their statement to the SEC Advisory Committee on Tender Offers that there will be "abuses" from time to time.[27] Markets are imperfect and impose unwarranted losses on individual participants from time to time. It is hard to know whether a regulation can cure an abuse; it is harder still to know whether effective abuse-prevention is worth the cost.

Analysis of Major Proposals for Change

The degree to which hostile takeovers are attempted and in fact succeed depends on the nature of management's reaction to tender offers as well as the type of strategies used by bidders. Furthermore, the range of actions that management and bidders can take is circumscribed by state and federal laws. In addition, the courts' interpretation of these laws as well as common law further limit the behavior of both bidders and defending managements.

Current Status of Takeover Regulation

Federal law. The major portion of regulatory power over corporate governance lies with the individual states. Since states are the grantors of most corporate charters, it is natural that state governments provide the legal framework within which corporations operate. Nevertheless, the federal government has found it desirable to participate in the regulation of corporate takeovers. The commerce clause of the Constitution provides the Congress with ample opportunities.

In 1968 Congress passed the Williams Act with the intent of protecting shareholder interests in corporate takeover contests. The Act mandates a minimum time limit for tender offers to remain open as well as disclosure statements of bidders' intentions.[28] The Williams Act is intended to insure that shareholders have the information and sufficient time necessary to make good decisions. The law is intended to maintain equal treatment toward both bidders and defending managements. By addressing only the informational issues of disclosure and time availability, it leaves most corporate control matters in the hands of the states. No significant expansion has occurred in federal regulation of corporate takeovers since 1968.

As the basic national law regulating corporate takeover activity, the Williams Act has had significant and controversial effects on the takeover process. Some believe that a minimum tender period and disclosure requirements improve information flows and make for a more rational "auction" for the defending company. In this view, regulation enhances the performance of the market to the benefit of shareholders.[29]

Others see these same requirements as hindering the ability of the market to efficiently allocate scarce resources. Thus, minimum tender periods benefit incumbent managers by giving them time to devise defensive strategies, thereby shifting the relative bargaining position away from the bidder and toward the target. In addition, the minimum tender period and disclosure requirements give information to other potential bidders who do not undertake the cost of generating it.[30] The end result is to increase the cost of corporate takeovers and supposedly to reduce their likelihood. But the latter is an outcome hard to square with recent experience. In any event, a 1980 study showed that average premiums obtained by stockholders of target companies rose from an average of 32 percent in the period prior to the Williams Act to an average of 53 percent in the nine years following its enactment.[31]

State regulation. The states remain the focal point for regulation of corporate control. The corporate charter, its bylaws, and the court-created business judgment rule[32] define the fiduciary responsibilities of management toward shareholders and thereby determine the basic ground rules for takeover activity.

Recently, states have been active in regulating takeover contests through direct legislation aimed at issues specific to takeover activity. By 1980, thirty-seven states had enacted laws regulating corporate takeovers, most of which were patterned after the Williams Act. In addition, thirty-four of the thirty-seven had so called "principal place of business" clauses in their takeover statutes.[33] These provisions apply the statutes not only to firms incorporated in the state, but also to firms which had their main office in the state, or where as little as 10 percent of the value of the corporation was owned by state residents. The apparent rationale for such protective clauses was to keep corporate activity in the state and thereby retain a major employer. The legal difficulty with this form of regulation is that it imposes costs on shareholders in other states and therefore abridges the flow of interstate commerce.

The Supreme Court in *Edgar* v. *MITE Corporation* (1982) addressed this issue. While that ruling did not eliminate all legislation based on principal place of business, it has limited the number of takeovers subject to state takeover statutes.[34]

Since the *MITE* decision, states have begun developing a second generation of state regulatory laws which give shareholders additional power to approve or reject changes in corporate control. These second generation laws attempt to skirt the interstate commerce problem by focusing on internal corporate procedures during takeovers. For instance, an Ohio law requires that the holders of a disinterested majority of shares approve a change in corporate control unless the company exempts itself from the law.[35] Hawaii requires that major stockholders of Hawaiian companies obtain the approval of a majority of shares they do not own before increasing their ownership beyond 10 percent.[36]

Currently, more than ten states have established such second generation laws. Four of these (Minnesota, Missouri, Indiana and Hawaii) have been declared unconstitutional on the grounds that they violate the commerce clause of the Constitution. The courts are defining ever more closely the balance between the federal government's power to regulate interstate commerce and the state's regulatory authority as grantor of corporate charters.

Proposals for Regulating Bidders' Tactics

Among current proposals to control bidders' tactics is the recommendation of the Securities and Exchange Commission to reduce the ten day "13(d) window" of the SEC Act. In January 1986 the SEC approved a proposal for legislation to reduce the current ten calendar day period to two calendar days for filing a disclosure statement by anyone accumulating more than a 5 percent share of a corporation's outstanding stock.[37] The change would alert the market, shareholders, and managers more quickly to possible raider activity, thereby reducing the ability of raiders to wage "blitzkrieg" on corporations prior to public knowledge.

A popular legislative proposal dealing with information flows is to require the bidder to provide community and employee impact statements outlining the probable effect of a takeover on these groups. Requiring such analyses would increase the cost of corporate takeovers and perhaps reduce their occurrence.

Another group of proposals concerning bidder activity would regulate the use of two-tier (or front-end loaded) tender offers. A two-tier tender offer is an offer to pay cash for the controlling interest in a corporation's stock and then acquire the remaining stock at a lower price, usually through an exchange of stock or a combination of cash and stock.

The use of two-tier offers has been criticized on the grounds that they coerce shareholders into accepting the first tier of the offer to avoid being saddled with the lower offer if the acquisition goes through. In response to this concern there have been calls for restricting or abolishing the use of two-tier tenders. One study, however, shows that a higher proportion of target shareholders accept any or all tender offers than two-tier tenders (73 percent versus 62 percent). Furthermore, half of all two-tier bids are made in friendly offers.[38]

Since corporate charters can be—and often are—amended to include fair price provisions, the case for legislating against two-tier offers is weak. Consistent with this reasoning, the SEC in January 1986 decided not to propose legislation on two-tier tenders. The Commission noted that "the marketplace, and state and federal courts are adequately addressing these issues."[39]

Proposals for Control of Defensive Tactics

Considerable attention has been paid to the control of defensive tactics, in part because many companies have been using one or another method of thwarting potential as well as actual hostile takeovers. By the end of 1985, 387 out of 500 companies included in the Standard and Poor's stock index had adopted at least one antitakeover provision. The major provisions adopted were the following:[40]

- 328 companies had received blank-check preferred stock authority, providing the board with considerable flexibility in terms of issuing shares of stock.
- 206 companies had moved to classified boards, with the terms of the directors staggered over a period of years.
- 170 companies had adopted provisions (aimed at minority shareholders) limiting shareholder rights to act by written consent, amend bylaws or call special meetings.
- 146 companies had voted in fair price provisions, which are aimed at deterring two-tier tender offers.
- 43 companies had adopted some type of poison pill.
- 33 companies had voted for antigreenmail provisions, which, in effect tell potential raiders that the board no longer has the authority to pay greenmail.

Most court rulings on defensive tactics have taken a broad interpretation of the business judgment rule and thus given management considerable power to reject takeover attempts. This in turn has brought a call for a narrower interpretation of the rule when applied to hostile corporate takeovers. Indeed, there have been circumstances under which the courts have narrowed the business judgment rule when they believed that defensive measures were too extreme or designed to entrench management.[41]

Control of poison pills. Stockholder Protection Rights Plans, popularly known as "poison pills," are designed to make a company unpalatably expensive to a hostile acquirer. In the landmark case of Household International, a "flip-over" pill adopted in 1984—and upheld by the Delaware Supreme Court in 1985—entitles the company's shareholders to buy $200 of an acquirer's stock for $100 upon a merger.[42] It would be triggered when a hostile suitor acquired a stake of at least 20 percent in the company. The exercise of such expensive shareholder rights would make any takeover highly improbable.

The court rejected the contention of a stockholder that the pill stripped shareholders of their rights to receive tender offers because the pill was adopted by the board of directors without a vote of the shareholders. The court held that Household's directors "reasonably believed Household was vulnerable to coercive acquisition techniques and adopted a reasonably defensive mechanism to protect itself." Specifically, the court said that the company's board of directors acted properly within the business judgment rule, which gives directors wide latitude to act in what they deem the best long-term interest of the shareholders.[43]

A 1986 decision of the U.S. Court of Appeals for the Seventh Circuit, however, narrowed the permissible uses of poison pills. It voided the pill adopted by CTS Corporation, an electronics manufacturer in Indiana, because it would make the company prohibitively expensive for any acquirer. CTS' "flip-in" version of the pill gave shareholders the right to buy a package of stock and debentures for 25 percent of their market price as soon as any shareholder acquired 15 percent or more of the company's stock. The large investor would not be allowed to participate in the plan.

The Court held that the pill could not be used against the Dynamics Corporation's offer to widen its holdings from 9.6 percent to 27.5 percent because it did not view such action as coercive. In contrast, the Delaware Court held in 1985 that Household International's poison pill discouraged a coercive two-tier offer, but encouraged other, broader tender offers.

Proponents of poison pill plans contend that they allow managements to negotiate more quickly and more effectively on behalf of shareholders. In this view, the presence of the pill protects shareholders from tender offers at unreasonably low prices as well as from partial offers, two-tier offers, and other "abusive" takeover practices.

The opponents of poison pills argue that they deter takeovers, and thus entrench management to the detriment of stockholders. As they see it, poison pill plans can effectively prevent shareholders from even considering the merits of a takeover proposal opposed by the board.

A staff study at the SEC has found that, in general, stock prices decline upon the announcement of the adoption of poison pill defenses. The pill is frequently employed to defeat takeover bids made at premium prices. On average, the rate of defeat for takeover attempts doubles from 23 percent to 47 percent if the firm has a poison pill in place. Also, shareholders of companies with poison pills that were ultimately taken over realized lower average increases in share prices than for takeovers generally. However, corporations that adopt poison pills in the absence of specific takeover threats generally do not experience significant reductions in their stock prices.[44]

It has been suggested that poison pills be subject to shareholder approval. This recommendation has been made by the Council of Institutional Investors, whose members manage over $160 billion in assets, mainly state and local pension funds.[45] Such a requirement could be imposed at either a state or federal level. However, federal intrusion in this area of corporate governance would depart from tradition and could well be viewed as an undesirable preemption of state corporation law. It also would delay a company's response to a takeover threat at a critical time.

The courts seem to be dealing with the various ramifications of this innovative type of corporate defense, without the need for additional legislation. This has been the position of the SEC. Chairman Shad has stated, "The propriety of poison pills is a matter of state corporate law. . . . To date, reliance on shareholders to protect their own interest through their voting rights, has worked well."[46]

Shark Repellents and Golden Parachutes

Shark repellents are provisions voted into the corporate charter or bylaws that are designed to deter hostile takeover bids. Specific types of shark repellents fall into four major categories: (1) staggered elections of corporate board of directors; (2) supermajority and disproportionate voting provisions; (3) fair-price amendments; (4) shareholder-approved poison pills.

Shark repellents have been criticized on the grounds that they work to the detriment of shareholders by deterring takeovers, yet shareholders agree to them. This apparent paradox can be explained because there may be gains to shareholders in approving these arrangements. For example, it may be in the shareholders' and managers' interests to agree to restrict the possibility of disrupting their relationship with a hostile tender offer.[47]

Staggering the elections of the board of directors is a simple, but potentially effective, means of discouraging certain types of hostile bids. For instance, if one-third of the board were elected each year, it would take an acquirer two years to take control of the corporation. This time delay between acquisition and effective control makes it more expensive for a potential bidder to undertake a takeover.

Fair-price provisions are corporate charter or bylaw amendments requiring a bidder to pay the same price for all shares. The intent of such provisions is to restrict the ability of bidders to make two-tier tender offers. By the end of 1985, 146 companies on the Standard and Poor's Stock Index had voted in fair-price provisions indicating that some shareholders do view two-tier tenders to be coercive. It seems apparent that policy toward two-tier offers and their defenses can appropriately be left to corporate shareholders and management.

The existence of disproportionate and supermajority voting-rights provisions presents a more complicated issue in takeover defenses. Supermajority provisions in bylaws require that certain decisions, such as approval of a merger or sale of major corporate assets, pass by "supermajority" vote (usually 2/3) of shareholders.

Disproportionate voting rights are created by a corporation offering different classes of common stock. One class may have full (one share one vote)
voting privileges while another may have only partial (one share 1/4 vote), or
no such privileges. The intent of these provisions is to direct full voting rights
to selected shareholders who favor management. For instance, MCI Commu-
nications Corporation has amended its charter to extinguish the voting rights
of any shareholder who owns more than 15 percent of the voting stock.[48]

At issue is the question of ownership of, and voting control over, the corporation. In the case of supermajority provisions, the discussion centers on the
appropriate percentage of shareholders required to make good decisions about
the future of the corporation.

Disproportionate voting-rights provisions have been approved by shareholders on many occasions. Yet some argue that ownership and voting privileges cannot be separated without damaging the system. One opponent of disproportionate voting rights put it succinctly:[49]

> It is important to note the unique nature of unequal voting rights. Corporate de-
> mocracy is a hollow concept if its changing constituents are unable to reconsider
> decisions made by their predecessors. . . . With one vote, shareholders disen-
> franchise themselves for all time.

The New York Stock Exchange currently delists any company with disproportionate voting shares. In spite of the NYSE policy, the other major exchanges have failed to follow suit. Regardless of the exchange policies, the
decision on the propriety of supermajority and disproportionate voting rights
ultimately falls on state legislatures and state courts as creators and interpret-
ers of charter laws. Furthermore, it may be appropriate for the states to address the entire issue with the intention of outlining a set of laws (such as one
share one vote) determining the voting rights of shareholders owning corporations chartered in the specific state.

Finally, golden parachutes are often included in the discussion of shark repellents. These are employment contract provisions that guarantee substantial
severance payments to top management if they lose their jobs as a result of a
change in control. These provisions supposedly give management an incentive to fight hostile takeovers harmful to the shareholders without having to
worry about the financial consequences of subsequently losing their jobs.
Such provisions have incurred considerable negative reaction from the press
because of the generous payments in several cases.

While golden parachutes do raise the cost of takeovers, these costs are usually known in advance and are small relative to the overall transaction. As
such, they really do not constitute an effective takeover defense. At times, it
appears that excessively generous ''parachutes'' encourage management to

welcome a change in control. Despite their popular notoriety, these provisions have become fairly standard among larger corporations.

Greenmail

Available studies suggest that shareholder wealth is reduced when management opposition to takeovers eliminates potential takeover bids. That is especially the case with "greenmail," whereby a company buys a block of its common stock from an active or potential bidder at a premium over the market price. Often the stockholder whose shares are repurchased had proposed an unfriendly takeover and the purchase is linked with an agreement to cease efforts to take over the company. Critics of these repurchases claim the practice is abusive because management is using the corporation's resources to buy out a potential bidder and thereby preclude stockholders from earning a premium for their shares.

Abnormal declines tend to occur in the market price of the stock of the repurchasing company after greenmail is paid. The sellers, in contrast, achieve significantly positive returns. However, the issue is not as clear-cut as it may seem. But some critics of regulation of greenmail contend that these targeted share repurchases can be beneficial because they reduce the expected cost of takeover attempts and thereby increase the likelihood of takeovers.

On balance, the case for outlawing greenmail is weak. Shareholders, if they want to, can amend corporate charters to restrict targeted repurchases. Several large companies have recently taken such action, which effectively signals to would-be takeover leaders that the firm will not be paying greenmail.

Tax Aspects of Takeovers

The Internal Revenue Code generally does not distinguish between friendly and hostile corporate acquisitions. With rare exception, the code neither encourages nor discourages hostile takeovers. Two exceptions are contained in the Deficit Reduction Act of 1984. Section 244A denies the dividend-received deduction for dividends received on debt-financed portfolio stock. Sections 280G and 4999 promulgate new rules on "golden parachutes."[50]

In 1986, the Internal Revenue Service issued a regulation that could slow corporate takeover activity. The new rule prohibits a company that paid more than fair market value for another firm from depreciating the excess amount. Instead, the rule requires that the acquiring firm assign the excess to goodwill which cannot be depreciated or deducted from taxable income.[51]

Three key technical features of the federal income tax do have substantial impacts on the pattern of takeover activity, even though that is not their intent: (1) the differing tax consequences of acquiring an entire corporation versus acquiring individual corporate assets and thus being able to mark up assets from book to current market values; (2) the disparate treatment of corporate "distributions" made in the form of interest, dividends, and long-term capital gains; and (3) the inability of corporations with limited taxable income to take full advantage of business tax preferences.

Indirectly, the different tax treatment of interest and dividends may have significant effects on the incentives for takeovers and subsequent changes in the capital structure of the firm whose control is shifting. Debt-financed takeovers increase share price to the extent that the tax advantages of debt financing are outweighed by the disadvantages such as increased risk of bankruptcy. This comes about because interest payments—but not dividends—are tax deductible by the corporation. Thus, until 31 December 1986, the combined individual and corporate tax on debt-financed investment is no more than 50 percent (the top individual rate in effect until 31 December 1986), while the combined tax on income distributed from equity-financed corporate investment was as high as 73 percent (with the top corporate rate at 46 percent).

As a result, the after-tax return on a dollar of income on debt-financed assets (50 cents) was, at the highest tax ratio, almost double the return on a dollar from equity-financed corporate investment (27 cents). When the new tax reform law becomes fully effective, however, the tax advantages of debt will decline. By 1988, the top individual rate will drop to 28 percent and the top combined rate will fall to 62 percent.

The new tax law also eliminates the so-called General Utilities doctrine, which allowed companies to avoid taxes when their assets are liquidated in a leveraged buyout. Previously, at the time of such a buyout, the assets of the target company are stepped up in value so that taxes are reduced because a large amount of assets is being depreciated. The new bill also requires that the company has to pay the full capital gains tax owed at the time of the buyout. Earlier tax law permitted spreading the tax over a period of years.

The new rules will not apply to companies with assets of less than $5 million until 31 December 1988. For companies that had adopted a liquidation plan, a plan to sell their stock by 1 August 1986, the new rules will not apply until 31 December 1987.[52] Although the tax rules are being changed, it remains to be seen how readily participants in takeovers adjust to them. If the past is a relevant guide, adjustments in pricing will occur more frequently than shifts in the frequency of takeovers, hostile or friendly.

With reference to current law, the ability on the part of new owners to write up the value of assets from book to market value yields increased depreciation charges and thus enhanced cash flow. Professor Warren Law contends that the increased depreciation and interest charges constitute the underlying rationale for most leveraged buyouts.

A 1986 study at the National Bureau of Economic Research provides some statistical perspective on the importance of the different aspects of tax policy. One-fifth of the mergers that took place between 1968 and 1983 involved a potential gain from the transfer of unused tax losses and credits. The average tax gain from these mergers was about 10 percent of the acquired company's market value. Gains this large are about the same size as the average premium paid for acquired firms in successful tender offers.[53]

The researchers concluded that other tax incentives—such as the ability to step up the basis of depreciable assets without being subject to capital-gains taxes—are quantitatively far less important. They also found only slight increases in leverage in the first two years following mergers, thus minimizing the use of the interest deduction provisions. However, their data only extend to 1983.

In the attention to the technical provisions of the Internal Revenue Code one should not overlook the root causes of tax-motivated or tax-supported mergers. These are (1) the double taxation of dividends, (2) the deductibility of interest, (3) business tax preferences and ways of utilizing them in the face of low earnings, and (4) net operating losses and similar tax attributes.

Thus, some of the bills introduced in the Congress to stem the merger boom are likely to have little effect if enacted. These include proposals to deny interest deductions on debt incurred to finance hostile takeovers and tax penalties on payments of greenmail (such as treating greenmail profits as ordinary income or subjecting such profit to a special 50 percent tax). Because such narrow proposals address the most glaring symptoms of the current wave of hostile mergers, their enactment might merely give rise to the development of new strategies of corporate acquisitions which would get around these obstacles.

The enactment of tax changes aimed at mergers per se might well reduce the frequency of involuntary takeovers, as desired by many members of Congress. But these laws also could reduce the number of economically desirable corporate acquisitions. The recently enacted tax-rate reductions may turn out to be more important in this regard than is generally realized.

There is one type of tax advantage which does seem to be a candidate for change. It arises in the case of dual-resident United States-United Kingdom "link" companies.[54] A link company is a U.S. corporation taxable in this country by reason of its residence and source of income, and simultaneously taxable in the United Kingdom by reason of being managed and controlled from that country.

Thus, a U.K.-based corporation can form a U.S. subsidiary for a nominal sum, have it borrow the cash portion of the purchase price, and have the subsidiary acquire a target company in the United States. The U.S. subsidiary has only its investment in the stock of the target company plus interest expense. If the parent is a profitable U.K. company, it can utilize the tax laws of both countries to obtain a double tax benefit from deducting the interest expense incurred in financing the acquisition.

For U.S. tax purposes, the U.S. subsidiary deducts its interest expense against future profits by filing a consolidated U.S. federal income tax return with the newly-acquired U.S. firm. Meanwhile, for U.K. tax purposes, the U.S. subsidiary is also taxable because it is deliberately managed and controlled in the U.K. Again, it deducts its interest expense, but this time against the profits of the U.K. parent firm. It accomplishes this feat by filing a group relief tax return which is akin to a consolidated U.S. corporate tax return. The key to the success of this arrangement is to have a profitable U.K. company be the parent of the U.S. acquirer company for the life of the debt financing the acquisition of the target.

At present levels of corporate income taxation, the double tax benefit reduces the effective cost of borrowing by 91 percent (46 percent U.S. corporate rate plus a 45 percent U.K. rate). Thus, the effective cost of borrowing at 10 percent would be less than 1 percent.

Some Observations

Takeovers are not without costs or dangers. Not every takeover succeeds in achieving the intended benefits. Indeed, the volume of subsequent divestitures shows that, in hindsight, many were misguided. Divestitures currently account for about one-third of both the number and dollar amount of all merger and acquisition transactions. The same lack of universal success, of course, can be attributed to virtually any other corporate investment or human action.

As a general proposition, any defensive tactic adopted by the corporation's stockholders should not be considered abusive, regardless of the extent to which it might deter takeovers. In this view, defensive moves can only be abusive if management uses its discretionary power to promote its own interests over those of the shareholders. In many instances it is difficult to distinguish between abusive and other tactics. Therefore, blanket rules to prohibit specific defensive tactics such as the adoption of "poison pills" can generate unintended and undesirable side effects.

Moreover, many efforts at regulation are ineffective. For example, in January 1986 the Federal Reserve System attempted to limit corporate takeovers using junk bonds. The new rule limited financing of hostile takeovers with debt to 50 percent in the case of "shell companies" (those without significant assets or operations). Since the issuance of the new Fed regulation, many raiders simply shifted to offering preferred stock, which has many of the characteristics of debt, but does not count as equity. In some cases, the company converted the equity into debt after the merger agreement was announced.

In other cases, the attacking company used a shell that had a modest amount of assets and activities. For example, Pantry Pride was the corporate vehicle used to acquire Revlon, notwithstanding the fact that its annual revenues of $110 million paled in comparison to Revlon's $2.4 billion.[55]

The experience with the Fed's junk-bond rule illustrates the futility of much governmental intervention due to the tendency of participants in competitive markets, such as the market for corporate control, to adjust to governmental action without fundamentally changing their ways of doing business.

Meanwhile, changes in the tax ground rules are likely to continue. Under the 1986 tax reform law, the Treasury Department will be studying the question of reforming subchapter C. Its report to the Senate Finance Committee and House Ways and Means Committee is due 1 January 1988.

Conclusions

Several large and contentious contests for corporate control have focused national attention on the subject of hostile takeovers. However, it is important to recognize that these highly visible transactions represent only a small fraction of the changes in control of American corporations carried out each year. Most takeovers continue to be friendly and approved by the boards of both companies involved. In many cases, the board of the target firm may have required a bit of coaxing—such as the threat to "walk away" and see the price of the target company's stock drop sharply.

Although much controversy exists in this area, many studies show that takeover contests are beneficial for stockholders of target companies. But direct evidence of net benefits—or net costs—to the economy as a whole ranges from meager to nil.

Yet, for well-financed groups to attempt hostile takeovers of private corporations is a legitimate undertaking. To clothe themselves with the public interest, however, is to stretch the point. "I am the champion of the small stockholder," declares one of the best-known of the new breed of multimillionaire corporate raiders. More modestly—and likely more accurately—another highly visible raider describes the group as "acting in pursuit of personal financial gain and not out of altruism. I do it to make money."[56]

There is no need—or justification—to argue that all takeover attempts are benign or that every effort to repulse them is laudable. Of course, some businesses and their shareholders clearly benefit from new management or even the threat of a change in management. But, as pointed out in the January 1985 Annual Report of the Council of Economic Advisers, "Contests for corporate control are not, however, motivated solely by opportunities to improve management."[57] Reasonable amounts of self-interest can be expected on the part of both those attempting corporate takeovers and those opposing them.

Perhaps the most significant factor to take into account in evaluating proposals for government to "do something" about hostile takeovers is historical. The long and intricate experiences of government involvement in business decision-making are not impressive. Whether that intervention is made by the judicial, legislative or executive branches, government often does more harm than good when it interferes in private economic matters.

In recent years, we have learned painfully and repeatedly about "government failure." That is, the presence of some shortcoming in the private business system (often called "market failure") is not sufficient cause for government to intervene. Thus, to justify added government regulation of the market for corporate control, it is also necessary to demonstrate that the various costs associated with government intervention are less than the benefits that are expected to be generated.[58]

Study after study has shown that much government regulation fails to meet this type of elementary but necessary benefit/cost test. As a result, such a strong supporter of corporate takeover efforts as President Reagan's Council of Economic Advisers has concluded that "it is preferable to allow individual companies to decide whether and how they want to protect themselves than to have the Federal Government dictate an inflexible nationwide policy."[59]

Moreover, as the managing director of Drexel Burnham Lambert has noted, business has a way of curing its own problems. "By the time we got to the issue of greenmail, greenmail was over."[60]

Powerful tools are available to those attempting to take over the control of American corporations. Concerns of fairness and the desire to maintain a balance of forces lead to the conclusion that the mechanisms available to repel hostile takeovers should not be diminished, especially unilaterally. The success of many hostile or uninvited tender offers demonstrates the strength of the attacker—and leads inevitably to questioning the need to weaken the defenders.

Indeed, the Williams Act, the primary federal statute governing corporate takeovers, is generally considered to represent such a balance between attackers and defenders. This law represents a compromise between: 1) the desire to assure adequate disclosure to investors and to afford target company shareholders and their managements a reasonable period of time in which to evaluate tender offers, and 2) the market's need to operate efficiently and with a minimum of government regulatory interference. While the Williams Act has served the purpose of assuring adequate dissemination of accurate information to investors, it has also imposed costs on the operation of the capital markets.

Another lesson of economic history is that government intervention begets more government intervention. If government should limit defensive maneuvers, that would tilt the balance and invariably lead to pleas to restrict offensive actions. Once again, more regulation would beget still more regulation.

There are many pros and cons on each side of the controversy over hostile takeovers of U.S. corporations. Opponents of the status quo are concerned that the threat of takeovers has forced many businesses to focus on short-term results, while proponents of takeovers respond that there is no factual basis for that common charge. Also, those advocating restrictions on takeovers express concern over the shifts from equity to debt that usually result from successful takeovers and the rapidly rising aggregate indebtedness of American companies. The response offered is that the market is the best judge of the proper level of indebtedness of individual business firms. That reply may not satisfy those who are concerned with the high and rising level of debt in the United States.

All in all, the business judgment rule—the presumption that the decisions of a board of directors will not be disturbed if they can be attributed to a rational business purpose—remains the most desirable approach to corporate governance. It is not necessary to conclude that corporate takeovers perform beneficial functions and are generally good for the economy. It is merely sufficient to acknowledge that current policy constitutes a workable compromise between the desires of target shareholders and managements and those who contend for corporate control.

Many new limitations on bidder activities have been proposed, but the need for additional restrictions on bidders has not been demonstrated. Target company shareholders already have protection from abuses by target managements in conjunction with contests for corporate control. State law, enforceable in the courts, governs the permissible terms of corporate charters, management contracts, and managers' and directors' fiduciary obligations. This also serves to check management abuses.

The balance between management's need to act expeditiously in the interest of the corporation and the shareholder's right to call that action into account should be resolved at the level closest to the problem and the relevant facts—by the corporation, its owners, and managers in the first instance; by state law, if necessary; and by federal law only as a last resort. This does not mean that inequities in the battle between management and the tenderers created by tax biases or existing regulations should be ignored. But the basic task of ensuring that the market for corporate control serves investors, employees, and other interested parties ultimately lies outside of government.

When faced with pressures to "do something," decision makers in the federal government should carefully consider the unintended effects that other federal policy decisions—notably in the tax area—can have on merger and acquisition activity. To the extent that these other government activities encourage more or less merger and acquisition activity than otherwise would have taken place in a free market, resources may be misallocated and some changes in policy may be desirable. Otherwise, the competitive marketplace provides the environment most conducive to free institutions and a strong, private business system.

It is intriguing to note the views of top executives of the most successful firms toward their shareholders. One recent study at the Harvard Business School, reported that none of the top executives of twelve successful American companies was very concerned about the current market value of the company's stock. One CEO stated this position very clearly:[61]

> The highest priority with me is perpetuation of the enterprise. I'd like to leave this joint in better shape than when someone passed me the baton. I have to take care of the shareholders in this, but I don't sweat the shareholders too much. Most investors in our industry are passive.

Another CEO expressed a similar viewpoint to a researcher for the Conference Board:[62]

> A year from now, 70% of my stockholders will have changed. On that basis, I put my customers, and my employees, way ahead of them.

The Harvard researchers concluded that the primary goal of the CEOs is the survival of the corporation in which they have invested so much of themselves psychologically and professionally. They concluded that the successful managers were committed "first and foremost, to the enhancement of *corporate* wealth, which includes not only the firm's financial assets reflected on the balance sheet but also its important human assets and its competitive positions in the various markets in which it operates."[63]

On reflection, if the raiders are opportunists, it is boards of directors and senior executives who have given them the opportunity. Too many CEOs and boards have focused on the ballet and the opera as the epitome of a corporation's responsibility to society. They seem to forget that a business is an economic institution, designed to provide goods and services for consumers in order to benefit the shareholders.

The irony is that some of the problems of the takeover "targets" have arisen from their desire to be more socially responsible. The modern business literature tells management to balance the desires of employees, customers, suppliers, public interest groups, and shareholders. For example, the Committee for Economic Development, in its influential report on the social responsibility of business, states that the professional manager regards himself as a "trustee" balancing the interests of many diverse participants and constituents in the enterprise. It is interesting to note that shareholders are only listed as one among those worthy groups—and they are listed last.

The heart of a positive response to unsolicited takeovers is not poison pills or shark repellents or government restraints on raiders. There is a third and often neglected force, the company's own board of directors.

Under law, all corporate power is exercised by or under the authority of the board. Directors really act as fiduciaries of the shareholders.[64] But the complaisant or rubber-stamp director has not totally vanished from the boardroom. Responding more fully to the desires of the owners of the business is the key to repelling takeover threats. Corporate officials, both board members and officers, often forget until the company's stock is in play that shareholders continually vote with their dollars.

The most important, and rarely performed, duty of the corporate board is to learn how to say "no." It is up to the board to veto proposed capital investments whose yield is below the cost of capital—even if some key executive is going to get upset because it was his or her pet project. It will continue to be difficult for the outside directors to exert such independence so long as an inside director (typically the CEO) remains as chairman of the board and is in charge of the agenda, the paper flow, and the proceedings.

The outside directors must assert themselves, especially in light of the increased liability that is imposed on them. They especially must learn to act on the knowledge that the inside directors who serve on the board with them are occasionally motivated by different concerns. Acquisitions may be good for executives whose compensation is related to the size of the company, but some may be poor investments for shareholders. A very generous corporate donation to the ballet may do wonders for the social life of the CEO, but it hardly benefits the shareholders.

The challenge to many boards is to pay out more cash for shareholders and to reduce outlays for low-yield projects.[65] The 1986 tax reform bill underscores that point. By equalizing the tax rates on capital gains and dividends, the new Internal Revenue Code deprives management of a traditional justification for retaining earnings in order to finance marginal projects.

If the board will not make the tough decisions that enhance the value of the corporation, the takeover artists will. Takeover mania is not a cause but a symptom of the unmet challenge. Outside directors are the heart of the critical third force in contests for corporate control. They need to bear in mind that the future of the corporation is in their hands—as long as they serve the desires of the shareholders.

Notes

1. Quoted in John Greenwald, "The Great Takeover Debate," *Time*, 22 April 1985, p. 44.
2. Quoted in Congressional Research Service, *The Role of High Yield Bonds (Junk Bonds) In Capital Markets and Corporate Takeovers*, A Report to the Subcom-

mittee on Telecommunications, Consumer Protection and Finance of the Committee on Energy and Commerce of the U.S. House of Representatives (Washington, D.C.: U.S. Government Printing Office, 1985), p. 26.

3. Alfred D. Chandler, Jr., "How the Heirs of Sloan and DuPont are Faring," *Across the Board*, May 1986, p. 28.

4. Peter F. Drucker, "Corporate Takeovers-What Is To Be Done?", *Public Interest*, Winter 1986, p. 3; see also Felix Rohatyn, "Junk Bonds and Other Securities Swill," *Wall Street Journal*, 18 April 1985, p. 30.

5. Quoted in Congressional Research Service, *op. cit.*, p. 27.

6. Michael C. Jensen, "Takeovers: Folklore and Science," *Harvard Business Review*, November/December 1984, p. 1,114.

7. Randall J. Pordena, "Takeovers: Good or Evil," *FRBSF Weekly Letter*, 3 January 1986, p. 2.

8. *Economic Report of the President, January 1985* (Washington, D.C.: U.S. Government Printing Office, 1985), p. 198.

9. "A Truce in the Takeover Wars?" *Regulation*, March/April 1985, p. 5.

10. Cited in David J. Ravenscraft and F. M. Scherer, *Mergers and Managerial Performance*, Working Paper No. 137 (Washington, D.C.: U.S. Federal Trade Commission, Bureau of Economics, 1986), p. 2.

11. F. M. Scherer, "Takeovers: Present and Future Dangers," *Brookings Review*, Winter/Spring 1986, p. 20.

12. Warren A. Law, "A Corporation Is More Than Its Stock," *Harvard Business Review*, May/June 1986, p. 80.

13. Ellen B. Magenheim and Dennis C. Mueller, *On Measuring the Effect of Acquisitions on Acquiring Firm Shareholders*, a paper presented to the Center for Law and Economic Studies, Columbia University, 13-15 November 1985.

14. Senate Finance Committee, *op. cit.*, p. 16; see also *Testimony of Warren A. Law Before the House Committee on Energy and Commerce*, Washington, D.C., 12 March 1985, p. 1.

15. Scherer, *op. cit.*, pp. 15–20.

16. Ravenscraft and Scherer, *op. cit.*, p. 2.

17. Stephen A. Rhoades, *The Operating Performance of Acquired Firms in Banking Before and After Acquisition*, Staff Paper (Washington, D.C.: Board of Governors, Federal Reserve System, 1985).

18. Edward S. Herman and Louis Lowenstein, *The Efficiency Effects of Hostile Takeovers: An Empirical Study*, paper presented to the Center for Law and Economics Studies, Columbia University, 1985.

19. *Ibid.*

20. Scherer, *op. cit.*, p. 20.

21. "A Twenty-Year Profile of Mergers and Acquisitions," *Mergers & Acquisitions*, January/February 1986, pp. 40, 42.

22. Murray L. Weidenbaum, *The Future of Business Regulation* (New York: Amacom, 1980), p. 100. For explanatory detail on this point, see pp. 99–102.

23. Martin Lipton and Andrew R. Brownstein, "Takeover Responses and Directors' Responsibilities—An Update," *Business Lawyer*, August 1985, pp. 1403–30.

24. *Ibid.*

25. Martin Lipton, "Takeover Abuses Mortgage the Future," *Wall Street Journal*, 5 April 1985, p. 12.

26. Frank W. Bubb, "Hostile Acquisitions and the Restructuring of Corporate America," *Freeman*, April 1986, p. 166.

27. "Separate Statement of Frank H. Easterbrook and Gregg A. Jarrell," Advisory

Committee on Tender Offers, *Report of Recommendations* (Washington, D.C.: U.S. Securities and Exchange Commission, 1983), pp. 70–121.

28. The Williams Act requires a tender offer to remain open for twenty business days. Section 13(d) of the Act requires that any person obtaining more than 5 percent of outstanding shares must file a disclosure statement with the SEC including: the name and background of the offeror, the offeror's source of funds and financial condition, the purpose of the tender offer (e.g., plans for mergers, liquidations, reorganizations and intended changes in management or board of directors) and any contacts between the target and the offeror in the past three years.

29. Louis Lowenstein, "Pruning Deadwood in Hostile Corporate Takeovers: A Proposal for Legislation," *Columbia Law Review*, Vol. 83, No. 2, March 1983, pp. 323–24.

30. Margaret E. Guerin-Calvert, Robert H. McGuckin and Frederick R. Warren-Boulton, *State and Federal Regulation in the Market for Corporate Control*, U.S. Department of Justice, Antitrust Division, Economic Analysis Group Discussion Paper (EAG 86-4), 21 January 1986.

31. Gregg Jarrell and Michael Bradley, "The Economic Effects of Federal and State Regulations of Cash Tender Offers," *Journal of Law and Economics*, October 1980, pp. 371–407.

32. The business judgment rule, based on common law, provides that, as long as managers have acted in "good faith" toward shareholders and if a rational business purpose can be attributed to their response, management will not be subject to judicial scrutiny. Furthermore, the burden of proof falls on the plaintiff, not on the defending management.

33. Guerin-Calvert, *et al., op. cit.,* p. 8.

34. *Ibid.*

35. "Study Describes New State Laws on Takeovers," *Update,* June 1985, p. 9.

36. "Laws in Hawaii Against Takeovers Are Ruled Invalid," *Wall Street Journal,* Vol. 4, 18 June 1986, p. 4.

37. John Shad, Chairman, Securities and Exchange Commission, Letter to Timothy Wirth, Chairman of House Telecommunications, Consumer Protection and Finance Subcommittee, 17 January 1986.

38. R. Comment, *The Economics of Any-or-All, Partial, and Two-Tier Tender Offers,* U.S. Securities and Exchange Commission, Release No. 34-21079.

39. Shad, *op. cit.*

40. "Antitakeover Measures Exist in Most Firms," *Update,* June 1986, p. 7.

41. For a summary of the business judgment rule and its evolution with regard to hostile takeovers, see Martin Lipton and Andrew R. Brownstein, "Takeover Responses: An Update," in *The Dynamics of Corporate Control II: Evolving Legal Standards Applied to the Frontiers of Corporate Strategy,* pp. 2–12.

42. Louis Perlmutter, *Takeovers: The Current Outlook,* a presentation to the Economic Club of Chicago, Chicago, Illinois, 3 March 1986, p. 3.

43. *Moran v. Household International* (In the Court of Chancery of the State of Delaware in and for New Castle County), 29 January 1985; Lipton and Brownstein, *op. cit.,* pp. 1403–30.

44. Mike Ryngaert, *The Effects of Poison Pills on the Wealth of Shareholders,* Securities and Exchange Commission Staff Paper, 5 September 1985, p. 36–37.

45. Fred R. Bleakley, "A Trustee Takeover on the Greenmailers," *New York Times,* 10 February 1985, p. 6F.

46. John Shad, *Major Efforts and Issues at the SEC,* in a speech to the Council of Institutional Investors, First Annual Meeting, Atlanta, Georgia, 29 October 1985, p. 11.

47. Charles Knoeber, "Golden Parachutes, Shark Repellents, and Hostile Tender Offers, *American Economic Review*, March 1986, pp. 155–67.

48. Cited in Lowenstein, *op. cit.*, p. 250.

49. T. Boone Pickens, Jr., "Need All Shareholders be Equal? Second Class Stock Impairs Market," *Wall Street Journal*, 13 February 1986, p. 30.

50. U.S. Senate, Committee on Finance, *Federal Income Tax Aspects of Hostile Takeovers and Other Corporate Mergers and Acquisitions* (Washington, D.C.: U.S. Government Printing Office, 1985).

51. "New IRS Rule Could Curb Takeovers by Increasing Tax Bills for Acquirers," *The Wall Street Journal*, 7 February 1986, p. 3.

52. "The Possible Conference Compromise," (Informal Notes), U.S. Congress, Joint Committee on Taxation, Washington, D.C., 16 August 1986, p. 24.

53. Alan Auerbach and David Reishus, *Taxes and the Merger Decision*, Working Paper No. 1855 (Cambridge, Mass.: National Bureau of Economic Research, 1986), pp. 24–25.

54. Letter from R. B. Weinel, Vice President, Ralston Purina Company, 19 March 1986.

55. Randall Smith, "Fed Rule Restricting the Use of Junk Bonds In Takeovers Is By Most Accounts Ineffective," *New York Times*, 18 August 1986, p. 43.

56. Quoted in "The Raiders," *Business Week*, 4 March 1985, pp. 80–81.

57. *Economic Report of the President, op. cit.*, p. 189.

58. See Murray L. Weidenbaum, *Business, Government and the Public*, Third Edition (Englewood Cliffs: Prentice-Hall, 1986), Chapter 2.

59. *Economic Report of the President, op. cit.*, p. 211.

60. "Roundtable," *Mergers & Acquisitions*, March/April 1986.

61. Gordon Donaldson and Jay W. Lorsch, *Decision Making at the Top: The Shaping of Strategic Direction* (New York: Basic Books, 1983), p. 28.

62. *Chief Executives View Their Jobs*, Report No. 871 (New York: Conference Board, 1985), p. 8.

63. Donaldson and Lorsch, *op. cit.*, p. 7.

64. Murray L. Weidenbaum, *Strengthening the Corporate Board* (St. Louis: Washington University, Center for the Study of American Business, September 1985.)

65. Jensen, *op. cit.*, pp. 109–21; see also Michael C. Jensen, "Agency Costs of Free Cash Flow, Corporate Finance and Takeovers," *American Economic Review* (forthcoming).

Appendix

Are New Laws Needed to Restrict Takeovers?

By Murray L. Weidenbaum

No Shortage of Existing Rules

The history of government regulation of business provides an important lesson: sensational cases make bad law.

There is great danger that the Congress will respond to the Ivan Boesky scandal with hastily enacted legislation which will do more harm than good.

The current wave of hostile takeovers has accentuated pressures to "do something."

But Congress should avoid repeating the errors of the past. Too often, committees of both houses have devoted 90 percent or more of their attention to discussing the problem and 10 percent or less to examining the proposed legislative solution. Nobody ever asks whether the proposed new law will work.

The key argument advanced by those who oppose corporate takeovers is that they are socially and economically detrimental. They charge that takeovers lead to forced liquidations—with the "raiders" reaping great profit in the process.

In this view, these threats force managers to look to the short-term in order to keep their current stock price high.

The standard response is that the stock market's reaction tells us that takeovers often enhance the company's value. The stock of the company being acquired goes up quickly on the mere announcement of a tender offer.

As for the charge that U.S. businesses are thinking short-term, the facts show that private-sector investment in research and development is now at an all-time high. The payoffs from those projects are far in the future and constitute strong evidence of the continuing long-run orientation of the companies.

In reality, hostile takeovers represent only a small fraction of the changes in control of American corporations. Most takeovers are friendly.

Beyond these facts, it is hard to prove that corporate takeovers actually do—or do not—promote economic efficiency. The large number of "post-merger divorces"—up to 40 percent of the acquisitions of the 1970s—certainly show that takeovers do not always work out well.

But, there is no need to argue that all takeover attempts are benign or that every effort to repulse them is motivated by management's desire to stay in control. Reasonable amounts of self-interest should be expected on the part of both those attempting corporate takeovers and those opposing them.

The most significant factor to take into account in evaluating proposals to regulate takeovers is historical: government often does more harm than good when it interferes in private business decision-making.

There is no need for a do-nothing approach. If the raiders are opportunists, we must ask, "Who gave them the opportunity?" The answer is boards of directors and senior executives who have not adequately served the interests of the owners of the business, i.e., the shareholders.

The heart of a positive response to unsolicited takeovers is not "poison pills" or "shark repellents" nor is it government restraints on raiders. Present law is fully adequate to deal with the takeover problem. The third and neglected force is the company's own board of directors. The full legal power in a company is lodged in the board.

Responding more fully to the desires of the owners of the business is the key to repelling takeover threats. Directors must really act as fiduciaries of the shareholders, as the law requires.

But the rubber-stamp director has not vanished from the boardroom. Corporate officials, both board members and officers, often forget until the company's stock is in play that shareholders continually vote with their dollars. Too many chief executives still say they "don't sweat the shareholders too much."

When it comes to representing shareholder interests, the most important duty of the board is to learn to say no. The challenge to many boards is to pay out more cash to shareholders and reduce outlays for low-yield projects.

The record is clear: if the board will not make the difficult choices that enhance the value of the corporation, the takeover forces will. Takeover mania is not a cause but a symptom of the unmet challenge.

Ivan Boesky is being punished for his wrongdoing under existing law. There is no shortage of pertinent statutes on the books. What is really needed are corporate directors who use the full authority the law gives them.

Notes

This 3 December 1986 article taken from *The Washington Times* is based on *Public Policy Toward Corporate Takeovers*, testimony given to the Subcommittee on Monopolies and Commercial Law of the House Committee on the Judiciary in Washington, D.C. on 18 November 1986. Reprinted by permission of *The Washington Times*.

About the Contributors

Kenneth W. Chilton is associate director of the Center for the Study of American Business (CSAB) at Washington University in St. Louis. Mr. Chilton is currently working on his Ph.D. in business. He holds a B.S. and an M.S. from Northwestern University. Mr. Chilton's research interests lie in the proper role for business and government in America, and more specifically, the effects of government regulation on the business system. In addition to a number of CSAB articles and reports, he has written "The Regulatory Environment for Entrepreneurship," a chapter in *The Environment for Entrepreneurship* (1984).

Richard E. Cook is a Ph.D. candidate in economics at Washington University and John M. Olin Fellow at the Center for the Study of American Business. He received his B.A. from Metropolitan State College in Denver and his M.A. from Washington University. His research interests are corporate governance, finance, and macroeconomics. He has authored "Testing Money Demand Using Interest-rate Futures," and coauthored *Learning to Compete: Feedback Effects of the Non-linear Economy* (Center for the Study of American Business, 1986).

Kenneth Lehn is assistant professor in the School of Business and research associate at the Center for the Study of American Business at Washington University in St. Louis. While on leave from Washington University, he served as deputy chief economist at the U.S. Securities and Exchange Commission in 1984-85. In 1986, he was a visiting assistant professor of economics at UCLA. Dr. Lehn received a B.A. in economics from Waynesburg College, an M.A. in economics from Miami University, and a Ph.D. in economics from Washington University. His research interests lie in the areas of industrial organization, law and economics, and corporate control. He has published in the *Journal of Law and Economics, Economic Inquiry*, and the *Journal of Political Economy*.

T. Boone Pickens is chairman and CEO of Mesa Petroleum Company. He describes himself as a shareholder advocate and a corporate activist and has recently founded the United Shareholders Association. Before his move to become an independent geologist, he was employed at a major oil company. Mr. Pickens has earned recognition for his management and entrepreneurial skills. In 1985, he was named Man of the Year by the Oil Trades Association and was the subject of a cover story in *Time*. Mr. Pickens's autobiography, was published by Houghton Mifflin in the Spring of 1987.

Annette Poulsen is acting chief economist at the Securities and Exchange Commission, where she has also held the position of deputy chief economist, since earning her Ph.D. in economics from Ohio State University. Dr. Poulsen's research interests lie in the areas of tender offers and Japanese banking in the U.S. She has coauthored several articles including "Shark Repellents and Stock Prices: The Effects of Antitakeover Amendments since 1980" forthcoming in the *Journal of Financial Economics*.

David J. Ravenscraft is an economist at the Bureau of Economics of the Federal Trade Commission. Previously, he held teaching positions at Northwestern University and the University of Illinois. Dr. Ravenscraft holds a Ph.D. in economics from Northwestern University, an M.A. from the University of Illinois, and a B.A. from Northern Illinois University. Currently, he researches the behavioral effects of mergers, takeovers, and sell-offs. He is the author of many working papers and publications including a forthcoming book with F. M. Scherer entitled *Mergers, Sell-offs, and Economic Efficiency* (Brookings).

F. M. Scherer is professor of economics at Swarthmore College. Dr. Scherer has held past positions as professor of economics at Northwestern University, and director of the Bureau of Economics at the Federal Trade Commission. He received his Ph.D. and M.B.A. from Harvard University, and an A.B. from the University of Michigan. Dr. Scherer's research interests lie in the areas of economics of mergers and the economics of industrial structure. He is the author of many articles and books, including *Industrial Market Structure and Economic Performance*, second edition (Rand McNally, 1980).

E. Thomas Sullivan is professor of law and research associate at the Center for the Study of American Business at Washington University in St. Louis. He has also held teaching positions at the University of Missouri and Georgetown University Law Center. Professor Sullivan received a J.D. from Indiana University School of Law. Among his many honors are listings in the *American Law Institute, Who's Who in American Law* and *Directory of American Scholars*. Professor Sullivan has written many books and articles including *Federal Limitations on Land Use Control* with G. Mandelker and J. Gerard.

Robert B. Thompson is professor of law and research associate at the Center for the Study of American Business at Washington University in St. Louis. He previously was employed as an attorney at Jones, Bird & Howell in Atlanta. Professor Thompson received a J.D. from the University of Virginia and a B.A. from Vanderbilt University. Among his numerous publications is a book with F. H. O'Neal entitled *O'Neal's Close Corporations* (1986).

Murray L. Weidenbaum is director of the Center for the Study of American Business and Mallinckrodt Distinguished University Professor at Washington University. A leave of absence from Washington University from January 1981 to August 1982 was spent serving as President Reagan's first chairman of the Council of Economic Advisers. Dr. Weidenbaum has held a variety of business, government, and academic positions. He joined Washington University in 1964 and was chairman of the Economics Department from 1966 to 1969. Dr. Weidenbaum received his Ph.D. in economics from Princeton University, his M.A. from Columbia University, and is a graduate of the City College of New York. He is widely known for his work on government regulation of business. His many publications include *Business, Government, and the Public,* third edition (Prentice Hall, 1986), *The Future of Business Regulation* (Amacom, 1980), and *The Economics of Peacetime Defense* (Praeger, 1974).

Index

173